D0984185

Beyond September 11

Beyond September 11

An Anthology of Dissent

Edited by Phil Scraton

Pluto Press
LONDON • STERLING, VIRGINIA

First published 2002 by Pluto Press
345 Archway Road, London N6 5AA
and 22883 Quicksilver Drive,
Sterling, VA 20166–2012, USA

www.plutobooks.com

British Library Cataloguing in Publication Data
A catalogue record for this book is available from the British Library

ISBN 0 7453 1963 7 hardback
ISBN 0 7453 1962 9 paperback

Library of Congress Cataloging in Publication Data
Beyond September 11 : an anthology of dissent / edited by Phil Scraton.
    p. cm.
Includes bibliographical references.
    ISBN 0–7453–1963–7 — ISBN 0–7453–1962–9
  1. Terrorism. 2. War on Terrorism, 2001– 3. Government, Resistance
to. I. Scraton, Phil.
    HV6431 .B495 2002
    973.931—dc21
                                                        2002005037

10   9   8   7   6   5   4   3   2   1

Designed and produced for Pluto Press by
Chase Publishing Services, Fortescue, Sidmouth EX10 9QG
Typeset from disk by Stanford DTP Services, Towcester
Printed in the European Union by Antony Rowe, Chippenham, England

Contents

Acknowledgements

This anthology could not have been produced without the willing co-operation of the authors and their response to tight deadlines. Barbara Houghton has been central to the production of the book, not only in liaising with authors, word processing, reformatting text and responding to numerous requests to accommodate changes, but also in her patient support throughout. Colleagues at the Centre for Studies in Crime and Social Justice, as ever, have encouraged and contributed much to the realisation of the project. At Pluto Anne Beech and colleagues have been enthusiastic and responsive in ensuring speedy production.

It is important to acknowledge formally: the *Guardian*, for contributions by Madeleine Bunting and Paul Foot; the *New Statesman*, for contributions by John Pilger; *The Nation* for the article by Naomi Klein; *Race and Class* for A Sivanandan's contributions; the *Independent* for Robert Fisk's personal account. Each article is fully acknowledged and referenced in the text.

Finally I could not have edited, and contributed to, this collection had it not been for the personal support and critical comments of my partner, Deena Haydon. My deepest thanks to her and to my friends and co-workers who have given so much over the last four months.

Phil Scraton
Merseyside
February 2002

Preface

So pervasive is the mass media that when dramatic, catastrophic events occur in Western societies, particularly the US, visual images are projected instantaneously on to a world stage. They are presented, indeed re-presented, to a global audience. This contrasts with the delayed or absent coverage of disasters and tragedies in the so-called Third World. By any standard, however, the magnitude and significance of September 11 was exceptional. Yet, like any transmitted event, meaning was constructed in the experiences of the beholder. While there could not be anything but incredulity, given the bold ferocity and appalling 'success' of the suicide mission, condemnation was not universal. For many throughout the world there was deep sadness and open outrage at the loss of civilians through wilful acts of mass murder; for others they were a cause for celebration. As those who hijacked and deployed domestic flights as bombs were condemned as terrorist killers, to others they were heroes who had sacrificed their lives in ultimate acts of heroism. This profound contrast in the responses of ordinary people across the globe could not, and cannot, be ignored.

The graphic, horrifying images of the 'bombing' and eventual collapse of the World Trade Center's twin towers left a lasting imprint on all who watched their repeated transmission. With powerful lenses, from close focus to wide angle, and with clear blue skies of late summer as the backdrop, not one moment of the disaster went unrecorded. This left an often voiced sense of unease that those who indulged in the coverage, as producers and as viewers, later felt they had been voyeurs. Yet the sheer scale of the disasters, in Manhattan, Washington and Pennsylvania demanded and received world attention. That, of course, had been a primary objective of the terrible mission. These were not casual targets. Inevitably, then, September 11 was portrayed as the day that 'changed history'. After these events 'life would never be the same'. Clearly that was, and remains, true for the bereaved, the survivors and the rescuers. Their lives and futures were altered suddenly and permanently; their hopes and plans devastated.

To represent more broadly those fateful moments or hours as 'world changing' masked the realities of international relations and the powerful interests that underpin them. However vicious, uncompromising and criminal, the attacks on the US were not without context. They were the end-product of historical, material circumstances. If they are to be understood it is necessary to put aside simplistic mono-causal explanations. The political imperative is to move beyond indignation, condemnation and retribution and face the complex political, economic and socio-cultural relations between and within nation-states to understand and confront regimes which spawn such acts. Yet, to seek explanation is not to deny culpability. To understand through contextualisation is not to appease or justify despicable acts of extreme violence. To pursue justice through international laws and conventions is not to betray the dead and their bereaved families. The events of September 11 shaped rather than changed contemporary history. If we fail to grasp material and social contexts, if we dismiss as irrelevant profound differences in their interpretation, we deny their meaning, neglect their significance and rationalise their truth.

In the rush to judgement of the immediate aftermath, the ease with which a label – terrorism – emerged and was applied as a self-evident classification was disturbing, although hardly surprising. In the clamour for vengeance, the speed with which previously little-known individuals, groups and organisations were ascribed 'monster' status was remarkable. And, in the misappropriation of 'justice' as a non-negotiable process, the legitimacy claimed, if not coerced, for the deployment of the most powerful weaponry on earth was breathtaking. As the bereaved and survivors were still reeling from the full, personal impact of the attacks, the US demanded of its people, its allies and all nation-states, unqualified approval for its self-serving 'war on terror'. The US alone decided on appropriate targets and its 'with us or against us' agenda condemned 'neutrals' to reclassification as 'enemies of the States'. Yet, consistent with a kind of Orwellian double-speak, it was a war that was not a war, suggesting, and eventually demonstrating, that the US would be bound neither by the rules of engagement associated with military action nor by the Geneva Conventions.

It was during the politics of the immediate aftermath, as the Bush agenda in the US transformed into the Blair agenda in the UK, that this anthology was conceived. As the destiny of Afghanistan's torturing Taliban regime was sealed, with unrestrained US support given to the torturing Northern Alliance to fight the ground war, the full implications of the potential of sustained and unlimited military intervention began to dawn. Still there was no workable or agreed definition of 'terrorism'. Neither was there any informed political debate on extending the 'war' in Afghanistan to other states. What qualified states for inclusion on the prescribed list of potential US targets? There was no political mandate for the 'war on terror' and no political accountability for prioritised targets or 'collateral damage'. At the same time, new anti-terrorist legislation was rushed through and enacted in the US, the UK and Europe. Apart from draconian law reform, existing legislation was used with harsh authoritarianism. In schools, colleges and universities, critical and rights-oriented debate was silenced with dissenters intimidated physically and professionally. The myth of academic freedom, usually disguised by liberal rhetoric and a pretence that the academy stands apart from vested military-industrial interests, was exposed.

What was deeply worrying about these developments was the ease with which opposition to the 'war on terror', in both political hubris and military action, was recast as betrayal. First a betrayal of those who died in Manhattan, Washington and Pennsylvania and second a betrayal of nationhood and 'civilised values'. The worst excesses of this media-hyped response were seen in headlines branding opponents of the military strategy as 'traitors'. Simultaneously, the 'evil' ascribed to Osama bin Laden, al-Qaida and the Taliban was transferred to Muslims living throughout the West, fuelling racism already endured by black and Asian communities.

In this context of vengeance and despair, of propaganda and reaction, I contacted academics, journalists, lawyers, activists and campaigners inviting short, informed articles reflecting critical responses to the Bush-Blair agenda. The brief was to write personally and/or professionally. This anthology, containing eight already published articles and twenty-six commissioned contributions, is not intended as a comprehensive coverage of all issues. Rather, it sets out to provide an accessible and detailed account of the implications of the responses to September 11 and its aftermath. It blends well-researched and closely observed political accounts with personal experiences.

What the collection achieves is a forum in which opposition to the 'war on terror', as constituted by President Bush in his September 2001 address to Congress and reaffirmed in his State of the Union speech in February 2002, has been voiced powerfully, authoritatively and without compromise. This anthology of dissent reflects deep concerns from within the US and allied states. The contributors, individually and collectively, present a profound, shared concern with what has been, continues to be and will be carried out in our names.

Phil Scraton
Merseyside
February 2002

INTRODUCTION: WITNESSING 'TERROR', ANTICIPATING 'WAR'

Phil Scraton

First thoughts

Trying to make sense – emotional, physical, political – of September 11, I return to my initial reactions and responses. Like so many others across the world, via satellite I witnessed truly horrifying scenes of scarcely believable atrocity. Filmed from every conceivable angle the second passenger aircraft imploded the twin tower. Its nose-cone, having passed through the building, was instantly engulfed in flames. At that 'live by satellite' moment, the collapse of the entire World Trade Center inevitable, the realisation dawned that the dual crashes were no coincidence. Both aircraft had been piloted, purposefully and accurately, into their targets. As news broke, telling of two other planes crashing, one into the Pentagon, the second out of control in Pennsylvania, the immensity and significance of these disasters became apparent. They had to be the dreadful end-product of effective and efficient collaboration involving groups working together, carefully planning and acquiring skills. These were not random targets. The World Trade Center, bomb damaged just eight years earlier, and the Pentagon represented hugely symbolic as well as material targets.

In a Verona hotel room we watched the dramatic live transmissions from downtown Manhattan. Firefighters and rescuers raced into the disaster zone passing dust-covered, ghost-like workers coming from the opposite direction – running or staggering for their lives. Cameras homed in on others trapped in offices high above the flames, some throwing themselves from windows to avoid choking or burning to death. As the towers collapsed, clouds of grey toxic dust covered all and everything in their path. Then came the first reports of agonised telephone calls made from one of the planes and by those facing death trapped in their offices. These were final goodbyes to loved ones. They reminded me of rescue workers recounting disaster scenes where the only sounds they could hear, as they listened for potential survivors, were those of mobile phones ringing from the debris as desperate relatives tried to make contact.

The carnage of September 11 could not have been anticipated. The total destruction of one of the world's largest building complexes, the deaths of between three and four thousand civilian workers

1

(estimated at 10,000 at the time) raised a terrifying question: where next? Throughout these early moments I was shocked. Shocked by the callous ferocity of the attacks, the randomness of death and suffering, the capacity and ability of the hijackers to puncture the US security network at so many levels, the ease with which they must have lived to prepare for their complex, devastating project. Individually and collectively, they had made a mockery of the world's most advanced and expensive intelligence services. Their acts – crimes against humanity – were derived from a reasoned hatred, a distorted fundamentalism that transformed belief, intellect and compassion into a mutant, predatory 'final solution' politics. Yet, to portray such men as psychopathic killers, whose 'lust for blood' emanates from individual or cultural pathology, diminishes the historical, political and economic contexts which fed and nurtured their absolute moral purpose.

Terrifying acts are not conceived in a political vacuum. They become broadly and popularly defined within the management and manipulation of 'identity'. Their status is ascribed through a familiar vocabulary that slips easily and casually from the tongue, grabs headlines and captures – then imprisons – imagination. It is a vocabulary which demonises, vilifies and distances: deliver 'us' from 'evil'; the 'massacre' of the 'innocent'; 'wicked' beyond 'humanity'; 'savages', not 'humans'; 'barbarism' versus 'civilisation'. In such accounts, so depraved are the perpetrators, so far removed are they from 'our' world, that they are aberrant and beyond redemption. They are 'other', not only outsiders and outlaws, but a sub-species. Their threat is not restricted to a collective rejection of 'our' Christian, social democratic values but extends to a commitment of our eradication. It is a dangerous construction invariably leading to an abandonment of the rule of law and established rules of engagement. If the 'enemy' is beneath contempt, the war against it can be unconditional.

The events of September 11 leave no doubts about the lengths to which some individuals, groups and organisations are prepared to go in the use of violence. Unique in terms of the operation, the claiming of so many civilian lives through co-ordinated acts of terror is hardly unusual. Terror is a strategy which ostentatiously denies the conventions of 'acceptable' conflict. Its purpose is to demonstrate as widely as possible a disregard for the boundaries or limits to formal combat. To strike terror into the heart of an identifiable community is to frighten people so deeply that they lose trust and confidence in all aspects of routine daily life. Yet, to demonise perpetrators, to represent their humaneness as monstrousness, creates and sustains a climate within which a deeper understanding of historical, political and cultural contexts is inhibited and is replaced by an all-consuming will to vengeance.

Following the devastation at the World Trade Center two highly visible and emotional expressions of grief and sympathy replaced the initial shock of the attacks. First was the presence in lower Manhattan of those in search of the missing. In scenes reminiscent of old, grainy and faded photographs of relatives at pitheads quietly awaiting news of loved ones lost underground, families and friends clustered together, as close as permitted to the area designated for all time as Ground Zero. They carried treasured photographs and written descriptions, many photocopied and pasted on walls, hoardings and makeshift notice boards. These became dignified shrines to lost lives.

Second, and displaying a kind of civic commitment to supporting the gruesome yet hapless search for survivors, was the ever-changing mass of people out on the streets applauding firefighters and rescuers as they changed shifts. Unable to assist directly, it was as if those who stood with banners and flags, many travelling long distances to be there, felt impelled to 'do something'. Undoubtedly, whatever the motives of individuals, this public recognition of the pain and loss endured by the rescue and recovery teams was much appreciated. Many firefighting precincts had lost officers, even entire crews.

How easy it is to hijack the spirit of grief, the heartfelt expressions of sympathy and the public displays of empathy. When, eventually, the US President – at first conspicuous by his absence – made his appearance in New York, the mood shifted to that of vengeance masquerading as the pursuit of justice in defence of global freedom. Returning to my emotions of those late September days, as firefighters posed Iwo Jima-style to plant the Stars and Stripes on the mountain of rubble that had claimed so many lives, I was not surprised by the attacks. Bush and his hawks, presumably with whom he had been planning a war schedule behind closed doors, reminded me of US insularity and the simplicity of a mindset that reduces complex political-economic and socio-cultural dynamics to the ranch barbeque discourse of 'good folks' and 'bad folks', to the civilised (meaning Western values) and the barbarians at 'our' gates, to allies and enemies. Suddenly the president with a dubious mandate to hold office, a man who when questioned did not know the name of the president of Pakistan, had been catapulted centre stage into a world political crisis.

Shocked, but not surprised; that was my initial reaction. Shocked by the 'success' of those terrible and terrifying missions, by the repeated failures of international surveillance and security systems and by the consolidation of deep religious convictions that could recast suicide and murder as a holy war. But not surprised. The insularity of a richly diverse and intricate union of states, which continually reveals itself as an aggressive political-economic and cultural coloniser, stifles critical and informed debate. The US projects its military-industrial complex, its command of material resources and cultural transmission with an absolute certainty that its WASP-ish dominant ideologies and lifestyles are both right and righteous. Through this combination of material and cultural absolutism all who supply resources, open their borders, agree to unfair terms of investment and buy into the American Dream are friends. The rest are foes.

And so ... to war

No country lightly commits forces to military action and the inevitable risks involved. The military action we are taking will be targeted against places we know to be involved in the al-Qaida network of terror, or against the military apparatus of the Taliban. The military plan has been put together mindful of our determination to do all we humanly can to avoid civilian casualties.

Tony Blair, UK Prime Minister, 7 October 2001

On 20 September George W Bush, heavily criticised for his invisibility throughout the immediate aftermath of the attacks on the US, addressed Congress. His nation had been 'awakened to danger and called to defend freedom'.[1] Shared grief had been 'turned to anger and anger to resolution'. 'Justice' would be delivered – whether 'we bring our enemies to justice or bring justice to our enemies'. In his sights were: al-Qaida – 'to terror what the Mafia is to crime'; Afghanistan's Taliban regime; and Osama bin Laden. Al-Qaida, with Osama bin Laden's direction, had recruited and trained 'thousands of ... terrorists in more than 60 countries'. To the Taliban Bush issued three non-negotiable demands: present the al-Qaida leadership to the US authorities; release all foreign nationals; provide access to all terrorist training camps. His message was unequivocal: 'hand over the terrorists' or 'share their fate'. The 'logic' was simple: in harbouring and supporting murderers, 'the Taliban regime is committing murder'. While not committing the US to the overthrow of the Taliban regime, this would be an inevitable consequence of its failure to meet US demands. Aiding and abetting 'terrorism' would provide legitimacy for military action.

Ominously, Bush expanded the dimensions of the US declaration of the 'war on terror': it 'begins with al-Qaida, but it does not end there. It will not end until every terrorist group of global reach has been found, stopped the defeated.' All nations that 'provide aid or safe haven to terrorists' would be pursued relentlessly on the basis of an ultimatum that either 'you are with us or you are with the terrorists'. There could be no third way, no neutral territories. In the long-term defence of US interests, in protecting its citizens, regimes tolerating or encouraging 'terrorism' would be designated 'hostile'.

Flexing the military muscle of global policing, Bush emphasised that it was not 'just America's fight'. What was 'at stake' was not only 'America's freedom'. It would be a long-term 'fight' for the 'world', for 'civilisation' and for 'pluralism, tolerance and freedom'. With reference to the Nato Charter he proclaimed that an 'attack on one is an attack on all', that the 'civilised world' was quickly 'rallying to America's side'. No room here for the 'clash of civilisations' thesis – it was the civilised against the rest. In 'grief and anger' had been forged 'our mission and our moment'. Defending the 'advance of human freedom, the great achievement of our time' now depended on US resolve and intervention.

And so the 'war on terror' was declared. Regardless of international mandate, formal political debate or democratic political process and in contravention of international law and conventions, Bush prepared the ground for the inevitable. The 'war' was not against Islam but against ubiquitous terrorism. With over 60 nation-states already proscribed as hostile, the long haul announced and the 'defence of civilisation' as the high moral purpose, the US was going to war. If states were not party to the Bush administration's solution, they would be regarded part of its problem. As far as the US government was concerned the attacks provided it with the authority and legitimacy to define, name and eliminate 'terrorist' organisations, their members and their associates.

Sitting in Congress was the UK Prime Minister, Tony Blair. He endorsed the Bush speech without qualification and the president did not disappoint: the US, he stated, had 'no truer friend than Great Britain' with the two states now 'joined together in a great cause'. Eight days later in his key speech to the Labour Party's annual conference Blair declared September 11 to be 'a turning point in history'.[2] Out of such 'tragedy', such 'evil', would emerge a force for 'lasting good'. The 'machinery of terrorism' would be destroyed 'wherever it is found'. 'Hope' would be given to all nations, with 'greater understanding between nations and between faiths' and 'above all, justice and prosperity for the poor and dispossessed ...' While longer-term objectives were aspirational, initial interventions would be directed against Osama bin Laden and the Taliban. Blair reiterated the Bush ultimatum: 'surrender the terrorists; or surrender your power. It's your choice.'

Blair stated that while the 'causes of terror' should be understood there could be no justification for September 11. It required a 'proportionate' and 'targeted' response. He juxtaposed the issue of civilian casualties with a reminder of 'what we are dealing with. Listen to the calls of those passengers on the planes. Think of the children on them, told they were going to die.' Civilian casualties to be avoided – yes; but only in the context of the civilian deaths in the September 11 attacks.

At home there was a need for urgent law reform 'not to deny basic liberties but to prevent their abuse and protect the most basic liberty of all: freedom from terror'. And, 'round the world', as he put it, there would also be change with governments 'coming together' and the 'power of community asserting itself'. 'Confidence is global' with state interdependence defining 'the new world we live in'. Mutual interests, 'woven together', represented 'the politics of globalisation ... driven by people'. Blair argued that the 'power of community' combined with 'justice' had to be mobilised to benefit all nations. The 'governing idea of modern social democracy is community' derived in 'the principles of social justice'. His mission statement was 'to deliver social justice in the modern world'.

And the first phase? In standing four square with the US, the objective was 'a fight for freedom' and 'a fight for justice too'. The moment had arrived, it had to be 'seized', 'let us re-order the world around us'. He presumed the 'moral power of the world acting as a community' ... 'now is the time for the strength to build that community'. What Blair constructed was the moral and political foundation, based on absolute confidence and certainty of a social democratic ideal present neither in the UK nor the US, for Bush's 'war on terror'. Effectively, self-righteously and in the soap-box rhetoric of 'community', 'justice', 'freedom' and 'equality' he took the moral high ground. Afghanistan would be bombed remorselessly, but it would be for its own, and the greater, good.

Suddenly the sleeping giants of Western democratic states were awakened to the repressive and torturing Taliban regime and the real potential of al-Qaida and Osama bin Laden, the latter previously seen as an ally and well-rewarded on the US payroll. A particularly patronising sequence occurred when Barbara Bush and Cherie Blair lectured the world on women's oppression under the Taliban. Why had it taken so long for the silencing, torturing and execution of women to become the concern of US and UK governments and their unofficial spokeswomen? The hypocrisy was tangible. Bush's war cry amounted to little more than moral indignation and vengefulness delivered through the rhetoric of universal justice and global peacekeeping. Arundhati Roy notes that Bush, in his self-anointed determination of the 'calling of the United States of America', identified a 'free nation' founded 'on fundamental values that rejects hate, rejects violence, rejects murderers and rejects evil'.[3]

Given this claim, Roy reflects on the litany of countries bombed by the US since 1945: China, Korea, Guatemala, Indonesia, Cuba, Belgian Congo, Peru, Laos, Vietnam, Cambodia, Grenada, Libya, El Salvador, Nicaragua, Panama, Iraq, Bosnia, Sudan, Yugoslavia and Afghanistan. In addition, a further list could be written of those countries where the US actively promoted and funded the overthrow of governments, most notably Chile, or destroyed political economies and reduced populations to starvation through trade embargoes and crippling sanctions. Bush envisions a world map dotted not with misery and suffering contributed to through the protection and promotion of US economic self-interest, but one where the 'Stars and Stripes' symbolises a calling to freedom, justice and equality.

Within a month of the attacks on the US, on October 7 slightly before 6 p.m. British time, the US and UK jointly launched cruise missiles against Afghanistan. Military action had been inevitable from the moment Bush issued his congress ultimatum. No one expected the Taliban to meet his demands. In going to war, despite UN protocols, the US claimed the endorsement of a 40-nation coalition. According to Bush 'carefully targeted' military action had been 'designed to clear the way for sustained, comprehensive and relentless operations to drive them [the 'terrorists'] out and bring them to justice'.[4]

As announced in Congress, however, military action would be the opening act in a more sustained, longer-term 'war on terror'. 'Today', affirmed Bush, 'we focus on Afghanistan, but the battle is broader.' He continued: 'Every nation has a choice to make. In this conflict there is no neutral ground. Today's operation is called Enduring Freedom. We defend not only our precious freedoms, but also the freedom of people everywhere.' The 'goal' was 'just' and no expense would be spared in the resourcing of a 'duty' to fight global terrorism. In supporting Bush, Tony Blair was confident that the 'cause is just'. The attacks on the US represented an 'attack on our freedom, our way of life and civilised values the world over ... our determination in acting is total'.

From its conception the Bush/Blair agenda for a 'war on terror' was flawed. Like so many social and societal reactions high on moral outrage, it had neither the intellectual grasp nor the political capacity to wage, let alone win, such a war. In the 'monstering' of Osama bin Laden, the Taliban and al-Qaida and their use of terror as a strategy, there was a serious failure to come to terms with the origins, definitions and manifestations of terrorism. Internationally it has proved difficult to establish a shared and operational definition of terrorism. This will always be so while states, both internally and externally, depend on repression and oppression in managing endemic structural inequalities. Civil rights and human rights struggles have not been confined to totalitarian regimes. Western social democracies, their political economies globalised around the inherent economic exploitation of advanced, and forever advancing, capitalism, are compelled to manage the consequences of the extreme relations of wealth and poverty. It remains, as it has been since democracy was grafted on to capitalism, a form of management underpinned ultimately by the authoritarian use of force and sanctioned state violence.

As Max Weber noted in capitalism's first period of international expansionism, the state holds the monopoly on the use of legitimate violence. While those who resist and fight totalitarian regimes, who sacrificed, for example, their relative peace to fight fascism in the Spanish Civil War, are celebrated for their heroism, those who use force against the excesses of 'democratic states' or their economic allies are castigated for their terrorism. Of course this should not reduce the issue to the simplistic 'freedom fighter or terrorist' question. What it does demand is that the complexity of definition, of relative motive, of historical and political context and of established objectives and 'just' targets is considered. It is a profound hypocrisy that social democratic states have researched, developed and supplied weapons of mass destruction on 'free market' principles in order to further their political and economic interests but then object when that weaponry is pointed in their direction. In all contexts, justifications for the use of violence remain a matter of political judgement and moral relativism.

Having been bankrolled and empowered by the US when it suited, the longer-term consequences of that action – the abusive totalitarianism of the Taliban and the networking of al-Qaida – were the sanctioning and bankrolling of the September 11 attacks. In utilising terror Osama bin Laden had learnt well: no distinction between military and civilian targets, strike fear at the heart of all communities. But, if this construction is applied universally to each and every intervention where fear and insecurity are instilled throughout communities or populations, then what of those states, proclaiming freedom and democracy, which have used and supported terror? From the saturation fire-bombing of a defenceless Dresden and the wilful destruction visited on surrendering German cities and towns at the close of the 1939–45 war to the catastrophic use of Agent Orange, Napalm and carpet-bombing in Vietnam and Cambodia, the sacrifice of civilians by the UK and the US epitomised the legitimation of terror. These indefensible acts exacted revenge and, quite literally, burnt reprisal into the collective memory of populations. Calculated and purposeful, such ends could not justify their means.

It is instructive that as the 'frontiers' of expanding capital were pushed back, using soldiers and missionaries to commit acts of physical atrocity and cultural genocide against aboriginal populations, 'terror' was introduced as a tactic to clear the way for economic settlement and exploitation. The 'infusion' of universal terror, to 'strike' or 'inspire' communities with terror, were essential strategies of domination at the heart of imperialist expansion. While today in Western societies much is made of the 'fear of crime' having consequences as debilitating as crime itself, the 'fear of atrocity' committed by the colonial powers was used ruthlessly as a powerful weapon in itself. There is no direct connection between contemporary state responses and those of earlier interventions, yet the legacy of political, economic and cultural domination – aided and abetted by the rule of law and its uncompromising enforcement – cannot be ignored. As the US and its allies congratulate themselves on freedom and justice as hallmarks of advanced democracies, they skip the long-term and unresolved consequences of colonisation and appropriation.

Their convenient denial over the 'unfree' within their populations, the victims whose inheritance and daily life are dictated, if not determined, by endemic social injustice and inherent structural inequality, has long roots. What cannot be denied is that 'infusing', 'inspiring' and 'striking' indigenous and enslaved communities with terror represents a deliberate strategy of domination that has not been forgotten. Indeed, it remains central to 'Third World' definition and status and to all struggles over land rights, territory and reservations. Whatever the claims for an academic, postmodern interpretation of the relativism of 'power', the contemporary world was given 'terrorism' derived in the 'absolute' and 'legitimate' power of political-economic interests central to the development, consolidation and sustenance of 'global' capitalism.

1. The direct quotes from US President George W Bush in this section are taken from his speech to Congress, September 20, 2001.
2. The direct quotes from UK Prime Minister, Tony Blair in this section are taken from his speech to the Annual Conference of the Labour Party, September 28, 2001.
3. Roy, Arundhati, 'Brutality smeared in peanut butter', *G2*, October 23, 2001.
4. *Guardian*, October 8, 2001.

AMERICA'S JIHAD: A HISTORY OF ORIGINS
Christian Parenti

As I write New York still smoulders, a massive round-up of Middle Eastern immigrants is under way and Afghanistan is being carpet-bombed with fuel-air ordnances known as 'daisy cutters' – the most powerful weapons next to tactical nukes. To understand America's new war on terror we must examine the role of the US in nurturing the very same Islamic military networks that are now global enemy number one. Political Islam has deep roots, which we cannot explore here, but it also has important, more recent origins that directly implicate US policy. Our story begins in Afghanistan.

The 'good' Jihad

In 1978 communist officers of the Afghan armed forces seized power from President Sardar Mohammed Daud. Though progressive in many respects – the communists favoured expanding education, gender equality and land reform – the new government nonetheless succeeded in alienating Afghanistan's largely autonomous tribal leaders.[1] Scattered rebellions soon began. Well aware of Soviet support for the Democratic Republic of Afghanistan the US immediately began discussing aid for the incipient rebellion. As early as March 30, 1979, Robert Gates, former director of the Central Intelligence Agency, attended a meeting at which Under-Secretary of Defense Walter Slocumbe asked whether 'there was value in keeping the Afghan insurgency going, [and] sucking the Soviets into a Vietnamese quagmire'.[2] Towards that end, America was soon channelling aid to the rebels. As former National Security Adviser to President Carter, Zbigniew Brzezinski explained in a 1998 interview with *Le Nouvel Observateur*, the US began aiding the tribalist and Islamic uprisings as early as July 3, 1979 – six months before the Soviet invasion.[3]

The fight really got going when Brezhnev – drunken, isolated and against the better judgement of his party – ordered the Soviet invasion of December 24, 1979. Soviet Special Forces, or SPETNAZ, commandos killed one communist leader, President Nur Mohammed Tarki, and replaced him with the more agreeable Babrak Karmal. For the next 13 years the Soviet Union bled into the Hindu Kush, sending in war material and fresh troops only to bring out zinc caskets and heroin-addicted vets. As the war progressed, the Red Army's tactics devolved: mines were dropped indiscriminately from planes and civilian populations bombed. In retrospect, the Afghan war was the long slow fuse that set off the USSR's implosion.[4]

The US side of this conflict was also massive, described by Fred Halliday as, 'the largest covert operation in the history of the CIA'.[5] From 1979 to 1992 the US channelled a minimally estimated three billion dollars to the various Mujahideen factions fighting the Russians and then the Najibullah regime. The Saudi dynasty sent an equal amount while additional aid flowed from China, Iran, assorted Islamic charities, drug-running operations, privatised CIA funding sources (such as the collapsed Bank of Commerce and Credit International) and various Arab millionaires (such as Osama bin Laden). Most of the arms were Soviet hand-me-downs purchased from the increasingly Western-oriented Egypt. Running the pipeline of arms, training, money, information and drugs in and out of Afghanistan was the Pakistani Inter Services Intelligence (ISI) agency. Described as a state within a state, the ISI almost doubled in size during the war and became the most religiously politicised apparatus of the Pakistani government.[6]

Throughout the Reagan years US funding for the Mujahideen steadily increased. Facilitated by innocuously named lobbying groups like the Afghan American Educational Fund, above-board appropriations for the largely secret campaign reached $250 million annually by 1985.[7] Much more issued from the CIA's black budget. It was always the most radically Islamic groups who received the bulk of the funding: fully a third of US monies went to the religious zealot and Pashtun, Gulbuddin Hekmtyar. (By the early days of the new Afghan war this feverishly anti-American warlord was trying to join the Taliban.)[8] US support of the anti-communist holy warriors was accompanied by a surge in stateside heroin consumption. According to one mid-1980s congressional investigation, narcotics sales in America were skyrocketing by $10 billion annually and overdose deaths had increased by 93 per cent between 1979 and 1983.[9]

Afghan international

By the early 1980s the Pakistani aid pipeline included substantial numbers of international volunteers. Many Muslim nations, particularly in the Middle East, began to see Afghanistan as not only a showdown between communism and capitalism but also as a convenient political dumping ground for frustrated clerical activists of the middle classes and the restive lumpen proletariat. Osama bin Laden's close comrade, the Egyptian surgeon turned terrorist, Ayman al-Zawahiri, is a perfect example: charged with conspiracy in the Sadat assassination, al-Zawahiri was arrested, tortured, and upon release fled to Afghanistan.

In 1986 the Afghan War escalated in three ways that would later feed into the global jihad. First, the US gave the Mujahideen Stinger anti-aircraft missiles, which largely crippled Soviet air power and brought an end to the war. Second, the US along with Britain's MI6 and the ISI, approved sending armed expeditionary forces into the Central Asian Republics of the USSR, penetrating the Red Bear's 'soft Islamic underbelly'. And third, the CIA gave direct support to the ISI's ongoing project of recruiting mercenaries and religiously motivated volunteers from around the world. By 1988 this meant there were recruiting centres in numerous American cities including New York, Detroit and San Francisco.[10]

Well before this, Osama bin Laden had already gone to Afghanistan, brought there by his friend Prince Turki, the head of

Saudi intelligence. The young bin Laden – tall, handsome, devout, and rich – was the next best thing to the real Saudi prince that the ISI had long requested. In Afghanistan, bin Laden's tasks included building infrastructure, co-ordinating logistics for the Mujahideen, dishing out funds and, later, fighting. As one of the leaders of the international volunteers, bin Laden kept track of the other recruits, registering their identities and contact information. From this roster, it is said, emerged al-Qaida.

However, more important than any one personality or organisation was the sheer number of angry, alienated young men from around the world who passed through the tempering fires of the Afghan War. Ahmed Rashid sums it up thus: 'With the active encouragement of the CIA and Pakistan's ISI who wanted to turn the Afghan jihad into a global war waged by all Muslim states against the Soviet Union, some 35,000 Muslim radicals from 40 Islamic countries joined Afghanistan's fight between 1982 and 1992. Tens of thousands more came to study in Pakistani madrasahs. Eventually more than 100,000 foreign Muslim radicals were directly influenced by the Afghan jihad.'[11] Many of these warriors were on wanted lists in their home countries and when the war ended they returned to official hostility or as political outlaws.

Catching the boomerang

By 1992 the Afghan communist President Najibullah had been driven from power, the USSR was no more, and the US began shutting down its end of the covert war. With no external enemy the Mujahideen coalition soon tore itself, and the cities of Afghanistan, to pieces. Cast to the wind, many of the Arab-Afghans, as the international vets were known, soon started armed jihads back home. In the Middle East, politicians and police braced themselves for the return of many thousands of angry, battle-hardened, religious warriors. Sure enough, the early 1990s brought a wave of low-intensity conflicts fuelled in equal parts by neo-liberal-created poverty, horrible government repression and the crystal clear religious solutions offered by extremist Political Islam.

In Algeria, the Islamic Salvation Front went to war when the government scuttled elections and cracked down on religious activists. In Egypt, well-practised police thugs rounded up scores of political Islamists and detained any Egyptian youths who returned home from long trips with Pakistani visas stamped in their passports. The Jordanian authorities, too, worried openly about the scores, or possibly hundreds, of Afghan vets now at a loose end and circulating among the mosques and organisations of the Muslim political scene.[12] Even the Philippines saw an influx of Abu Syyaf Afghan vets who set themselves up a mini jihad-cum-gangster paradise in the south of the archipelago.

Mildly concerned experts of the Western policy establishment began writing about the 'new arc of crisis'. This phrase, coined in the 1970s by Brzezinski, originally referred to the imagined possibility of Soviet expansion into the Middle East. The real 'arc of crisis' was much broader as Islamists scattered from the Afghan War took up the gun in Georgian Abkhazia, Chechnya, Tajikistan, Algeria, Egypt and even Bosnia.[13] Many of these new micro-wars threatened American allies and interests, but some of the conflicts were also useful to US foreign policy makers. Scholars such as Peter Gowan, David Gibbs and Michel Chossudovsky have sketched well the logic of US new post-Cold War imperialism. While the ideology of socialism and class struggle have largely disappeared, threats to US corporate interests and political power still remain, the old matter of containing other capitalist powers that might rival America at the regional level now come to the fore.[14]

Take, for example, Bosnia. As Peter Gowan casts it, the battle for Bosnia was organic in origin at the same time as it served as a proxy theatre in which the US and the 'friendly' nations of Europe jockeyed for influence. Could Europe go it alone? Would NATO and, with it, American influence over the EU disappear? Whoever could control the crisis of the Balkans would determine these questions and the future of Euro-Atlantic relations.[15] One of the details in the struggle was a 1992 influx of devout Saudi-influenced Wahabbist Mujahideen veterans recruited by the ruling Party of Democratic Action of Bosnia. These fundamentalist warriors from Chechnya, Saudi Arabia, Egypt and Pakistan fought alongside the same government forces that were soon receiving covert US training. According to international observer troops, the Mujahideen in Bosnia grew from a few hundred to around 6,000 in 1995.[16]

The Christian Science Monitor described a typical recruit: 'Riyad Quayyum, [is] a wiry and determined-looking Pakistani construction engineer who has lived in Saudi Arabia for the past 16 years. He is leaving Jiddah for Bosnia next week, one of hundreds of Muslims from the Arab world and beyond who have chosen to work and fight alongside the Bosnians ... Mr. Quayyum was an anti-aircraft expert in the Pakistani army, and during a stint with the

Mujahideen guerrillas in Afghanistan he operated hand-held Stinger ground-to-air missiles.'[17]

The Islamic party dominating the Bosnian government was a US ally, and in some way surrogate. Thus American policy makers remained ambivalent towards ever more numerous jihadists. When the US finally prevailed, demonstrating that Europe was still dependent on NATO and NATO on the superiority of US air power, and orchestrated the Dayton resolution to the war, removing the implacably anti-America Mujahideen volunteers became a public demand and precondition for saving the Izetberavitch government.[18]

The same dynamic – anti-American Islamists *indirectly* advancing American strategic interests – played out in Kosovo. There the KLA, primarily a gangster outfit, accepted the services of many Arab-Afghan 'guests' in its fight against the Serbs. In fact, according to testimony in the trial of Claude Kader – an Algerian-born French national and Afghanistan-trained Mujahideen vet who worked under the cover of the Albanian-Arab Islamic Bank – both bin Laden and al-Zawahiri are reported to have visited Albania in 1996 and 1997. Who knows if this is true? But the influence of Middle Eastern Islamic extremism in Kosovo is real. Anyone who travels in the countryside of that province cannot miss the many new and strangely shiny mosques which, locals and aid workers say, are Wahabbist and funded by Osama bin Laden and other Arab fundamentalists.[19]

The point is not that the US was cosy with right-wing Political Islam in this second phase of the story. Rather, American policy towards the jihadists was wrought with contractions. The United States did not take the jihadist threat seriously, because it found much of their activity useful. Thus the KLA received US arms and training and Secretary of State Madeleine Albright shook hands with KLA godfather Hashim Thaci, while America's special envoy to Bosnia, Robert Gelbard, described that force as 'Islamic terrorists'.[20] The same ambivalence was seen, though on a different scale, not long before September 11, when the Bush White House called off an FBI investigation of two US-based bin Laden siblings. According to the BBC and other sources, both Bush senior and junior were business partners with various members of the bin Laden family and all were connected through various oil defence-contracting interests including the Carlyle Group. President Bush quite logically feared that the FBI investigations of Osama's siblings would lead to bad publicity about historic and quite above board ties between his family and the bin Ladens.[21]

But there was, and is, something else blinding American leaders. Consider again the comments of Brzezinski when asked if he regretted the Afghanistan War. His response was blunt: 'Regret what? That secret operation was an excellent idea. It had the effect of drawing the Russians into the Afghan trap and you want me to regret it? ... What is most important to the history of the world? The Taliban or the collapse of the Soviet Empire? Some stirred-up Moslems or the liberation of Central Europe and the end of the Cold War?'[22] Brzezinski's comments reflect the arrogance and false security provided by the racist imagination of empire: their crises, over yonder, will never hurt us.

Capital triumphant

There is one more strand of US history that demands our attention: the global triumph of capital. How has the new post-socialist world of market hegemony, led as it is by American might, shaped the deep reservoir of rage that makes Osama bin Laden's poster so popular among the Muslim poor? Even if Osama is rich and the hijackers were middle class, their actions resonate with the millions of wretchedly poor. The World Bank's Development Report for 2000/2001 estimates that there are about 2 billion people living in 'abject poverty'. That means they lack even the very basics – adequate food, shelter and clean water. As for the Middle East, in Egypt the World Bank reports that 30 per cent of the people subsist on less than $2 a day; in Yemen it's 35 per cent. It gets worse. Roughly 40 per cent of the Middle East's population is under 17 years old, and one-fifth of all young men there are unemployed. The average per capita income of the region is about $2,100 annually.[23]

The US, leading the rest of the global North's rich nations, has created this horror: for decades imposed poverty-generating neo-liberal policies that force states to privatise resources and slash public spending. This raises unemployment – increasing poverty, disease, forced migration and environmental degradation. Fuelling such poverty is the debt crisis. Cheap credit from the oil boom of the 1970s went sour as interest rates rose and commodity prices plummeted in the early 1980s. Since then scores of developing countries have been trapped in a downward cycle of usurious borrowing and repayment that enriches Northern banks at the expense of an ever-poorer Southern majority. Over the past 17 years the South has transferred a net total of $1.5 trillion to Northern creditors. According to Saskia Sassen of the London School of

Economics, 'There are now about 50 countries that are hyper-indebted and unable to redress the situation.' The International Monetary Fund requires these 'Highly Indebted Countries' to pay 20 to 25 per cent of their export earnings towards debt servicing. 'In contrast,' writes Sassen, 'the Allies cancelled 80 per cent of Germany's [Second World War] debt and only insisted on 3–5 per cent of export earnings debt service.'[24] In Egypt, the home of Mohammed Atta who piloted the first jet into the World Trade Towers, the government spends a mere 4 per cent of its budget on health care. As a result 8.5 per cent of Egypt's children die before the age of five.

Rebellion in the post-hope era

With redistributive agendas of the Nasserite or Marxist variety vanquished, all that remains are the 'socialisms of fools' – nationalism, anti-Semitism, racism and messianic Political Islam. Into the cauldron of poverty come Osama bin Laden's demands: America out of the Holy Land; justice in Palestine; a return to the pure and righteous society of the Islamic imagination. To get the point across bin Laden's promo videos splice shots of Israeli troops beating children with rousing jihadist training sequences of young men fighting back while the chorus sings: *revolt! revolt!* The US may well smash al-Qaida in Afghanistan but what new generation of activists will the global war breed? Will there be yet more blowback in ten years? If one is lulled into comfort by the repression of radical Islam, consider again the comments of al-Zawahiri from twenty years ago. On trial from inside a cage full of Islamic prisoners, al-Zawahiri speaking English, shouted this message to the press:

Now we want to speak to the whole world! Who are we? We are Muslims! We are Muslims who believed in their religion! We tried our best to establish this Islamic state and Islamic society! We are here, the real Islamic Front against the Zionism, communism and imperialism! We suffered the severest inhuman treatment! And there they kicked us, they beated us, they whipped us with the electric cables! They shocked us with electricity! And they used their wild dogs, and they hanged us over the edge of the dogs with our hands tied at the back! There they arrested the wives, the mothers, the fathers, the sisters and the sons in a trial to put the psychological pressure over these innocent prisoners![25]

Are we surprised that al-Zawahiri is enraged with the US? His captors, the Egyptian security forces were financed and trained by the US. Should we be surprised when the next generation strikes back at the empire or its citizens? America's open-ended jihad is precisely the type of policy that will compound the existing problems from which emerged the four suicidal jet-bombs of September 11. Only global justice, that is economic redistribution and real development, can compete with the messianic nihilism of radical Islam.

1. Goodson, Larry P., *Afghanistan's Endless War: State Failure, Regional Politics, and the Rise of the Taliban* (Seattle: University of Washington Press, 2001). Goodson gives a good account of how the Mujahideen formed. By his accounting there were seven Sunni groups and four Shia groups by 1989 with more Shia groups and some post-communist militias emerging later for a total of twelve groups by the early 1990s.
2. Gates, Robert, *From The Shadows: the ultimate insider's story of five presidents and how they won the cold war* (New York: Touchstone Books, 1997).
3. 'Zbigniew Brzezinski: How Jimmy Carter and I started the Mujahideen', reprinted on the *CounterPunch* web site, October 8, 2001; original form, *Le Nouvel Observateur* (France), January 15–21, 1998, p. 76.
4. Kotz, David, Weir, Fred, *Revolution from Above: The Demise of the Soviet System* (New York: Routledge, 1997).
5. In the March 25, 1996, *New Republic.*
6. Rashid, Ahmed, *Taliban: Militant Islam, Oil and Fundamentalism in Central Asia* (New Haven: Yale University Press, 2001); Kremmer, Christopher, 'Made By The USA: A $6 billion Rebel Group That Haunts Its Former Masters', *Sydney Morning Herald*, September 18, 2001; Burke, Jason, 'Ordeal in Arden: Frankenstein the CIA created Mujahideen trained and funded by the US are among its deadliest foes', *Observer*, January 17, 1999. There are in fact extremely anti-American, Wahhabist elements in the ISI which was effected by the Mujahideen as much as it effected its proxies. See for example, Gupt, Shishir, et al., 'The Tussle Within: The Double Game', *India Today*, November 12, 2001.
7. Atlas, Terry, 'U.S. Aid Pipeline to Afghan Rebels Springing Leaks', *Chicago Tribune*, February 3, 1985.
8. Ehrlich, Richard, 'Anti-Soviet rebels far from united', *The Toronto Star*, February 20, 1988.
9. Robinson, Mike, 'Narcotics Traffic Grossed $110 Billion in 1984, Panel Reports', *The Associated Press*, Wednesday, March 6, 1985.
10. Rashid, 'Chapter Ten: Global Jihad', *op. cit.*; Cooley, 'Chapter Five: Recruiters, trainers, trainees', *op. cit.*
11. Rashid, Ahmed, 'The Taliban: Exporting Extremism', *Foreign Affairs* 78, no. 6, November–December 1999: 25–35. The Afghan Mujahideen sent 300 guerillas with knowledge of Soviet weaponry to help the US efforts during the Gulf War. See 'Cheques and Balances of War', *Australian Financial Review*, February 14, 1991.

12. 'Arab war veterans pose threat in Mideast', *The Toronto Star*, December 19, 1992.
13. Philips, Alan, 'New "arc of crisis" fuels fears over Muslim aggression', *Daily Telegraph*, October 8, 1992.
14. Gowan, Peter, 'The Euro-Atlantic Origins of NATO's Attack on Yugoslavia', in Tariq Ali, ed., *Masters of the Universe? NATO'S Balkan Crusade* (Verso Books, 2000); Gibbs, David N., 'Washington's new interventionism: U.S. hegemony and inter-imperialist rivalries', *Monthly Review*, September, 2001; Chossudovsky, Michel, 'Who is Osama Bin Laden?' *Humanist*, Volume 61, Issue 6, November 1, 2001.
15. Gowan, *op cit.*
16. Harris, Francis in Zagreb and Fox, Robert, 'International: Arab fighters link up with Muslim units in Bosnia', *Daily Telegraph*, September 4, 1992.
17. Gwyn, Richard, 'Balkan dominoes could tumble into one very big war', *Toronto Star*, November 27, 1992; Ford, Peter, 'Islamic Conference Yields Cautious Words', *Christian Science Monitor*, December 4, 1992.
18. 'Islamic forces will go home, Bosnia vows US links exit of Mujahideen to peace treaty', *Boston Globe*, December 9, 1995.
19. Based on author's interviews and conversation in July and August 2000. Lest one get the wrong idea, there is no apparent Wahabbist influence on the everyday life of Kosovo Albanians. Rather than being devout Muslims the province's youthful population worships the gods of fashion, music, the automobile and nationalism.
20. Christoff Kurop, Marcia, 'European Jihads: Al Qaeda's Balkan Links', *Wall Street Journal*, November 1, 2001.
21. 'Bush thwarted FBI probe against bin Ladens', *Agence France Presse*, November 7, 2001.
22. 'Zbigniew Brzezinski: How Jimmy Carter and I started the Mujahideen', reprinted on the *CounterPunch* web site, October 8, 2001; original form, *Le Nouvel Observateur* (France), January 15–21, 1998, p. 76.
23. *World Development Report 2000/2001: Attacking Poverty* (Oxford: World Bank/Oxford University Press, 2001).
24. Sassen, Saskia, 'A message from the global south', *Guardian*, September 12, 2001.
25. Transcript, Public Broadcasting System, 'Frontline: Looking for Answers', Program #2002, original airdate: October 11, 2001.

AN UNCONSCIONABLE THREAT TO HUMANITY
John Pilger

A war in the American tradition

The Anglo-American attack on Afghanistan crosses new boundaries. It means that America's economic wars are now backed by the perpetual threat of military attack on any country, without legal pretence. It is also the first to endanger populations at home. The ultimate goal is not the capture of a fanatic, which would be no more than a media circus, but the acceleration of Western imperial power. That is a truth the modern imperialists and their fellow travellers will not spell out, and which the public in the West, now exposed to a full-scale jihad, has the right to know. In his zeal, Tony Blair came closer to an announcement of real intentions than any British leader since Anthony Eden. Not simply the handmaiden of Washington, Blair, in the Victorian verbosity of his extraordinary speech to the Labour Party conference, put us on notice that imperialism's return journey to respectability was well under way. Hark, the Christian gentleman-bomber's vision of a better world for 'the starving, the wretched, the dispossessed, the ignorant, those living in want and squalor from the deserts of northern Africa to the slums of Gaza to the mountain ranges of Afghanistan'. Hark, his unctuous concern for the 'human rights of the suffering women of Afghanistan' as he colluded in bombing them and preventing food reaching their starving children.

Is all this a dark joke? Far from it; as Frank Furedi reminds us in the *New Ideology of Imperialism*, it is not long ago 'that the moral claims of imperialism were seldom questioned in the West. Imperialism and the global expansion of the Western powers were represented in unambiguously positive terms as a major contributor to human civilisation'. The quest went wrong when it was clear that fascism, with all its ideas of racial and cultural superiority, was imperialism, too, and the word vanished from academic discourse. In the best Stalinist tradition, imperialism no longer existed. Since the end of the Cold War, a new opportunity has arisen. The economic and political crises in the developing world, largely the result of imperialism, such as the bloodletting in the Middle East and the destruction of commodity markets in Africa, now serve as retrospective justification for imperialism. Although the word remains unspeakable, the Western intelligentsia, conservatives and liberals alike, today boldly echo Bush and Blair's preferred euphemism, 'civilisation'. Italy's Prime Minister, Silvio Berlusconi, and the former liberal editor, Harold Evans, share a word whose true meaning relies on a comparison with those who are uncivilised, inferior and might challenge the 'values' of the West, specifically its God-given right to control and plunder the uncivilised.

If there was any doubt that the World Trade Center attacks were the direct result of the ravages of imperialism, Osama bin Laden, a mutant of imperialism, dispelled it in his videotaped diatribe about

Palestine, Iraq and the end of America's inviolacy. Alas, he said nothing about hating modernity and miniskirts, the explanation of those intoxicated and neutered by the supercult of Americanism. An accounting of the sheer scale and continuity and consequences of American imperial violence is our élite's most enduring taboo. Contrary to myth, even the homicidal invasion of Vietnam was regarded by its tactical critics as a 'noble cause' into which the United States 'stumbled' and became 'bogged down'. Hollywood has long purged the truth of that atrocity, just as it has shaped, for many of us, the way we perceive contemporary history and the rest of humanity. And now that much of the news itself is Hollywood-inspired, amplified by amazing technology and with its internalised mission to minimise Western culpability, it is hardly surprising that many today do not see the trail of blood.

How very appropriate that the bombing of Afghanistan has been conducted, in part, by the same B52 bombers that destroyed much of Indochina 30 years ago. In Cambodia alone, 600,000 people died beneath American bombs, providing the catalyst for the rise of Pol Pot, as CIA files make clear. Once again, newsreaders refer to Diego Garcia without explanation. It is where the B52s refuel. Thirty-five years ago, in high secrecy and in defiance of the United Nations, the British government of Harold Wilson expelled the entire population of the island of Diego Garcia in the Indian Ocean in order to hand it to the Americans in perpetuity as a nuclear arms dump and a base from which its long-range bombers could police the Middle East. Until the islanders finally won a high court action last year, almost nothing about their imperial dispossession appeared in the British media.

How appropriate that John Negroponte is Bush's ambassador at the United Nations. This week, he delivered America's threat to the world that it may 'require' to attack more and more countries. As US ambassador to Honduras in the early 1980s, Negroponte oversaw American funding of the regime's death squads, known as Battalion 316, that wiped out the democratic opposition, while the CIA ran its 'contra' war of terror against neighbouring Nicaragua. Murdering teachers and slitting the throats of midwives were a speciality. This was typical of the terrorism that Latin America has long suffered, with its principal torturers and tyrants trained and financed by the great warrior against 'global terrorism', which probably harbours more terrorists and assassins in Florida than any country on earth. The unread news today is that the 'war against terrorism' is being exploited in order to achieve objectives that consolidate American power. These include: the bribing and subjugation of corrupt and vulnerable governments in former Soviet central Asia, crucial for American expansion in the region and exploitation of the last untapped reserves of oil and gas in the world; Nato's occupation of Macedonia, marking a final stage in its colonial odyssey in the Balkans; the expansion of the American arms industry; and the speeding up of trade liberalisation. What did Blair mean when, at the Labour Party Conference in Brighton, he offered the poor 'access to our markets so that we practise the free trade that we are so fond of preaching'? He was feigning empathy for most of humanity's sense of grievance and anger: of 'feeling left out'. So, as the bombs fall, 'more inclusion', as the World Trade Organisation puts it, is being offered the poor – that is, more privatisation, more structural adjustment, more theft of resources and markets, more destruction of tariffs. On Monday, the Secretary of State for Trade and Industry, Patricia Hewitt, called a meeting of the voluntary aid agencies to tell them that 'since September 11, the case is now overwhelming' for the poor to be given 'more trade liberation'. She might have used the example of those impoverished countries where her cabinet colleague Clare Short's ironically named Department for International Development backs rapacious privatisation campaigns on behalf of British multinational companies, such as those vying to make a killing in a resource as precious as water.

Bush and Blair claim to have 'world opinion with us'. No, they have élites with them, each with their own agenda: such as Vladimir Putin's crushing of Chechnya, now permissible, and China's rounding up of its dissidents, now permissible. Moreover, with every bomb that falls on Afghanistan and perhaps Iraq to come, Islamic and Arab militancy will grow and draw the battle lines of 'a clash of civilisations' that fanatics on both sides have long wanted. In societies represented to us only in caricature, the West's double standards are now understood so clearly that they overwhelm, tragically, the solidarity that ordinary people everywhere felt with the victims of September 11. That, and his contribution to the re-emergence of xeno-racism in Britain, is the messianic Blair's singular achievement. His effete, bellicose certainties represent a political and media élite that has never known war. The public, in contrast, has given him no mandate to kill innocent people, such as those Afghans who risked their lives to clear landmines, killed in their beds by American bombs.

These acts of murder place Bush and Blair on the same level as those who arranged and incited the twin towers murders. Perhaps never has a prime minister been so out of step with the public mood, which is uneasy, worried and measured about what should be done. Gallup finds that 82 per cent say 'military action should only have been taken after the identity of the perpetrators was clearly established, even if this process took several months to accomplish'. Among those élite members paid and trusted to speak out, there is a lot of silence. Where are those in Parliament who once made their names speaking out, and now shame themselves by saying nothing? Where are the voices of protest from 'civil society', especially those who run the increasingly corporatised aid agencies and take the government's handouts and often its line, then declare their 'non-political' status when their outspokenness on behalf of the impoverished and bombed might save lives? The tireless Chris Buckley of Christian Aid, and a few others, are honourably excepted. Where are those proponents of academic freedom and political independence, surely one of the jewels of Western 'civilisation'? Years of promoting the jargon of 'liberal realism' and misrepresenting imperialism as crisis management, rather than the cause of the crisis, have taken their toll. Speaking up for international law and the proper pursuit of justice, even diplomacy, and against our terrorism might not be good for one's career. Or as Voltaire put it: 'It is dangerous to be right when the government is wrong.' That does not change the fact that it is right.

This war of lies goes on

There is no victory in Afghanistan's tribal war, only the exchange of one group of killers for another. The difference is that President Bush calls the latest occupiers of Kabul 'our friends'. However welcome the scenes of people playing music and shaving off their beards, this so-called Northern Alliance are no bringers of freedom. They are the same people welcomed by similar scenes of jubilation in 1992, who then killed an estimated 50,000 in four years of internecine feuding. The new heroes have so far tortured and executed at least 100 prisoners of war, and countless others, as well as looted food supplies and re-established their monopoly on the heroin trade.

This week [November 19], Amnesty International made an unusually blunt statement that was buried in the news. It ought to be emblazoned across every front page and television screen. 'By failing to appreciate the gravity of the human rights concerns in relation to Northern Alliance leaders,' said Amnesty, 'UK ministers at best perpetuate a culture of impunity for past crimes; at worst they risk being complicit in human rights abuse.' The truth is that the latest crop of criminals to 'liberate' Kabul has been given a second chance by the most powerful country on earth pounding into dust one of the poorest, where people's life expectancy is just over 40. And for what?

Not a single terrorist implicated in the attacks on America has yet been caught or killed. Osama bin Laden and his network have almost certainly slipped into the tribal areas of the North-West Frontier of Pakistan. Will Pakistan now be bombed? And Saudi Arabia, and Egypt, where Islamic extremism and its military network took root? Of course not. The Saudi sheikhs, many of them as extreme as the Taliban, control America's greatest source of oil. The Egyptian regime, bribed with billions of US dollars, is an important American proxy. No daisy cutters for them. There was, and still is, no 'war on terrorism'. Instead, we have watched a variation of the great imperial game of swapping 'bad' terrorists for 'good' terrorists, while untold numbers of innocent people have paid with their lives: most of one village, whole families, a hospital, as well as teenage conscripts suitably dehumanised by the word 'Taliban'.

It is perfectly understandable that those in the West who supported this latest American tenor from the air, or hedged their bets, should now seek to cover the blood on their reputations with absurd claims that 'bombing works'. Tell that to grieving parents at fresh graves in impoverished places of whom the sofa bomb-aimers know nothing. The contortion of intellect and morality that this triumphalism requires is not a new phenomenon. Putting aside the terminally naive, it mostly comes from those who like to play at war: who have seen nothing of bombing, as I have experienced it: cluster bombs, daisy cutters, the lot.

How appropriate that the last American missile to hit Kabul before the 'liberators' arrived should destroy the satellite transmitter of the Al-Jazeera television station, virtually the only reliable source of news in the region. For weeks, American officials have been pressuring the government of Qatar, the Gulf state where Al-Jazeera is based, to silence its broadcasters, who have given a view of the 'war against terrorism' other than that based on the false premises of the Bush and Blair 'crusade'.

The guilty secret is that the attack on Afghanistan was unnecessary. The 'smoking gun' of this entire episode is evidence of the

British government's lies about the basis for the war. According to Tony Blair, it was impossible to secure Osama bin Laden's extradition from Afghanistan by means other than bombing. Yet in late September and early October, leaders of Pakistan's two Islamic parties negotiated bin Laden's extradition to Pakistan to stand trial for the September 11 attacks. The deal was that he would be held under house arrest in Peshawar. According to reports in Pakistan (and the *Daily Telegraph*), this had both bin Laden's approval and that of Mullah Omah, the Taliban leader. The offer was that he would face an international tribunal, which would decide whether to try him or hand him over to America. Either way, he would have been out of Afghanistan, and a tentative justice would be seen to be in progress. It was vetoed by Pakistan's President Musharraf who said he 'could not guarantee bin Laden's safety'. But who really killed the deal?

The US ambassador to Pakistan was notified in advance of the proposal and the mission to put it to the Taliban. Later, a US official said that 'casting our objectives too narrowly' risked 'a premature collapse of the international effort if by some luck chance Mr bin Laden was captured'. And yet the US and British governments insisted there was no alternative to bombing Afghanistan because the Taliban had 'refused' to hand over Osama bin Laden. What the Afghani people got instead was 'American justice' – imposed by a president who, as well as denouncing international agreements on nuclear weapons, biological weapons, torture and global warming, has refused to sign up for an international court to try war criminals: the one place where bin Laden might be put on trial.

When Tony Blair said that this war was not an attack on Islam as such, he was correct. Its aim, in the short term, was to satisfy a domestic audience then to accelerate American influence in a vital region where there has been a power vacuum since the collapse of the Soviet Union and the emergence of China, whose oil needs are expected eventually to surpass even those of the US. That is why control of Central Asia and the Caspian basin oilfields is important as exploration gets under way.

There was, until the cluster bombing of innocents, a broad-based recognition that there had to be international action to combat the kind of terrorism that took thousands of lives in New York. But these humane responses to September 11 were appropriated by an American administration, whose subsequent actions ought to have left all but the complicit and the politically blind in no doubt that it intended to reinforce its post-Cold War assertion of global supremacy – an assertion that has a long, documented history. The 'war on terrorism' gave Bush the pretext to pressure Congress into pushing through laws that erode much of the basis of American justice and democracy. Blair has followed behind with anti-terrorism laws of the very kind that failed to catch a single terrorist during the Irish War.

In this atmosphere of draconian controls and fear, in the US and Britain, mere explanation of the root causes of the attacks on America invites ludicrous accusations of 'treachery'. Above all, what this false victory has demonstrated is that, to those in power in Washington and London and those who speak for them, certain human lives have greater worth than others and that the killing of only one set of civilians is a crime. If we accept that, we beckon the repetition of atrocities on all sides, again and again.

The truths they never tell us

Polite society's bombers may not have to wait long for round two. The US Vice-President, Dick Cheney, warned that America could take action against '40 to 50 countries'. Somalia, allegedly a 'haven' for al-Qaida, joins Iraq at the top of a list of potential targets. Cheered by having replaced Afghanistan's bad terrorists with America's good terrorists, the US Defense Secretary, Donald Rumsfeld, has asked the Pentagon to 'think the unthinkable', having rejected its 'post-Afghanistan options' as 'not radical enough'. An American attack on Somalia, wrote the *Guardian*'s man at the Foreign Office, 'would offer an opportunity to settle an old score: 18 US soldiers were brutally killed there in 1993 ...'. He neglected to mention that the US Marines left between 7,000 and 10,000 Somali dead, according to the CIA. Eighteen American lives are worthy of score-settling; thousands of Somali lives are not.

Somalia will provide an ideal practice run for the final destruction of Iraq. However, as the *Wall Street Journal* reports, Iraq presents a 'dilemma', because 'few targets remain'. 'We're down to the last outhouse', said a US official, referring to the almost daily bombing of Iraq that is not news. Having survived the 1991 Gulf War, Saddam Hussein's grip on Iraq has since been reinforced by one of the most ruthless blockades in modern times, policed by his former amours and arms suppliers in Washington and London. Safe in his British-built bunkers, Saddam will survive a renewed blitz – unlike the Iraqi people, held hostage to the compliance of their dictator to America's ever-shifting demands.

In this country, veiled propaganda will play its usual leading role. As so much of the Anglo-American media is in the hands of various guardians of approved truths, the fate of both the Iraqi and Somali peoples will be reported and debated on the strict premise that the US and British governments are against terrorism. Like the attack on Afghanistan, the issue will be how 'we' can best deal with the problem of 'uncivilised' societies. The most salient truth will remain taboo. This is that the longevity of America as both a terrorist state and a haven for terrorists surpasses all. That the US is the only state on record to have been condemned by the World Court for international terrorism and has vetoed a UN Security Council resolution calling on governments to observe international law is unmentionable.

Recently, Denis Halliday, the former Assistant Secretary General of the UN who resigned rather than administer what he described as a 'genocidal sanctions policy' on Iraq, incurred the indignation of the BBC's Michael Buerk. 'You can't possibly draw a moral equivalence between Saddam Hussein and George Bush [Senior], can you?' said Buerk. Halliday was taking part in one of the moral choice programmes that Buerk compères, and had referred to the needless slaughter of tens of thousands of Iraqis, mostly civilians, by the Americans during the Gulf War. He pointed out that many were buried alive, and that depleted uranium was used widely, almost certainly the cause of an epidemic of cancer in southern Iraq. That the recent history of the West's true crimes makes Saddam 'an amateur', as Halliday put it, is the unmentionable; and because there is no rational rebuttal of such a truth, those who mention it are abused as 'anti-American'. Richard Falk, Professor of International Politics at Princeton, has explained this. Western foreign policy, he says, is propagated in the media 'through a self-righteous, one-way moral/legal screen [with] positive images of Western values and innocence portrayed as threatened, validating a campaign of unrestricted political violence'.

The ascendancy of Rumsfeld and his deputy, Paul Wolfowitz, and associates Richard Perle and Elliot Abrams means that much of the world is now threatened openly by a geopolitical fascism, which has been developing since 1945 and has accelerated since September 11. The present Washington gang are authentic American fundamentalists. They are the heirs of John Foster Dulles and Alan Dulles, the Baptist fanatics who, in the 1950s, ran the State Department and the CIA respectively, smashing reforming governments in country after country – Iran, Iraq, Guatemala – tearing up international agreements, such as the 1954 Geneva accords on Indochina, whose sabotage by John Foster Dulles led directly to the Vietnam War and five million dead. Declassified files now tell us the United States twice came within an ace of using nuclear weapons.

The parallels are there in Cheney's threat to '40 to 50' countries, and of war 'that may not end in our lifetimes'. The vocabulary of justification for this militarism has long been provided on both sides of the Atlantic by those factory 'scholars' who have taken the humanity out of the study of nations and congealed it with a jargon that serves the dominant power. Poor countries are 'failed states'; those that oppose America are 'rogue states'; an attack by the West is a 'humanitarian intervention'. (One of the most enthusiastic bombers, Michael Ignatieff, is now 'Professor of Human Rights' at Harvard.) And as in Dulles's time, the United Nations is reduced to a role of clearing up the debris of bombing and providing colonial 'protectorates'.

The twin towers attacks provided Bush's Washington with both a trigger and a remarkable coincidence. Pakistan's former foreign minister, Niaz Naik, has revealed that he was told by senior American officials in mid-July that military action against Afghanistan would go ahead by the middle of October. The US Secretary of State, Colin Powell, was then travelling in central Asia, already gathering support for an anti-Afghanistan war 'coalition'. For Washington, the real problem with the Taliban was not human rights; these were irrelevant. The Taliban regime simply did not have total control of Afghanistan: a fact that deterred investors from financing oil and gas pipelines from the Caspian Sea, whose strategic position in relation to Russia and China and whose largely untapped fossil fuels are of crucial interest to the Americans. In 1998, Dick Cheney told oil industry executives: 'I cannot think of a time when we have had a region emerge as suddenly to become as strategically significant as the Caspian.'

Indeed, when the Taliban came to power in 1996, not only were they welcomed by Washington, but their leaders were flown to Texas, then governed by George W Bush, and entertained by executives of the Unocal oil company. They were offered a cut of the profits from the pipelines; 15 per cent was mentioned. A US official observed that, with the Caspian's oil and gas flowing, Afghanistan would become 'like Saudi Arabia', an oil colony with no democracy and the legal persecution of women. 'We can live with that', he said. The deal fell through when two American embassies in East Africa were bombed and al-Qaida was blamed. The Taliban duly moved to the top of the media's league table of demons, where the normal exemptions apply. For example, Vladimir Putin's regime in Moscow, the killers of at least 20,000 people in Chechnya, is exempt. Last week, Putin was entertained by his new 'close friend', George W Bush, at Bush's Texas ranch. Bush and Blair are permanently exempt – even though more Iraqi children die every month, mostly as a result of the Anglo-American embargo, than the total number of dead in the twin towers, a truth that is not allowed to enter public consciousness. The killing of Iraqi infants, like the killing of Chechens, like the killing of Afghan civilians, is rated less morally abhorrent than the killing of Americans.

As one who has seen a great deal of bombing, I have been struck by the capacity of those calling themselves 'liberals' and 'progressives' wilfully to tolerate the suffering of innocents in Afghanistan. What do these self-regarding commentators, who witness virtually nothing of the struggles of the outside world, have to say to the families of refugees bombed to death in the dusty town of Gardez, long after it fell to anti-Taliban forces? What do they say to the parents of dead children whose bodies lay in the streets of Kunduz? 'Forty people were killed', said Zumeray, a refugee. 'Some of them were burned by the bombs, others were crushed by the walls and roofs of their houses when they collapsed from the blast.' What does the *Guardian*'s Polly Toynbee say to him: 'Can't you see that bombing works?' Will she call him anti-American? What do 'humanitarian interventionists' say to people who will die or be maimed by the 70,000 American cluster bomblets left unexploded? For several weeks, the *Observer*, a liberal newspaper, has published unsubstantiated reports that have sought to link Iraq with September 11 and the anthrax scare. 'Whitehall sources' and 'intelligence sources' are the main tellers of this story. 'The evidence is mounting ...' said one of the pieces. The sum of the 'evidence' is zero, merely grist for the likes of Wolfowitz and Perle and probably Blair, who can be expected to go along with the attack. In his essay, *The Banality of Evil*, the great American dissident Edward Herman described the division of labour among those who design and produce weapons like cluster bombs and daisy cutters and those who take the political decisions to use them and those who create the illusions that justify their use. 'It is the function of the experts, and the mainstream media,' he wrote, 'to normalise the unthinkable for the general public.' It is time journalists reflected upon this, and took the risk of telling the truth about an unconscionable threat to much of humanity that comes not from faraway places, but close to home.

This is an edited version of articles first published in the *New Statesman* on October 15, November 19 and November 26, 2001.

THE THREAT OF UNITED STATES' RUTHLESSNESS
Madeleine Bunting

Defending the middle

No one culture has evolved the perfect formulation of human values. Any good liberal must agree with that. The limitations are apparent of the liberal model of an individual pursuit of happiness. Can that guide us through an environmental crisis and grotesque economic inequality? What liberal hasn't pondered how to reinvigorate social solidarity, or revitalise concepts of the common good? These are familiar symptoms of the crisis in Western thought. Because we are at war, we do not have to abandon our capacity for humility and self-criticism, nor the search in other cultures for the inspiration for new thinking.

This last is what the liberal fundamentalist rejects, satisfied that he or she has nothing to learn from deep engagement with other cultures. Lurking in that is a rigid belief in universal values established in the eighteenth century in the American and French revolutions. It is a dangerous trap to conflate liberalism as a political doctrine with liberalism as an all-encompassing rationalist principle. The former is the best method of politically organising pluralistic societies that humanity has evolved. The latter is a homogenising cultural imperialism.

Liberal fundamentalism has too often discredited the precious human rights tradition. All societies fall well short of the UN Declaration of Human Rights (UNDHR), but it was Western, liberal countries that divorced political and civil rights from economic and social rights and elevated the former as a Cold War weapon. The politically motivated promotion of some rights over others has deeply irritated many Muslims who accuse the West of hypocrisy, and are alienated by a language of rights and individualism which doesn't reflect their ethical tradition's emphasis on responsibility and the collective good. The UNDHR attempted to accommodate both perspectives by synthesising individual rights and communal values, which the world has been interpreting ever since. But the US turned its back on this, preferring to stay with its narrower formulation; it abused the rest of the world for not following its lead.

It may seem strange to debate the nature of liberalism during a humanitarian catastrophe in Afghanistan. But crisis and conflict have had a crucial role in formulating our conception of justice, as Francesca Klug points out in her book on the history of human rights, *Values for a Godless Age*. HG Wells sent a letter to *The Times* in 1939, with a draft declaration, arguing that it was important that people knew why and what they were fighting for: 'At various crises ... it has been our custom to produce a declaration of the principles on which our public and social life is based, a restatement of the spirit in which we face life.' The *Daily Herald* set aside a daily page to debate his declaration; it was translated into 30 languages and dropped over occupied Europe. If there is to be a new disposition between Muslims and the West after this war – and there needs to be – there's no better time to start thinking about it than now.

A grubby, vengeful war

When Tony Blair took Britain into the US war with Afghanistan, he assured us that it was a three-pronged strategy – the military, diplomatic and humanitarian would be pursued in tandem. Each was equally important. After ten days of intensive bombing, Blair's pledge was exposed as the politically expedient sham it always was. It was third way wishful thinking of the worst kind to imagine that a military attack on such a desperately poor country as Afghanistan was compatible with humanitarian needs.

Sophistry such as George Bush's, that this was not a war against the Afghan people but against the Taliban, now looks absurd. You can't blow up fuel dumps, as the US has done in Herat and Kabul, without crippling the distribution of aid. You can't bomb a country from high altitude without hitting depots and spreading fear amongst truck drivers and warehouse labourers. So it is disingenuous of Clare Short, the Secretary of State for International Development, to say that the bombing is not stopping aid getting into the country. The point is that the aid is piling up in warehouses but not reaching the hungry stomachs that need it, a problem exacerbated by the fact that thousands have fled the cities for the countryside for fear of the bombs.

What makes the humanitarian situation so frightening is the scale. Over 7 million people are believed to be at risk. What the war risks doing is turning a desperate, fragile situation into one of the biggest humanitarian disasters of recent decades. The attacks of September 11 came at a terrible moment for Afghanistan; just as aid would have been stepped up to stockpile for the winter, it was reduced to a mere 20 per cent of its previous capacity. Now there is only a one-month window to get enough aid into remote villages before entry routes become impassable for the winter. This is the horrible reality of fighting a war in such a devastated, impoverished country. It is a ludicrous fantasy of recent years to believe that war can be conducted without significant civilian loss of life.

War is always vicious, and what the twentieth century showed was that the vast majority of its victims are now women and children; at the beginning of the twentieth century, only 20 per cent of war's casualties were non-combatants and by the end of the century, that had shifted to 80 per cent. Unicef is predicting that the staggeringly high infant mortality rates in Afghanistan (25 per cent) will rise because of the war and claim another 100,000 children's lives this winter. Other vulnerable groups of the population, such as the elderly, will also be disproportionately hit as the Afghan population undertakes a desperate struggle to survive. Some are already reduced to eating leaves and grass.

Faced with these facts, Bush's airdrops of yellow food packs, like his initiative that American children donate a dollar each for Afghan children, is an offensive piece of political posturing which convinces no one outside of the US. It may reassure the American people of their noble fight, but the reality of this grubby, vengeful war is beginning to become apparent. Blair and Bush would do well to consider the political consequences of a famine: across a broad swathe of the Muslim world, the US military action will be held responsible for every one of the deaths.

This raging colossus

Over the past few days, I've been ordered on to a strict diet of my words. A stream of emails arrived from American readers with plenty of advice (get laid, get pregnant, shut your fat legs, shut up) and prognostications for my future (you'll be fired). One told me that I made them feel sick: 'untouched by our tragedy, yet [you] feel the right to criticise our country's actions'. One asked if 'you have a molecule of shame or humility within your entire being?' and promised to pray for me. Another asked: 'How stupid do you feel now? ... this is one of the best wars ever fought' and another asked:

'As the US war on terror becomes increasingly successful, could the world say "thank you"?'

Thank God for the volume of seawater which puts these kinds of nutters on another continent. It's not so much the fine line in misogynistic abuse from US patriots, but the intolerance of debate and diversity of opinion which is really frightening. The truth is that this kind of emotional intensity also seeped into the war on this side of the Atlantic – entrenched camps for and against are waging a bitter war of words over the heads of a majority who are worried and confused, but see no alternative to war.

Fear drives this kind of emotional intensity. It is a pitifully short time, only two months, since we learned of a ruthlessness born of fanaticism which we had not thought possible; our perception of human nature is having to readjust painfully to the revelation of a capacity for calmly premeditated brutality. I'm sure that fear has influenced my continuing conviction that waging war on Afghanistan is unlikely in the long term to defeat that kind of ruthless Islamist terrorism, and is very likely to have disastrous consequences for the poor benighted country itself. I very much hope I will be proved wrong.

It must have been so comforting to have been swept up in the emotional euphoria of VK day. It was the ultimate Disney ending after a month of nation-builders' storytelling. If only it were that simple. But even on VK day, the excited reporters and commentators surrounded by a telegenic rabble of boys curious at television cameras found no echo among anxious Afghan women, most of whom remained behind their burkas. Nor did the VK story last long, quickly replaced by the tension of warlords struggling to position themselves; in Jalalabad, young men jostled around the cameras, their eyes, cartridge belts and guns all gleaming, poised for what they know best – waging war.

And yet, it's not even those Jalalabad warriors who made events so troubling, but the growing appreciation of just how ruthless and ambitious the US is likely to become in its war against terrorism. What was starkly revealed was that the US had only one interest in this war in Afghanistan: capturing bin Laden and destroying al-Qaida; that imperative outstripped all considerations of Afghanistan's future. So the timing of the attack was decided by US military preparedness rather than any coherent political strategy for the region, and the US war aim determined the crucial switch in tactics around

November 4 when the US decided to throw its weight behind the unsavoury Northern Alliance by bombing the Taliban frontlines.

For the US, the whole country of Afghanistan is collateral damage. Or, to put it another way, a little hors d'oeuvre before they move on to the next course – Somalia, Yemen or, most worryingly of all, Iraq? The latter is already being openly touted in Washington as a possibility for the 'second stage' and tension is growing in the Gulf region. Meanwhile, as far as the US is concerned, the UK with its nation-building agenda, the UN and everyone else is welcome to spend their soldiers' lives on the onerous task of clearing up the mess the US bombing has left behind, freeing it to concentrate on the next task.

All this strengthens the view that what we have to fear from September 11 is not just Islamist fanaticism, but the US response to it. Indeed, the latter could well prove a far greater threat to the stability of many countries, further stoking the Islamist fanaticism it seeks to extinguish. The template has been developed in Afghanistan: lavish bribery of neighbours, unchecked deployment of vicious military hardware, keep US soldiers out of it and use others to do the fighting. It is a foreign policy of brute force and it draws legitimacy within the US from a lethal combination of three factors: a profound sense of righteous anger, the reality of unchallenged economic and military power and a pervasive ignorance of and indifference to the rest of the world.

To increase the danger, the US actions are unchecked by fear of another superpower and, at present, unchecked by its usually vibrant civil society where debate about the purposes or methods of the war against terrorism has been cowed into virtual silence in the mainstream. The result is that an ugly ruthlessness is creeping into US political culture. For example, 'physical interrogation' or torture is proposed in the columns of *Newsweek* while President Bush signs an order allowing military tribunals of suspected terrorists in private and without a jury, for the first time since the Second World War.

In time we may come to see the disastrous timing of a right-wing presidency intent on asserting US unilateralism assuming power shortly before September 11: that tragic catastrophe provided the moral mandate at home and the freedom for manoeuvre from allies for such a unilateralist policy. For all the US needed Western support for its war, we seem to have been singularly unsuccessful in extracting in return any compromises on US unilateralism. Putin's protestations on NMD were brushed off, and barely a murmur was raised in criticism of the US's failure to deliver its climate change plan while the world went ahead in Marrakesh.

From the start, this administration was unabashed, denying any sense of responsibility to anyone other than its own citizens. Now, everyone has the almighty headache of how they are to tiptoe round and placate this raging colossus. Blair, white with exhaustion, opted for the role of chief cheerleader, and while it may incense some that Britain, like every other country, was reduced to such impotence, the harsh reality is that it was AOS – all options stink. Bush will use and discard Blair, and the British prime minister is likely to be one among many casualties.

The Labour Party has traditionally been deeply split over the conduct of US foreign policy. Vietnam, Central and Latin America and the Iran-Contra affair all provoked intense controversy. That was bad enough, but we were not involved in playing the supporting role. At the risk of further incensing my American correspondents, the manipulation of the CIA in Central America could come to seem like child's play compared with what we are likely to glimpse over the next decade.

This is an edited version of *Comment* articles first published in the *Guardian* on October 15, October 18 and November 19, 2001.

'TERRORISM', 'WAR' AND DEMOCRACY COMPROMISED
Paul Foot

Samson the terrorist

The most powerful case for individual terrorism comes from the Old Testament. It is the story of Samson, the mighty warrior who was betrayed by his lover, and then blinded and imprisoned by his enemies, the Philistines. Moshe Machover, an Israeli dissident, provided the relevant passage from the Book of Judges, Chapter 16, reminding me that the story is widely taught to Israeli children 'as an act of heroism on Samson's part'. Moshe prefers to read it as a 'useful antidote against Islamophobia and Judaeo-Christian arrogance'.

Certainly the Philistines in the story, as they taunt and mock the tortured warrior, come across as almost exact replicas of the Murdochs, the Conrad Blacks, the BBC foreign news chiefs and everyone else who refuses to understand the difference in the Middle

East between the violence of conquerors, exploiters and oppressors on the one hand and the violence of the conquered, exploited and oppressed on the other.

On the night of their triumph over Samson, the Philistine leaders celebrated and got drunk. 'And it came to pass, when their hearts were merry, that they said: "Call for Samson, that he may make us sport." And they called for Samson out of the prison house, and he made them sport: and they set him between the pillars. And Samson said unto the lad that held him by the hand: "Suffer me that I may feel the pillars whereupon the house standeth, that I may lean upon them."

'Now the house was full of men and women; and all the lords of the Philistines were there; and there were upon the roof about three thousand men and women that beheld while Samson made sport. And Samson called unto the Lord and said: "O Lord God, remember me, I pray thee, and strengthen me, I pray thee, only this once, O God, that I may be avenged of the Philistines for my two eyes."

'And Samson took hold of the two middle pillars upon which the house stood, of the one with his right hand and of the other with his left. And Samson said: "Let me die with the Philistines." And he bowed himself with all his might; and the house fell upon the lords and upon all the people that were therein. So the dead which he slew at his death were more than they which he slew in his life.'

I agree with Moshe that this story is a moving reminder to tyrants that their power and arrogance can never be taken for granted, but I think it would be a pity if all those Israeli schoolchildren, or anyone else for that matter, took it as an argument for individual terrorism. As a guide to that question, I much prefer the advice of Leon Trotsky who became a socialist largely out of hostile reaction to the individual terrorism and assassinations practised by so many rebels against Russian tsarism in his youth.

All his life, Trotsky argued against individual terrorism. He sympathised with the motives of the terrorists, and demanded their release from captivity. But he eloquently resisted what he called the 'seductive symmetry' of the argument that if terror is feasible for rulers, it is appropriate for those who challenge their rulers. Terror, he argued, is essential to arbitrary power, but not to the opponents of arbitrary power, for three main reasons. First, it leads almost inevitably to the deaths or injuries of innocent people, many of them victims of exploitation and arbitrary power. Second, terrorist acts are followed inevitably by more violence and more oppression from the authorities. Third, most crucially, acts of terror divert the attention of the masses away from collective action. They spread the illusion that single acts of violence, especially if they are dramatic or courageous, can replace the collective action of the masses.

According to Trotsky, 'The more the attention of the masses is focused on terrorist acts, the more those acts reduce the interests of the masses in self-organisation and self-education. But the smoke from the explosion clears away, the panic disappears, life again settles into the old rut, the wheel of capitalist exploitation turns as before; only police repression grows more savage and brazen. And as a result, in place of the kindled hopes and artificially aroused excitement comes disillusion and apathy.'

The conclusion was plain. 'In our eyes, individual terror is inadmissible precisely because it belittles the role of the masses in their own consciousness, reconciles them to their powerlessness and turns their eyes and hopes towards a great avenger and liberator who some day will come and accomplish their mission.' Trotsky wrote that nearly 100 years ago, long after the Old Testament. And he was even closer to the truth than Samson was.

A shabby excuse for democracy

There is not a shred of a case for the military action in Afghanistan, yet in the 'debate' in the House of Commons on October 8 not a single voice was raised against it. There was no motion and no vote. And although a few MPs are against the war, the only sign of dissidence was an isolated question from Alan Simpson warning that 'bombing will produce more terrorists than it kills'.

Clare Short, International Development Secretary and member of the War Cabinet (how far she has come from her humanitarian welfare work in Birmingham, where she started!) congratulated them on a 'high quality debate' whose main feature was 'a deep consensus'. It didn't seem to occur to her or anyone else that deep consensus is the curse of high quality debate, or that a single evening's discussion, full of gushing praise for Blair and Bush, cut short so that MPs, in the middle of the crisis, could slink off to continue their grossly extended holidays, was a pathetic apology for parliamentary democracy. Jenny Tonge, who only a few days previously had drawn applause from delegates at the Liberal Democrat party conference for her advice to the government to bomb Afghanistan with bread not bombs, enthusiastically supported the bombs option. 'The die has been cast', she said, drawing deeply on the well-worn Liberal thesaurus of clichés. 'The decision has been taken, I am sure, with far better intelligence than I have. Therefore, I support that decision and that action.'

No doubt the superior intelligence that convinced her was every bit as accurate as the intelligence that foresaw the New York atrocity and guarded against it. Geoffrey Robinson said he believed in the 'now widespread acceptance of the inevitable military action'. Perhaps he should read his own journal, the *New Statesman*, which sets out clearly and almost unanimously the case against the inevitability of military action.

Opponents of the bombing were challenged to provide alternatives. David Winnick said, 'The question for colleagues who oppose military action is simple. What alternative do they propose? The murderous network that we face can, like fascism, be appeased or fought. It is as simple as that.' Stephen Pound asked, 'If not this action, what action should be taken?'

There are plenty of answers to these questions, but very few got a decent airing in the debate. I cite a few. Stop subsidising the government of Israel. Stop appeasing the war criminal Sharon. The continuous breaches by Israel of United Nations resolutions, the constant seizure of other peoples' territory, the apparently everlasting persecution of the Palestinian people have been sustained by more economic and military aid from the US and Britain than has been bestowed on any other country on earth. Appeasement of Israel has been the lynchpin of US and British policy in the Middle East, and is obviously connected, at whatever distance, to the terrorist attacks on September 11. Yet the crucial importance of Palestine to the issue was emphasised by only one MP in the debate – John Austin.

Stop appeasing the Russian government over its murder and torture of the people of Chechnya. This subject got an honourable mention from Ian Taylor, who rejoiced that 'not least because of the events in Chechnya, Moscow is very much on side in attempting to find a solution to what has been going on in Afghanistan'. Stop bombing Iraq – hardly mentioned in the debate. Stop cuddling up to feudal and sexist dictatorships such as Pakistan and Saudi Arabia which are every bit as foul as the Taliban. Geoffrey Clifton-Brown said, 'One thinks with admiration of the bravery of General Musharraf of Pakistan.' No one seemed to disagree, or even protest that the brave general came to power in a military coup against an elected government.

Above all, stop siding with the rich of the world against the poor. From the Tory front bench Bernard Jenkin complained that the events of September 11 'shattered the illusion of a safe and comfortable world'. That world, including even North Essex, was neither safe nor comfortable. Its distinguishing characteristic was the vast wealth of the irresponsible and greedy few and the indescribable poverty, hunger and thirst of the many. That doesn't excuse the fanatical and suicidal terrorism of September 11. But it helps to explain it. And if the gap between rich and poor is allowed to grow, terrorism will grow too.

These alternatives do not require dropping a single bomb or killing a single innocent person. Every one of them would do more to combat terrorism than all the cruise missiles dropped on Kabul and Kandahar. Yet it was the bombing, not the alternatives to bombing, which secured the unanimous acclaim of the mother of parliaments.

Who now are Britain's guilty men?

The first I heard of Adam Ingram was when I spotted his name on a blacklist leaked to me at the *Daily Mirror* in 1987. The list, compiled by the Economic League, long since defunct, named 'subversives' who might cause trouble if employed. I was dismayed that my own name was not on the list and that Adam Ingram's was. He was a newly elected MP and seemed to have spent most of his early political life in the not entirely subversive environment of the East Kilbride Labour Party. I protested vigorously in the *Mirror* about this smear.

Now, however, Mr Ingram is minister for the armed forces, and likens those of us who oppose the war in Afghanistan to appeasers of Hitler in the 1930s. This theme was taken up by the government's chief whip, Hilary Armstrong, in her historic interview with Labour MP Paul Marsden. Last week the question – can opponents of the current war be compared to appeasers of Hitler? – was asked on the BBC's *Question Time*, but none of the five panellists answered it.

So here are one or two features about the situation in Afghanistan that seem to distinguish it from the situation in Europe in the late 1930s, and appear to have eluded Adam Ingram and Hilary Armstrong. By 1939, the population of Germany had grown to 86 million. The chief reason for its rapid growth was the annexation of the Rhineland (1936), Austria (1938), Czechoslovakia (1938) and Poland (1939). Afghanistan by contrast has a population (at most) of 25 million, at least a third of whom are starving. The population figures are going down all the time because hundreds of thousands of people are fleeing the country. As far as I can discover, the number of countries invaded or even threatened by Afghanistan is nil.

In 1939, Hitler and his colleagues had built the most powerful military machine in the world on the back of one of the three largest economies in the world. The German army had 100 divisions. In reserve, Hitler's special forces, the SA and SS, had 1.5 million members. The German Luftwaffe, only a few planes in 1933, could take on any other air force in the world. By contrast the Afghan armed forces rely almost entirely on third-rate weapons and museum-piece planes stolen years ago from the Russians or donated by the Americans.

While Hitler's forces aimed at annexation and attack, the Afghan armed forces are absorbed in defence against opponents in a civil war. While Hitler's armies, backed by the entire state machine of Germany, constituted a constant threat to all neighbouring states, the Afghan army does not threaten any other state. Indeed, the threat from Afghanistan does not come from the state at all, but from terrorists sheltered by the state. In these circumstances, any comparison between appeasement of Hitler in 1939 and opposition to the war in Afghanistan is crass to the point of imbecility. Pulverising an already pulverised country does not harm the terrorists harboured there – it builds support for them in other impoverished countries. It does not preserve the frightful images of September 11 – it obscures them in daily military blunders in Afghanistan.

These extracts are edited from Paul Foot's columns in the *Guardian* on September 18; October 16; October 30.

THE POLITICS OF MORALITY
Phil Scraton

If any government sponsors the outlaws and killers of innocents they have become outlaws and murderers themselves. And they will take that lonely path at their own peril.

George W Bush, October 7, 2001

Just three weeks into the bombardment of Afghanistan and US Republican senator, former challenger for the presidential nomination, John McCain defended the morality of the 'just war'. 'Shed a tear' for the suffering of the innocent, 'for all that will be lost when war claims its wages from us' and then 'get on with the business of killing our enemies as quickly as we can, and as ruthlessly as we must'.[1] The US had been attacked by 'a depraved, malevolent force that opposes our every interest and hates every value we hold dear'. Annihilation of all regimes that 'sponsor' terrorism was the clear objective for the full 'fury' of US military power. For McCain, as for Bush, the morality of uncompromising action rested on who struck the first blow: 'We did not cause this war. Our enemies did, and they are to blame for the deprivations and difficulties it occasions.' 'Loss of innocent life' and the 'geopolitical problems' brought about by US military action were entirely the responsibility of US 'enemies'. In order to assist in repairing the 'damage of war' the US first had to 'destroy the people who started it'. This bullish logic came as no surprise. It released the US and its allies from responsibility and accountability. They could bomb and destroy with impunity.

It was ironic, however, that Colin Powell, the military leader who came to prominence through action in the Balkans, appeared as the dove on the president's shoulder. Indeed, he seemed to grasp immediately that the bombing of relatively defenceless and already rubble-strewn cities and towns could prove to be the motivation for the emergence of further al-Qaida-style groups and for the long-term escalation of terror strategies. What was a surprise was Blair's naivete in toeing the Bush line. However qualified the language of Blair's conference speech, whatever the memorable sound bites on community, justice and civilisation, his support was unhesitating and unequivocal. How could he underestimate the realities of destruction, the killing of innocents, the impending starvation and the bitter consequences? Unleashing the tiger, the vicious, racist and homophobic messages scrawled on the bombs dropped by the US, amounted to short-term political opportunism to satiate the hunger for revenge. Voices of dissent were attacked remorselessly as terrorist sympathisers or appeasers. The Bush-Blair warning to nation-states that they were 'either with us or against us' extended to their citizens.

A confrontation between a little-known back-bench MP, Paul Marsden, and the Blair government's Chief Whip, Hilary Armstrong, provided a dramatic illustration of how dissenters would be treated. Marsden's objection, shared by a number of MPs and many constituents, was that the prime minister held no mandate to prosecute a war on the electorate's behalf without, at the very least, a parliamentary debate and vote. While Parliament would have given overwhelming support for military action, Marsden argued that denying an informed debate effectively silenced dissenting voices. Not an MP of left-wing credentials and destined to defect to the Liberal Democrats, Marsden broke ranks with his leadership both in the House of Commons and in numerous high profile media interviews.

Armstrong, keen to maintain the impression that within Labour ranks there was unanimity of purpose, told Marsden that he needed a few lessons in 'communication skills'.[2] She demanded a 'guarantee' that he would 'not talk to the media unless you speak to me first'. In the ensuing bitter exchange Armstrong dismissed Marsden's concerns over military action and the silencing of dissent. War, she stated, 'is not a matter of conscience'. Further, and more disturbing was a charge directed at, and undoubtedly beyond, Marsden: 'It was people like you who appeased Hitler in 1938.'

Apart from the misreading of the politics of 'appeasement', the exploitation of this comparison – not confined to Armstrong's outburst to Marsden – was profoundly offensive. It suggested that through raising valid, reasoned and humanitarian questions and doubts about the 'war on terror' in general and about bin Laden, al-Qaida and the Taliban regime in particular, critics not only had sympathy with Hitler and Nazism, but also with their atrocities. While Armstrong objected to her 'heat-of-the-moment' words being taken literally, the allegations of appeasement had a wider political and public constituency.

Blair and his senior ministers were quick to dissociate themselves from the Armstrong outburst. Yet, whatever Marsden's intentions and subsequent actions, members of the parliamentary Labour Party were left in no doubt that opposition to the Bush–Blair agenda would be neither respected nor tolerated within the Party's mainstream ranks. 'Opposers' had been classed as appeasers. There was no place for personal conscience. In other words, the morality of a 'just war' was the only 'morality'; a moral position established through the denial of conscience and the absence of discourse. To gain some understanding of the politics of morality which has come to play such a significant part in Blair's leadership, it is necessary to consider his longer-term 'crusade' for 'moral renewal'.

In February 1993 on Merseyside two ten-year-old children abducted and killed a two-year-old. It was an exceptional case. Yet, as politicians, media commentators and professional 'experts' disguised their adult prejudices as informed opinion, the atypical was elevated to the typical through a concerted appeal to stereotypes. The age of 'innocence' was over, 'evil' had prevailed. James Bulger's terrifying death was portrayed consistently as the severe end of a continuum of children's worsening behaviour. Its casual randomness was presented as evidence of societal complacency regarding the state of childhood and child-rearing. In this discourse a crisis in 'the family' was identified as nurturing a crisis in 'authority'. Its legacy was a 'crisis in childhood'.

Politicians of all persuasions competed for air-time and press interviews – determined, as Prime Minister John Major infamously put it, to 'punish a little more and understand a little less'. The Shadow Home Secretary produced his own, equally trite, sound bite. Tony Blair's mission statement, 'tough on crime and tough on the causes of crime', could be interpreted as progressive or reactionary. For Blair the issue was not political, nor legal, nor social, nor cultural, nor economic; it was *moral*. Presumably aware of the brutal circumstances in which the child died, Blair commented that they were 'like hammer blows against the sleeping conscience of the nation'.[3] Being 'tough' on causes and consequences, seemingly with no place for context, would challenge the 'moral vacuum' prevalent in British society. Learning, understanding and teaching the 'value of what is right and what is wrong' offered the only lasting safeguard against a spiralling descent into 'moral chaos'.

Six years later Prime Minister Blair delivered a rhetorical and impassioned speech to the Labour Party conference. Under his wing, guided by 'New' Labour 'Third Way' modernisers, his Party had been 'reborn'; socialists reincarnated as social democrats. Alongside this transformation, British strength and nationhood had been 'renewed'. 'Ours', he trumpeted, 'is a moral cause, best expressed through how we see our families and our children.' The appeal was for 'strong families cherished by a strong community'. It constituted 'a new, national moral purpose for this new generation'. A society 'without prejudice' but 'with rules, with a sense of order' could be delivered only through 'a partnership between government and the country …'. Such a partnership would 'lay the foundations of that moral purpose'.[4]

Tony Blair's 1999 morality tale responded to a media-hyped national outcry over two pre-teenage pregnancies. Again, the exceptional was utilised, even exploited, to play the morality card, a card that self-evidently trumps all others. For Blair 'morality' is a taken-for-granted state of well-being. It does not need explanation, it defies relativity and it presumes consensus. His very certainty over 'right' and 'wrong' exposes the simplicity and simple mindedness of moral absolutes. There are no grey areas, no contradictions and no different 'ways of seeing'. From this position it becomes all too easy to slide into the prejudice of 'otherness'; rejecting the 'moral' definitions, decisions and actions of others. While Blair's moral certainty might be attractive to Christian social democrats, his promotion of moral purpose and moral renewal is vacuous when devoid of context. Yet still he proclaims morality, still he envisions nationhood and, connected to these constructions, he defines and prescribes the boundaries of 'civilisation'.

As the fallout from the Marsden affair continued, the conduct of the war was increasingly questioned and scrutinised. Television news broadcast the devastation wreaked on civilians. Deaths, maiming and enforced homelessness were the visible evidence of the on-the-ground inaccuracy of the bombing. If the elimination of 'terror' was the objective it seemed a terrible irony that terror was etched deep in the faces of the children who had endured the first waves of military action. Red Cross warehouses were hit, not once but twice, and UN workers were killed when a bomb flattened their offices. Former Labour defence minister Peter Kilfoyle, hardly regarded a moderate, voiced his concerns over the 'indiscriminate damage' caused by the bombing.[5] He criticised the government's 'confusion' over 'its war aims and objectives'. Less than a month into military action and a 'wobble' in public and political confidence was clearly evident.

On October 27, at his Chequers weekend retreat, Tony Blair briefed journalists on a speech to be given to the Welsh Assembly a few days later. Immediately before his departure for the Middle East, he would affirm Britain as 'a very moral nation with a strong sense of right and wrong'.[6] Its inherent 'moral fibre' would 'defeat the fanaticism of these terrorists and their supporters'. To that end it was essential that Britain should 'stay the course' in support of the US. The morality of the military action lay in opposing and eliminating the 'maniacal and fanatical view of the world' held by al-Qaida, the Taliban and their supporters. He continued, 'Never forget why we have done this, never forget how we felt when we watched planes fly into the trade towers, never forget those answering phone messages, never forget how we imagined how mothers told their children they were going to die, never forget the firefighters and police who died trying to save others.'

By the time Blair delivered the speech, no doubt informed by reaction to the briefing, much of the assertiveness and superior tone

regarding Britain as a 'moral nation' had evaporated, making way
for a less self-righteous slant. He stated that 'they [meaning bin
Laden and al-Qaida] have one hope: that we are decadent, that we
lack the moral fibre, or will, or courage, to take them on'. In accom-
modating critics of the war, he commented that 'no one who raises
doubts is an appeaser or a faint heart'.[7] The government messages
were now mixed. Blair was heavily criticised for briefing to a speech
'of high emotion and Churchillian defiance' which was then watered
down. Yet while he acknowledged the right to criticise the war
strategy, his Foreign Secretary, Jack Straw, lambasted the media for
fermenting opposition.

A day later and Tony Blair was in Syria. It provided President
Bashar al-Assad with a unique platform to condemn the US-led
military action. While rejecting terrorism, he considered it necessary
to 'differentiate between terrorism and war'.[8] Drawing a distinction
between 'resistance and terrorism' he classified Hamas, Hezbollah
and the PLO not as terrorists but as resistance fighters. Resistance,
he argued 'is a social, religious and legal right ... safeguarded by UN
resolutions'. He went on to denounce Israel's use of 'state terrorism'.
This led directly to how, in the current crisis, the West had constructed terrorism; not as 'a network' but in the identity of Osama
bin Laden. Terrorism 'does not have a certain head, either as a person
or in terms of an organisation'. Whatever claims were made for
'behind the scenes' diplomacy, Blair (seen by many as some kind of
US envoy to the Middle East) suffered political humiliation from the
rostrum of a leader already openly hostile to US intervention and
supportive of the Palestinian cause.

While Syria's human rights record remains abysmal, with political
dissent and media criticism sufficient to bring imprisonment to
activists and journalists, Blair's visit lent credibility to its regime
albeit in the context of diplomacy. In his defence, his trip to Syria
and to Saudi Arabia, Jordan, Israel as well as his meeting with Yasser
Arafat were about establishing a dialogue. Obviously, he was under
no illusions about the likely response at each meeting. Yet there was
no public 'dialogue' with President Bashar al-Assad. Rather, Blair was
served a reminder, reinforced by his reception in Saudi Arabia, that
constructing and popularising a 'war on terror', derived in defining,
then occupying, the moral high ground, misrepresented the
complexity of competing interests and material struggles. Replacing
moral relativism with moral certainty followed a familiar pattern of
cultural imperialism. Assad was given a rare opportunity to lecture

the West on the naivete and offensiveness of its crusading rhetoric, on the deep resentment felt throughout the Middle East concerning inferred superiority of Western 'civilisation' and on the Israeli settlement programme including the occupation of Palestinian areas. He grasped the worldwide, front-page opportunity with both hands.

So concerted was the subsequent criticism of the wisdom of Blair's visit to Syria that his communications director, Alistair Campbell, briefed journalists and gave a forthright 'no regrets' response.[9] Nothing, it seemed, had been learnt from the episode. Campbell, typically direct, referred to the meetings with Arab leaders as 'eyeball to eyeball'. He reminded reporters that the 'battle that we are engaged in is with a combination of a dictatorship and a bunch of terrorists'. Far from calming the situation, Campbell's briefing simply fuelled what Ahdaf Soveif notes as a 'general incredulity' among Arabs 'at Tony Blair's gung-ho stance and Britain's seeming eagerness to be part of the conflict'.[10]

The problem, according to Tony Blair, his Chief Whip and his Director of Communications and Strategy, was not the short- or long-term consequences of military intervention against 'terrorism', whatever the impending outcome in Afghanistan. It lay with those political commentators and journalists who refused to grasp the issues, deliberately misled their audience and who undermined the moral, civilising objectives of the combined political, humanitarian and military strategies. Following the 'liberation' of Kabul from Taliban rule, and its handover to the notoriously divided Northern Alliance, Alistair Campbell attacked the 'corrosive negativism' of newspaper and broadcast journalism. The media had underestimated the intelligence of the 'British people'. Kabul's fall could not be interpreted as 'anything other than a very good day for the coalition, for Afghanistan and for its people'.[11]

That the Taliban had been routed beyond question was a positive development. It was a regime of execution, torture and terror legitimated within by its own combination of moral certainty and religious interpretation. Yet its presence, growth and consolidation was indebted to the initial support and eventual indifference of the West. Campbell's 'anything but good' statement overlooked the more profound contextual issues of recent history: the role of the US, of the CIA in particular, in Afghanistan; the appropriateness and consequences of ruthless bombardment; the suitability of the Northern Alliance as the foundation on which to establish democratic rule; the viability of a 'new world order' comprising a community of nations with a Bush-led US administration at the helm; the full implications throughout the Middle East and Asia of a permanent 'war on terror'; the significance and outcomes of the authoritarian shifts within the US, the UK and Europe including special powers and internment; the Palestinian question.

As the UK government expressed delight at the speed of the Taliban's demise the lecture given just weeks earlier by Syrian President Bashar al-Assad to Prime Minister Blair seemed forgotten. Whether Western states liked it or not, he articulated a position held by many, and growing, throughout the Middle East and Asia. His message could not have been more direct: if you engage in a politics there are no certainties, there are no absolutes. And that position was courageously adopted by some of the families bereaved by the September 11 attacks. Writing to the US president as the bombing of Afghanistan began Phyllis and Orlando Rodriguez stated: 'Your response to the attack does not make us feel better about our son's [Gregory] death … It makes us feel our government is using our son's memory for justification to cause suffering for other sons and parents in other lands.'[12]

1. McCain, John, 'Hit them even harder', *Guardian*, October 30, 2001, p. 17.
2. The transcript of this meeting, as recorded by Paul Marsden, first appeared in the *Mail on Sunday*, October 21, 2001.
3. *Guardian*, February 20, 1993.
4. *Observer*, September 5, 1999.
5. *Guardian*, October 29, 2001.
6. *Observer*, October 28, 2001.
7. *Guardian*, October 31, 2001.
8. *Guardian*, November 1, 2001.
9. *Guardian*, November 3, 2001.
10. Soveif, Ahdaf, 'Nile Blues', *G2*, November 6, 2001, p. 2.
11. Campbell, Alistair, Letter to the Editor, *Guardian*, November 15, 2001.
12. *Observer*, October 14, 2001.

REPRESENTATIONS OF TERROR IN THE LEGITIMATION OF WAR

Eileen Berrington

Initial reports of major disasters and their tragic circumstances powerfully define the key issues, shaping understanding and constructing a collective memory. Flying hijacked passenger airliners into each of the World Trade Center (WTC) towers and, almost simultaneously, the Pentagon, constituted acts beyond imagination. Happening, as they did, in the heart of the most advanced telecommunications system in the world, these unfolding disasters were covered internationally via live broadcasts. While footage of the first WTC explosion came from an amateur hand-held video, media professionals filmed the second from every conceivable angle. By the time newspapers were published people throughout the world had witnessed the scenes of death and destruction, seen people jumping from windows and heard of victims frantically contacting families moments before their certain death.

Inevitably the images published in the press reflected the intensity of the disasters, the horror of survivors and the distress of victims' families. Given the instantly recognisable Manhattan skyline, the collapsed buildings of the WTC, plumes of smoke and the intensity of the flames became the focus of attention. As if to emphasise the significance of the WTC at the economic heart of global capitalism, the *Sun* proclaimed September 11 as the DAY THAT CHANGED THE WORLD. The full-page photograph showed the WTC in flames shortly after the second aircraft exploded. The *Daily Star* used a similar picture, the image cropped, bringing the flames and smoke into close-up. The paper offered its readers a SPECIAL EDITION ON THE WORST TERRORIST OUTRAGE IN HISTORY. IS THIS THE END OF THE WORLD? asked the front page, adding, BIG APPLE HORROR PUTS US ON THE BRINK OF WAR.

The *Daily Mail* led with a distance shot across the Hudson River, depicting the volumes of smoke but no flames. The headline was stark: APOCALYPSE NEW YORK. SEPTEMBER 11, 2001. The *Daily Express* promised THE MOST COMPLETE AND UP-TO-DATE COVERAGE. Its front page used a close-up of the WTC engulfed in flames and smoke, adding a white overlay: DECLARATION OF WAR. The *Guardian*, *Independent* and *The Times* used the same image – black smoke rising from the towers, flames and falling debris. The newspapers' respective headlines were A DECLARATION OF WAR; DOOMSDAY AMERICA THOUSANDS KILLED AFTER HIJACKED AIRLINERS DESTROY WORLD TRADE CENTER AND SMASH INTO PENTAGON and WAR COMES TO AMERICA.

On September 13 the *Independent* led with THE AMERICAN DREAM IN RUINS and a picture of the 'smouldering debris' at the WTC site. America was involved in a dual search – for survivors and for those who had carried out the attack. A strap above the paper's masthead carried the pronouncement DOOMSDAY: THE AFTERMATH. GOOD WILL PREVAIL OVER EVIL, promised *The Times*, while the *Guardian* announced that US RALLIES THE WEST FOR ATTACKS ON AFGHANISTAN. There was a small photograph of Mohamed Atta, one of the dead hijackers. All three papers included inner supplements with lengthy discussion and photographs. The *Mirror* included 'a 36-page picture record' of the disaster. President Bush was featured on the front page alongside stark headlines: WAR; BUSH VOWS TO CRUSH A NEW AND DEADLY ENEMY and BLAIR BACKS HIM AND FEARS 100S OF BRITS DEAD.

Early the following week, when the military action promised in the immediate aftermath by President Bush had not yet materialised, Osama bin Laden's image appeared on front pages. I WANT HIS HEAD ON A PLATTER, declared the US vice-president, Dick Cheney (*Mirror*, September 17). The *Daily Star* issued a warning to Afghanistan: GIVE HIM UP OR WE BOMB YOU, as BUSH AND BLAIR UNITE TO FIGHT. A simulation of a 'Wild West' poster appeared the following day with a picture of Osama bin Laden, WANTED DEAD OR ALIVE (*Mirror*, September 18). President Bush's picture was incorporated into the paper's masthead. The *Daily Star* used the same headline, adding that there was a FIVE MILLION DOLLAR REWARD. Bin Laden was 'in the sights' of Britain's élite military force: SAS WE'LL TAKE HIM OUT (*Daily Express*). The *Sun* took a very different approach, using a colour picture of a vigil in Las Vegas. A photogenic four-year-old was on her father's shoulders, with 'Tears in her eyes' and 'the Star-Spangled Banner in her hand'. GOD BLESS AMERICA, proclaimed the headline, asking readers to FLY THE FLAG and observe three minutes' silence at 11 a.m.

The imagery, tone and style of reporting provided only one context and outcome: 'terrorism' and 'war'. An attack of such magnitude on the United States would have global repercussions. Even in a largely secular society there was an assumption that people would understand the biblical references and ideological associations. While they might not have the degree of religious significance they once had, such imagery is embedded in popular culture, through films, drama and fiction. The difference now was that this was reality and that on September 11 there was no all-American hero saving the day.

Yet even at this early stage in the reporting process there was sensationalism, dramatisation and exaggeration of events that were in themselves so horrific that they needed no embellishment. The same processes were discernible in official statements by President Bush, senior officials and a range of (Western) world leaders, notably the UK prime minister, Tony Blair. This was 'an attack', 'terrorism'; it was 'unprovoked'. Therefore the US was justified, even compelled, to respond with aggression. That this could be interpreted as retaliatory action for any number of instances of Western, but particularly US, military or political intervention or oppression around the world did not figure in political, popular or populist discourses. Events on September 11 were firmly categorised within the context of war atrocities. In terms of media coverage, therefore, there was recourse primarily to the conventions and templates relating to war reporting rather than those typically associated with reporting disaster or tragedy.

Reporting war and conflict follows particular, general patterns, depending on who is depicted as 'victim' or 'aggressor'. So in the West, events involving Western aggression or military intervention are typically represented as regrettable but necessary to preserve or restore some greater good. Armed conflict is seen as a last resort, as an obligation on the part of powerful Western democracies to support the powerless and oppressed, to protect or restore freedom and democratic processes. The 'other side', therefore, becomes automatically aligned with injustice, 'wrong' and 'evil'. There are expectations that the domestic media will adopt a 'patriotic' stance. Accounts of civilian deaths or injuries caused by Western military action are denied if possible, or recontextualised where denial becomes unsustainable. Phrases like 'collateral damage' dehumanise and depersonalise, particularly when placed alongside the personal biographies of 'our' casualties – servicemen (and, occasionally, women) and their families.

Expectations of media compliance and acquiescence are often underpinned by formal and informal means. For example, during the Falklands/Malvinas conflict between Britain and Argentina in 1982, the Ministry of Defence reluctantly agreed to permit a small number of carefully selected journalists to accompany the Task Force to the South Atlantic. All reports were sent via the Ministry; there were no independent means of transmission. Decisions about withholding or forwarding information, therefore, ultimately lay with the military, but the process was ideologically legitimised under the auspices of national and operational security. This was the formal means of exercising control over the information supply.

But journalists also became caught up in jingoism and nationalism. Increasingly, many found themselves identifying with their 'comrades' – the military personnel with whom they travelled, lived and on whom their survival depended. As David Morrison has commented, journalists in such situations are 'not removed from the pressures and forces of the drama that is going on around them'. So some journalists become, or see themselves as, participants in rather than detached observers of conflict. Self-censorship is a feature of reporting, creating additional opportunities for sanitised news representations through informal means, while further limiting the representation of alternative views.

In addition, there are some news events where, even without such strictures and difficulties, it is difficult to express 'alternative' views without appearing callous or insensitive. Reporting that appears to 'side with the enemy' leads to accusations that journalists, publications or programmes are apologists for the inexcusable; supporters of terrorism and unpatriotic. During their Falklands coverage and discussion, the BBC programme *Panorama* was robustly attacked for presenting 'Argentine' views. Did the programme makers not know where their loyalties ought to lie? In a similar vein, discussion of September 11 in a special edition of BBC1's *Question Time* led to an apology to the former US ambassador to Britain by the BBC director-general. Expression of anti-American views by some members of the audience was 'regrettable'. Live transmission was 'inappropriate' and the programme should have been recorded and edited before screening to prevent offence.

It is significant that despite the uniqueness of September 11 newspaper reports fit easily into the established frames and templates of journalism. In addition to the conventions of war reporting, the use of ideological cues and the invocation of folk devils and moral panics are immediately apparent. Certain words, phrases and images, through repetition, conjure up a range of emotions and associations. They become a form of mental shorthand and, quite literally, word association. Right from the start particular key themes were foregrounded. 'Middle Eastern' terrorists are popular folk devils who feature in news, current affairs and foreign policy, but are also the subject of cultural transmission. 'Us' against 'them', 'good' *versus* 'evil', democracy intervening to free the enslaved – all are popular themes in film and TV entertainment. Given Western, globalised media ownership and control, it is of little surprise that the 'good guys' are overwhelmingly white and/or American; that the 'bad guys' are typically depicted as visibly 'foreign', by appearance, accent or through stereotyped 'cultural' characteristics. Audiences have come to expect that the 'good guy', because he is invariably a man, no matter how heavily outnumbered and lacking in firepower, will prevail and will, through force, restore 'order' and rescue the helpless.

Media reporting is quick to personalise stories. In relation to crime there are individuals whose behaviour attracts such widespread condemnation that 'folk devil' is too benign a label to apply. Those committing particularly horrific crimes are frequently demonised and dehumanised, their crimes explained as 'evil' acts by 'evil' people. Yet even within this category, there are those whose offences are seen as demonstration of the essence of who they are and what they represent. These are 'the monsters' of their time – groups (for instance, 'paedophiles') and individuals, such as Pol Pot, Colonel Qaddafi and Saddam Hussein. After September 11 there were new monsters, whose names, Osama bin Laden and the al-Qaida network were very quickly on every presenter's lips and in newspapers across the world. There was now a direct, focused target for blame and retribution; vague 'Middle Eastern terrorism' was supplanted as the US military gaze and the world's attention became firmly fixed on Afghanistan. Bin Laden's image became instantly familiar and recognisable; his name tripped increasingly easily off the tongue both in the US and in Britain.

What is omitted from news representations, however, is as significant as what is highlighted. Early accounts failed to inform audiences that bin Laden's training camps, where it was alleged the September 11 atrocities had been nurtured if not actually planned, owed their existence to US political intervention. While Afghanistan was under Soviet occupation, the CIA actively encouraged and financially supported 'freedom fighters' in their struggles against their oppressor. The film *Rocky 3*, starring Sylvester Stallone, arguably one of the most easily identifiable symbols of American military muscle, is dedicated to the 'brave people' of Afghanistan. Britain also played its part in creating bin Laden the 'monster', with the SAS providing specialised training for his followers.

Political alliances change when former 'brothers-in-arms' become powerful and no longer reliant on outside intervention or support. They develop new allegiances; enemies become friends and vice versa. Decontextualised news reports blur the history and origins of conflict (for example, different versions and explanations of the situation in 'Northern Ireland'). No explanation is offered or, initially, at least, demanded, other than that Osama bin Laden and the 'extremist' Islamic Taliban rulers of Afghanistan are to blame. Bin Laden and his associates must be hunted down and 'brought to justice'. There is an immediate call for alignment – those governments who support bin Laden, however marginally, become equally culpable. They too are enemies of the US state. They become potential targets of retributive justice in whatever form the US decides it will be administered. First news reports included discussion and debate over which world leaders had and, more significantly, had not, aligned themselves with the US. Expressions of sympathy were no longer sufficient; battle lines were being drawn.

Popular stereotypes and assumptions are easily invoked. In relation to the possibility of further attacks, there were a number of distinguishing features to 'assist' in identifying potential enemies, based on nationality, perceived identity, culture and the politics of appearance. Were people whose ethnic origins were Middle Eastern 'trustworthy' or were they 'enemies within'? Even if they were US citizens, was that enough? Which was the defining influence that would guide their actions and cement their loyalty – nationality or religion? Under such conditions, racism – never far from the surface – finds fertile ground. The familiar rhetoric and fear of 'strangers in our midst' are invoked. Resentment, suspicion and hostility grow, and are encouraged, however indirectly and inadvertently, by media messages and political pronouncements. Violence, threats and intimidation become a feature of interpersonal relations. The consequences can be catastrophic, as evidenced in Rwanda, Sri Lanka and throughout the former Yugoslavia, where the euphemism 'ethnic cleansing' obscures the reality of politics of racism and prejudice and their devastating effects.

As the weeks passed there was a gradual, albeit limited, emergence of alternative views within mainstream media reporting. This offered a degree of challenge to initial one-dimensional, simplistic, unsophisticated accounts that offered one explanation alone, assuming a unanimous response from audiences. What happened on September 11 was exceptional and horrific. Such actions cannot be justified. The difficulty lies in locating what happened in its wider context, not to be disrespectful or lacking in sympathy, but in terms of understanding. Simplistic depictions of 'good' and 'evil' provided the US with the legitimacy to invade and attack. Rational, considered analysis offers scope for alternative ways of seeing and responding. Was military action to exact retribution, revenge or 'justice' the only viable response?

At the time of writing, there is a dawning awareness that the show of force by the US and its close allies has not achieved its promised objective. Osama bin Laden has been neither captured nor killed, despite the defeat of Afghanistan's Taliban rulers. Instead, the outcomes of the military assault are civilian casualties, further division, hostility and resentment. This creates or exacerbates the conditions within which the kind of views that underpinned what happened on September 11 will flourish. In any conflict, each side has its own victims, martyrs and sense of grievance. No single nation-state has the monopoly on nationalism, patriotism or self-sacrifice.

'EITHER YOU ARE WITH US, OR YOU ARE WITH THE TERRORISTS': THE WAR'S HOME FRONT
Jude McCulloch

The declaration of 'war on terrorism' and the United States' military attack on Afghanistan in the wake of September 11 led to a chorus of dissent and cautionary warnings around the world. There is no doubting that the attack on Afghanistan had the potential to result in the deaths of hundreds of thousands of Afghans, whose only sin was to live in one of the world's most impoverished countries under one of the world's harshest and most repressive regimes. The inevitable civilian deaths fuelled anti-Western and particularly anti-American sentiment, inspiring attacks of the type that the military strikes are apparently aimed at preventing. With the calamity surrounding the international situation it is little wonder that the repressive domestic security measures that are part of the 'war on terrorism' have received little attention. Nevertheless these domestic developments demand attention: they pose a serious threat to freedom from state terror and are likely to prove just as counter-productive in repressing 'terrorism' as the international military strategy. In addition they impact on people's ability to engage in dissent and build an anti-war movement powerful enough to halt escalating military action.

Since the mid-1970s, and particularly post-Cold War, terrorism – along with the 'war on drugs' and organised crime – has provided the main rationale for major changes to national security arrangements in English-speaking democracies. These changes have seen sections of the military increasingly integrated into 'internal security', the militarisation of police, and the granting of more resources and powers to agencies involved in gathering intelligence on citizens. Traditionally the police and military have had separate roles, with the police involved in domestic law enforcement and peacekeeping, and the military confined to use against external enemies in times of war. This separation is important because the military operate under a philosophy of maximum force aimed at killing and defeating an enemy whereas the police are duty bound to use only minimum force against individual suspects protected by due process rights. Martial law implies the suspension of legal rights, while using the military against citizens and a close ideological and operational alliance between the police and military are usually associated with repressive regimes. The 'war on terrorism' marks an escalation and intensification in the militarisation of law enforcement and the decline in civil liberties. Measures implemented or seriously contemplated in the United Kingdom, United States and Australia include detention without trial, removal of the right to silence and legal representation, eavesdropping on lawyer–client communications, use of torture and drugs to force confessions, increased surveillance and reduced privacy protections, and vastly expanded resources to those sections of the military and paramilitary police involved in 'homeland' security.

By linking increases of the state's coercive capacities to shocking acts of violence like the September 11 attacks, governments cynically exploit popular fear, anxiety and paranoia. Within the binary frameworks of 'with us or against us' and 'good versus evil' opponents of government policy – journalists, academics, politicians, public figures and activists – are vilified, censured, marginalised and punished, so that criticism is muted if not silenced altogether. It is clear, however, that domestic 'anti-terrorist' measures are not simply a response to events but are instead proactive measures coinciding with the trend towards an increasingly repressive state. History demonstrates that 'anti-terrorist' measures announced after bombings, hijackings, and assassinations have sometimes been implemented in secret by government months and even years previously. At the very least the measures fit comfortably with government policy directions and demands for greater powers and resources by police, military and security agencies. Events like those of September 11 simply provide an opportune political climate to announce changes that might otherwise be rejected as too draconian.

Another result of publicly linking repressive measure to events like the hijack/bombings in the United States is that it creates the false impression that the measures will be confined to dealing with these types of violent and extreme events. However, in police, military and security circles terrorism is not confined to violent and extreme acts but extends to include dissent and political and industrial activism of all kinds. According to counter-terrorist theory it is 'but a short step from a march to a bomb': terrorism and political activism are seen as part of a continuum. Legislation recently passed in the United States defines domestic terrorism as any dangerous or unlawful activity that is intended 'to influence the policy of a government by intimidation or coercion'. The definition is broad enough to encompass a whole range of political activities. In Australia, consistent with the continuum view of terrorism, the military has contingency plans to set up detention centres to counter threats, including 'mass demonstrations', 'industrial political and social disturbances' and 'terrorism'. Counter-terrorist theory also maintains that community, non-government, and activist organisations frequently – knowingly or otherwise – serve as fronts for terrorist organisations. Terrorism thus provides a pretext for spying on, harassing, incarcerating and even killing people engaged in doing things that many take for granted as rights available to citizens in a democracy. In addition, measures initially justified on the need to counter terrorism are progressively normalised and integrated into everyday policing and security operations.

In Australia, consistent with trends in the United Kingdom and United States, 'counter-terrorist' paramilitary police are now used regularly in a range of policing operations. The paramilitary units train with the military, include former members of the military and use a range of military equipment and weaponry. Since their establishment in the mid-1970s, apart from using extreme levels of force in their own operations, the units have had a profound impact on the overall nature of policing, acting as trainers and role models for other police. Paramilitary tactics that emphasise confrontation and high levels of force have become routine, with the result that weapons and methods that were once justified on the basis of countering terrorism are now seen as part of normal police response. One symptom of the militarisation of policing in Australia has been an increase in the number of fatal shootings by police, as police have become more philosophically attuned and more tactically adept at the soldier's craft of killing. Another symptom is the increasingly militarised approach to demonstrations. Protesters are not seen as citizens who may be breaking the law and subject to arrested and charge, but instead as 'the enemy within', to be defeated by use of overwhelming force.

'Counter-terrorist' police are regularly involved in spying on community and activist groups and recording the identity of those attending demonstrations. If military detention centres are established, police intelligence gathered at demonstrations and through surveillance and infiltration of social movements will be used to screen and clear 'persons of good character'. The whole tone of the military document outlining the arrangements for detention indicates that 'good character' and dissenting political opinions are considered mutually exclusive categories. Amendments to the Australian Defence Act, passed in the lead up to the Sydney 2000 Olympics, although promoted as necessary to deal with terrorist threats surrounding the Games, open the way for the federal government to call out the troops in the case of political demonstrations or industrial disputes.

States, through the military and the police, have enormous capacity to coerce citizens and inflict violence on individuals. The history of counter-terrorism demonstrates that it is frequently a source of terror far greater in viciousness and pervasiveness than the terror it is ostensibly countering. After the military regime was ousted in Argentina in the early 1980s a commission of inquiry concluded that the 'terrorism' of the military regime was 'infinitely worse' than the terror they were allegedly combating. Despite this, commentators, scholars and the media tend to adopt the categories of terrorism and counter-terrorism promoted by government with the result that state terrorism – murder, police violence, sexual assault, torture, illegal arrests and detention, and legal arrest and detention based on political activity, ethnicity, race or class background (in other words kidnapping or hostage-taking) – are ignored altogether or at least permitted to masquerade as 'counter-terrorism'. The state's ability to label people as terrorists or terrorist sympathisers, no matter how absurd or far-fetched, works to position those so labelled as non-citizens, outside the moral community, to whom human rights bear no relevance.

Apart from the reality that 'counter-terrorism' is terrorism, it may also inspire the type of terrorist acts it is said to be preventing. When more peaceful avenues for political dissent are cut off or repressed, movements will not disappear but may instead become more clandestine and violent. It is well established that in Northern Ireland the incarceration of hundreds of Republicans without charge under internment in 1971 moved many away from political protest and civil disobedience and created support for the IRA. The British military's tactics directed at 'getting the hard men', created 'more hard men to get'. Apart from exacerbating existing tensions, the intensification of state violence under the guise of counter-terrorism can motivate revenge attacks. On the second anniversary of the death of more than 80 people, including 27 children, at Waco, Texas in an assault by the FBI, Timothy McVeigh blew up a federal building in Oklahoma City, killing 168 men, women and children. In a letter to Gore Vidal, McVeigh explains that: 'Foremost, the bombing was a retaliatory strike: a counter-attack ... From the formation of such units as the FBI's "Hostage Rescue" and other assault teams amongst federal agencies during the 80s, culminating in the Waco incident, federal actions grew increasingly militaristic and violent, to the point where at Waco, our government – like the Chinese – was deploying tanks against its own citizens ... For all intents and purposes, federal agents had become "soldiers".'[1] Such revenge actions are themselves likely to lead to further 'anti-terrorist' measures – President Clinton signed the Anti-Terrorism Act in the wake of the Oklahoma City bombing – resulting in an escalating cycle of attack and counter-attack.

Increasing state repression is not primarily a response, much less a solution to terrorist attacks and threats. The escalation of state repression is associated with globalisation, the waning of a nationally defined capitalist class and the ascendancy of a new international class with global interests. The military capacity of nations is being turned inwards because it suits the interests of multinational capital. Internal tensions have intensified as nation-states increasingly abandon principle of social and wage justice in an effort to attract and retain mobile international capital. Conflict is also arising between nation-states and those participating in organised resistance against the decline in living standards, degradation of the environment and increasing inequality within and between states. Citizens responding to and resisting the negative impacts of globalisation are the 'enemy within' which states seek to put down by the use of force. While many understand that globalisation involves a 'race to the bottom' in terms of labour and environmental standards it is less widely understood that it involves a similar downward race in terms of the value states put on the lives of citizens. The blurring of the line between the police and military, common in emerging democracies and militarised states, is a growing feature of established democracies where paramilitary policing is on the rise and the military is taking a greater role in 'internal security'.

The history of state terror illustrates that counter-terrorism is used to punish, intimidate and disappear politically inconvenient citizens. In the 'war on terrorism' politically inconvenient citizens will include peace and anti-war activists. In the words of President Bush, 'Either you are with us, or you are with the terrorists.' In the same way that social justice aspirations and anti-war sentiment were previously associated with communism, such sentiments will be equated with terrorism during the new war: anti-terrorism is the new McCarthyism.

1. Letter by Timothy McVeigh quoted in Gore Vidal (2001) 'The meaning of Timothy McVeigh' in *Vanity Fair*, September 2001, pp. 129–35; 191–97 at p. 192.

RESISTANCE AND TERROR: LESSONS FROM IRELAND
Bill Rolston

In November 2001, Tony Blair came under pressure for ignoring domestic issues while jetting around the world as ambassador for the US bombing of Afghanistan. In response, a new spin was put on his involvement, pulling together the domestic and international. Toby Harnden of the *Daily Telegraph* announced that 'America is to draw on Britain's 30 years of experience in dealing with the IRA in its battle against terrorism'.[1]

US Homeland Security Director Tom Ridge pointed out that Britain 'is a country that unfortunately has had a real-world experience with political terrorism', thereby emphasising that the focus of any such advice would be on the actions of the state in countering political insurgency in Ireland. And there is a lot of experience on which to draw – internment without trial, low-intensity intelligence operations targeting selected communities, arming and supporting counter-gangs of loyalists, undercover operations, including shoot-to-kill activities, spying on a wide range of individuals and groups, plastic bullets, distortion of the legal process by abolishing juries and changing rules of evidence, the criminalisation of political opponents and so on.

There is another story to tell, that of the individuals and communities at the receiving end of that war effort. But it is a story which Ridge is unlikely to hear from his British allies. That story would tell of repressive laws and state actions, and of the resistance of communities in the face of overwhelming odds. The revelation of this other story would muddy the waters, for it would show that, despite the propaganda, good is not all on the side of the state, nor are the insurgents inherently evil. At very least, a rounded story shows that reality is much more complex than propaganda would have it. But more importantly, it would reveal an obvious conclusion about the British experience of fighting insurgency over three decades (and more) in Ireland: namely that, despite the impressive array of weaponry involved, it did not work. The IRA was not beaten. In the end, the only hope for peace and conflict resolution came from talking.

The writing was on the wall as regards a solely military solution to the conflict in the North of Ireland for a long time. The British strategy of containment – ensuring that the worst of the conflict was confined to a limited number of geographical areas solely in the northern part of the island of Ireland – was never totally successful. The IRA campaign was carried to England and continental Europe. In addition, Britain was frequently subjected to international criticism over its policies and actions in Ireland. At an early stage, a case brought by the Irish government to the European Court of Human Rights over the treatment of internees in 1971 led to Britain being found guilty of torture. Over three decades, Britain was in fact found guilty of violations by the European Court more times than all the other members of the European Union combined. Most recently, in April 2000, Britain was found guilty of contravening Article 2 of the European Convention (the right to life) concerning a number of cases, including the undercover British army killing of eight IRA volunteers and one civilian in Loughgall, County Armagh, in May 1987. Frequent reports from international civil liberties organisations – such as Amnesty International, Liberty, the Cobden Trust, British Irish Rights Watch, the International Association of Democratic Lawyers – have criticised Britain over a wide range of issues, from the use of plastic bullets to collusion with loyalist paramilitaries in the death of prominent Belfast lawyer Pat Finucane. Finally, even British-sponsored reports managed to break through the walls of containment. Thus, the investigation of Manchester Assistant Chief Constable John Stalker of a number of controversial deaths by the Royal Ulster Constabulary (RUC) in 1982 was so close to revealing a policy of shoot-to-kill which emanated from the top of the RUC (if not higher) that Stalker was removed from the job, publicly vilified, and his report never published.[2]

Despite all this, it took a long time for the realisation to emerge that the military option was doomed to failure, not least because central to the British state's militarist mindset in relation to Ireland was the attempt to control the language and terms of the discussion. Listen to Douglas Hurd, once Secretary of State for Northern Ireland, as he denies the rationality of those opposing imperial power: 'I believe that, with the Provisional IRA and some of the Middle-Eastern groups, it is nothing really to do with a political cause any more. They are professional killers. That is their occupation and their pleasure and they will go on doing that. No political solution will cope with that. They just have to be extirpated.'[3] War is about winning, preferably outright, about destroying the enemy, and that destruction takes place in the first instance at the symbolic level. Meaning and definition become a theatre of war no less than the actual battlefield itself.

In many ways, the British were successful in this propaganda war. One measure of this was the extent to which the critical faculties supposedly central to many areas of civil society – including the media and academia – atrophied. More often than not, criticism of the state and its actions was at best muted. A tyranny of 'balance' was concocted whereby, for example, the interview with a victim of state violence had to be placed alongside the official spin of the powerful organisation perpetrating the violence. In a situation where to be judged as sympathetic to 'the men of violence' was dangerous, in career terms and otherwise, it became *de rigueur* for academics and commentators to preface their comments with a condemnation of violence. The sum total of all those statements over the years did nothing to isolate the causes of violence; but they were not really meant to. Instead, they were a nod of deference to the powers that be, signifying loyalty and thereby being granted the right to speak.

Likewise, in the media censorship became endemic. Often it was self-censorship, which, as respected journalist and broadcaster Mary Holland once noted, had become an art form in British media coverage of the Irish conflict. More than 70 programmes are known to have been cut or delayed in the period up to 1988.[4] At that point direct state censorship came to the fore, and from 1988 to 1994, British broadcasting regulations prevented the broadcasting of the direct speech of spokespersons of a number of organisations, most notably Sinn Féin, even though their words could be dubbed or subtitled. At one level, such a policy appeared ridiculous, but it was no less successful for that. The easiest option for broadcasters was not to bother interviewing Sinn Féin representatives, with the result that the number of such interviews declined drastically. The ban played a crucial role in containment by making the possibility of open debate difficult. As veteran political campaigner Bernadette McAliskey, herself gagged as a result of the ban, put it, the ability of people in Britain 'to understand what is going on is seriously impeded by the fact that, from the beginning, the people who are attempting to make a judgement are of necessity deprived of one side of the argument'.[5]

The end result of this cumulative censorship was the demonisation of individuals and communities. Sinn Féin vice-president Máire Drumm, murdered by loyalists, became 'the grandmother of hate'. According to the *Sunday Times*, 'Her friends and enemies are already offering many an epitaph, but there is none more chilling than removing the final 'm' of her surname and spelling Maire Drumm backwards: MURDER I AM'.[6] For the *Liverpool Echo*, Republican activist Mairead Farrell, shot dead by the SAS in Gibraltar, was 'the angel of death'; 'She could have been a model. Instead she was a killer. The reckoning for IRA commander Mairead Farrell – the girl with the looks of a film star and a heart of ice – came at the wrong end of an undercover soldier's gun.'[7] In the *Daily Telegraph* and other outlets, South Armagh was 'bandit country' because of its inhabitants' staunch republican convictions. Of course, all this fitted neatly with the wider state agenda. Politically motivated insurgents were denied any political ideology and were reclassified as criminals; 'A crime is a crime is a crime', said Prime Minister Margaret Thatcher. In 1981 ten republican prisoners starved themselves to death in order to put that lie to rest. The BBC entered the affray when a heads of department meeting noted that news chiefs were unhappy with broadcasting the only photograph they had of the first of the hunger strikers, Bobby Sands; 'a smiling photograph gave a misleading impression of a convicted felon' noted the minutes.[8]

Despite the propaganda onslaught, few conventional wars, and even fewer violent political conflicts, are won outright. In fact, the ending of such political conflict often begins with the realisation that there is no outright victory. Conflict resolution thus depends on the denial of the first premise of state propaganda: even the enemy is a human being, with the result that people have to talk and listen and be given the space for both. Such sentiments run counter to the binary thinking which underlies war and war propaganda.

In the Irish context, as early as the late 1970s elements in both the British military and the IRA, the two main protagonists, realised that neither side could win militarily. In 1977 veteran republican Jimmy Drumm marked a break from traditional Provisional IRA strategy by arguing that the British were not about to withdraw and that 'a successful war of liberation cannot be fought exclusively on the backs of the oppressed in the Six Counties, nor around the physical presence of the British army'.[9] It was a long, tortuous path from this to the 1994 IRA ceasefire. For its part, elements in the British military establishment had begun reassessing at about the same time. In 1978, Brigadier James Glover in his intelligence analysis of the IRA concluded that it was not composed of easily defeated 'mindless hooligans' but of militarily capable and politically astute combatants with a great deal of popular support.[10] But it was years before the hawks in the British Establishment, not all of whom wore uniforms, came to accept this. In fact, it has to be said that some 'securocrats' have not yet come to terms with the new script. The IRA was neither going to win outright nor be beaten. With this mutual realisation, the stage was set for the slow emergence and development of the current peace process.

The beginning of a non-military way out of conflict is the acknowledgement that there are reasons for insurgency. In the Irish case those reasons are found in a long history of imperial conquest, colonialism, repression, state-sponsored sectarian division and anti-Irish racism. This experience led to resistance. And resistance was no garden party; it involved violence, death, destruction and, indeed, terror. Horrible as some of the atrocities which resistance gave rise to, they have to be put in two contexts. First, the state was at it too, responsible for its own spectacular atrocities and its day-to-day reign of terror over centuries. Second, the question which needs to be considered, but rarely is, is how people, often young women and men, who were themselves intelligent, rational, loving and lovable could become involved in a war of resistance. Edward Said has raised this in relation to the Middle-East: '... speaking now as one Palestinian – I have been horrified at the hijacking of planes, the suicidal missions, the assassinations, the bombing of schools and hotels; horrified both at the terror visited upon its victims, and horrified by the terror in Palestinian men and women who were driven to such things'.[11]

Indeed, there are lessons from Ireland well worth learning in relation to the US/British 'war against international terror'. But there is little sign that either the US or Britain is open to learning those lessons. Instead, they are repeating the mistakes made in Ireland, presuming that military might is all, and going flat out to win the propaganda war. There is no space for dialogue. When Tony Blair was asked if bin Laden and al-Qaida could be 'dealt with', he replied: 'Well, you defeat them. I mean, you can't negotiate with them ... We have to take action and shut the whole of that terrorist network down. I mean, eliminate it, eradicate it.'[12] The propaganda war follows suit; everything is the fault of one man, the demented and evil Osama bin Laden. Even if some British military advisers realised that such a singular focus can be counterproductive – Ministry of Defence director of policy Simon Webb told the House of Commons defence committee, 'I think we need to be careful that we don't make too much of him. I personally think we should be careful about building people up too far', the danger being that he becomes even more of an icon in the Arab world[13] – it is unlikely that such advice is heard or heeded on the other side of the Atlantic. And even if it is, there is the availability of other demons such as Saddam Hussein.

With propaganda comes censorship. The US and British administrations each sought to prevent the broadcast of footage of bin Laden acquired from Al-Jazeera television, and later the station's building in Kabul was (coincidentally?) bombed. And few in any position of political or moral authority are asking fundamental questions. Why does a 'terrorist organisation' such as al-Qaida exist, and how does it recruit such popular support? Why do educated and intelligent young men and women bring themselves to kill and be killed for a cause? Why do communities of ordinary men, women and children support these young men and women, either quietly in the privacy of their own homes, or publicly on the streets and materially by providing safe houses, etc.? Why, in short, should anyone see them as freedom fighters rather than terrorists? At the official level, instead of attempts to answer such questions, we have the crude propaganda of George W. Bush: 'America has a message for the nations of the world. If you feed a terrorist or fund a terrorist, you're a terrorist.'[14]

As any commentator who viewed the Irish war with an open mind could testify, the IRA was only able to sustain a campaign lasting 30 years by dint of its popularity. There was a set of grievances, an analysis and the promise of a solution, albeit violent. Above all, those who volunteered to wage that war and those communities which provided them with food, shelter, safe houses and moral sustenance could not be dismissed as irrational or non-political. Likewise in relation to the US/UK crusade. The Islamist cause, of which al-Qaida is one extreme representation, is fuelled by rational political analysis. Israel continues to have the support of the US despite the most horrific of actions against the Palestinians. Iraqi children continue to starve as a result of sanctions imposed or tolerated by powerful Western states.

And on a wider level, Muslim and other refugees around the globe are seen increasingly as at least a problem, or worse, a threat in the West. And all this and more is underwritten by crude propaganda which begins with the presumption that those who object are the problem. In the light of this, it is little wonder that some intelligent young people will strap explosives to themselves, that others will turn to other forms of terror, that some will travel across half a continent to take up weapons, while others will form 'extremist' political parties. And backing them up will be countless ordinary decent people who will support them in whatever way they can because there is no other promise of a solution on offer.

What happened in New York, Washington and Pennsylvania was horrible, but it is too simple to put it all down to the evil machinations of one criminal mastermind, or worse still, to a whole religious tradition. There have been too many victims in the lead up to and aftermath of September 11, and not all of them have been American or British. A lasting monument to their memory would be neither war nor revenge, but the understanding, debate and dialogue which could lead to a resolution of the conflict and the reassurance that there will be no more victims.

1. *Daily Telegraph*, November 8, 2001.
2. On state killings, including the Loughgall victims and Pat Finucane, as well as the Stalker affair, see Rolston, Bill, *Unfinished Business: State Killings and the Quest for Truth*, Belfast: Beyond the Pale Publications, 2000.
3. Cited in *Belfast Telegraph*, March 9, 1989.
4. For a complete list, see Curtis, Liz, 'A Catalogue of Censorship 1959–1993', in Rolston, Bill and Miller, David (eds), *War and Words: The Northern Ireland Media Reader*, Belfast: Beyond the Pale Publications, 1996.
5. *Conflicting Reports: Reporting the Conflict in Northern Ireland*, Report of a Conference, London: British Irish Rights Watch, 1993.
6. *Sunday Times*, October 31, 1976.
7. *Liverpool Echo*, March 7, 1988.

8. Quoted in Curtis, Liz, *Ireland, the Propaganda War*, London: Pluto Press, 1984, p. 204.
9. Kelley, Kevin, *The Longest War: Northern Ireland and the IRA*, Dingle: Brandon, 1982, p. 265.
10. *Ibid*, pp. 295–6.
11. Said, Edward, *The Question of Palestine*, London: Routledge and Kegan Paul, 1980, p. xii.
12. Cited in *Irish News*, November 7, 2001.
13. Cited in the *Guardian*, November 8, 2001.
14. Cited in the *Guardian*, November 27, 2001.

SEPTEMBER 11 AFTERMATH: WHERE IS THE WORLD HEADING?

Noam Chomsky

The new millennium has begun with two monstrous crimes: the terrorist attacks of September 11, and the reaction to them, surely taking a far greater toll of innocent lives.

The atrocities of September 11 are widely regarded as a historic event, and that is most definitely true. But we should be clear about exactly why it is true. These crimes had perhaps the most devastating instant human toll on record, outside of war. The word 'instant' should not be overlooked; it is unfortunate, but true, that the crimes are far from unusual in the annals of violence that falls short of war. The aftermath is only one of innumerable illustrations. The reason why 'the world will never be the same' after September 11, to borrow the phrase now commonly used, lies elsewhere.

The scale of the catastrophe that has already taken place in Afghanistan, and what may follow, can only be guessed. But we do know the projections on which policy decisions are based, and from these we can gain some insight into the question of where the world is heading. The answer is that it is heading along paths that are well-travelled.

Even before September 11, millions of Afghans were being sustained – barely – by international food aid. On September 16, the *New York Times* reported that Washington had 'demanded [from Pakistan] the elimination of truck convoys that provide much of the food and other supplies to Afghanistan's civilian population'. There was no detectable reaction in the US or Europe to the demand that enormous numbers of destitute people be subjected to starvation and slow death. In subsequent weeks, the world's leading newspaper reported that 'The threat of military strikes forced the removal of international aid workers, crippling assistance programs'; refugees reaching Pakistan 'after arduous journeys from Afghanistan are describing scenes of desperation and fear at home as the threat of American-led military attacks turns their long-running misery into a potential catastrophe'. 'The country was on a lifeline,' one evacuated aid worker reported, 'and we just cut the line.'

The UN World Food Program and others were able to resume some food shipments in early October, but were forced to suspend deliveries and distribution after the bombing, resuming them later at a much lower pace, while aid agencies levelled 'scathing' condemnations of US air drops that are barely concealed 'propaganda tools'.

The *New York Times* reported, without comment, that the number of Afghans needing food aid was expected to increase by 50 per cent as a result of the bombing, to 7.5 million. In other words, Western civilisation is basing its plans on the assumption that they may lead to the slaughter of several million innocent civilians – not Taliban, but their victims. On the same day, the leader of Western civilisation once again dismissed with contempt Taliban offers of negotiation and their request for some credible evidence to substantiate the demands for capitulation. His stand was regarded as right and just, perhaps even heroic. The UN Special Rapporteur on the Right to Food pleaded with the US to end the bombing that was putting 'the lives of millions of civilians at risk', renewing the appeal of UN High Commissioner of Human Rights, Mary Robinson, who warned of a Rwanda-style catastrophe. Both appeals were rejected, as were those of the major aid and relief agencies. And virtually unreported.

The Food and Agricultural Administration (FAO) had warned in late September that over 7 million people might face starvation unless aid was immediately resumed and the threat of military action terminated. After bombing began, the FAO issued even more grave warnings of a humanitarian catastrophe, and advised that the bombing had disrupted planting that provides 80 per cent of the country's grain supplies, so that the effects next year will be even more severe. All unreported. These unreported appeals happened to coincide with World Food Day, which was also ignored, along with the charge by the UN Special Rapporteur that the rich and powerful easily have the means, though not the will, to overcome this 'silent genocide'.

The airstrikes have turned cities into 'ghost towns', the press reported, with electrical power and water supplies destroyed, a form of biological warfare. Seventy per cent of the population were reported to have fled Kandahar and Herat, mostly to the country-side, where in ordinary times between 10 and 20 people are killed or crippled every day by land mines. Those conditions are now much worse. UN mine-clearing operations were halted, and unexploded US ordnance adds to the torture, particularly the lethal bomblets scattered by cluster bombs, which are much harder to clear.

The fate of these miserable people will never be known, or even investigated, if past precedents are a guide. Careful enquiry into con-sequences is reserved for crimes that can be attributed to official enemies. In such cases, enquiry properly considers not only those immediately killed but the far vaster numbers who die as a result of the policies that are condemned. For our own crimes, if there is any enquiry at all, standards are entirely different. The effects of criminal acts are disregarded. In the case of Afghanistan, whatever happens, if investigated at all, will be blamed on something else – the drought, the Taliban – but crucially not those who have consciously and pur-posefully implemented crimes that they expect will cause mass slaughter of innocents.

Only those entirely ignorant of modern history will find any of this surprising. The victims, after all, are only 'uncivilised tribes' – Winston Churchill's contemptuous reference to Afghans and Kurds when he insisted upon the use of poisoned gas to inspire a 'lively terror' among them 80 years ago. But in this case too, we will learn little about the aftermath. Ten years ago Britain instituted an 'open government' initiative. Its first act was to remove from the Public Records Office all files concerning the use of poison gas against the uncivilised tribes. If it is necessary to 'exterminate the indigenous population', so be it, as the French Minister of War declared while announcing that the process was under way in Algeria in the mid-nineteenth century, not for the last time. It is all too easy to proceed. What is happening to Afghans now is conventional, a central theme of modern history. It is therefore natural that it should arouse little interest or concern, even report.

The crimes of September 11 are indeed a historic turning point, but not because of their scale; rather, because of the choice of target. For the US, this is the first time since the British burned down Washington in 1814 that the national territory has been under attack, or even threatened. There should be no need to review what has happened to those who were in the way or disobedient in the centuries since. The number of victims is huge. For the first time, the guns have been pointed in the opposite direction. That is a historic change.

The same is true, even more dramatically, of Europe. Europe has suffered murderous destruction, but from internal wars. Meanwhile, European powers conquered much of the world, not very politely. With rare and limited exceptions, they were not under attack by their foreign victims. The Congo did not attack and devastate Belgium, nor the East Indies the Netherlands, nor Algeria France. The list is long and the crimes horrendous. It is not surprising, therefore, that Europe should be shocked by the terrorist atrocities of September 11. But while these do signal a dramatic change in world affairs, the aftermath represents no change at all.

It has been rightly emphasised by US and other world leaders that confronting the terrorist monster is not a short-term task, but a lasting one. We should therefore consider carefully the measures that can be taken to mitigate what has been called, in high places, 'the evil scourge of terrorism', a plague spread by 'depraved opponents of civilisation itself' in 'a return to barbarism in the modern age'.

We should begin, surely, by identifying the plague and the depraved elements that have been returning the world to barbarism. The curse is not new. The phrases I quote are from President Ronald Reagan and his Secretary of State, George Shultz. The Reagan administration came to office 20 years ago proclaiming that the struggle against international terrorism would be the core of US foreign policy. They responded to the plague by organising campaigns of international terrorism of unprecedented scale and violence, even leading to a World Court condemnation of the US for 'unlawful use of force' and a Security Council resolution calling on all states to observe international law, which the US vetoed, also voting alone with Israel (and in one case El Salvador) against similar General Assembly Resolutions. The World Court order to terminate the crime of international terrorism and pay substantial reparations was dismissed with contempt across the spectrum; the UN votes were scarcely even reported. Washington reacted at once by escalating the economic and terrorist wars. It also issued official orders to the mercenary army to attack 'soft targets' – undefended civilian targets – and to avoid combat, as it could do, thanks to US control of the skies and the sophisticated communication equipment provided to the terrorist forces attacking from neighbouring countries.

Those orders were considered legitimate as long as pragmatic criteria were satisfied. One prominent commentator, Michael

Kinsley, regarded as the spokesperson of the left in mainstream discussion, argued that we should not simply dismiss State Department justifications for terrorist attacks on 'soft targets': a 'sensible policy' must 'meet the test of cost-benefit analysis', he wrote, an analysis of 'the amount of blood and misery that will be poured in, and the likelihood that democracy will emerge at the other end' – 'democracy' as Western élites understand the term, an interpretation illustrated quite clearly in the region. It is taken for granted that they have the right to conduct the analysis and pursue the project if it passes their tests.

And it did pass the tests. When Nicaragua finally succumbed to superpower assault, commentators across the spectrum of respectable opinion lauded the success of the methods adopted to 'wreck the economy and prosecute a long and deadly proxy war until the exhausted natives overthrow the unwanted government themselves', with a cost to us that is 'minimal', leaving the victims 'with wrecked bridges, sabotaged power stations, and ruined farms', and thus providing the US candidate with 'a winning issue': ending the 'impoverishment of the people of Nicaragua' (*Time* magazine). We are 'United in Joy' at this outcome, the *New York Times* proclaimed, proud of this 'Victory for US Fair Play', a *Times* headline read.

The civilised world was 'United in Joy' again a few weeks ago as the US candidate won the Nicaraguan election after stern warnings from Washington of the consequences if he did not. The *Washington Post* explained that the victor had 'focused his campaign on reminding people of the economic and military difficulties of the Sandinista era' – that is, the US terrorist war and economic strangulation that devastated the country. Meanwhile the president instructed us about the 'one universal law': all varieties of terror and murder 'are evil' – unless, of course, we are the agents.

Prevailing Western attitudes towards terrorism are revealed with great clarity by the reaction to the appointment of John Negroponte as UN ambassador to lead the 'war against terrorism'. Negroponte's record includes his service as 'proconsul' in Honduras in the 1980s, where he was the local supervisor of the international terrorist campaign for which his government was condemned by the World Court and Security Council. There is no detectable reaction. Even Jonathan Swift would be speechless.

I mention the case of Nicaragua only because it is uncontroversial, given the judgements of the highest international authorities. Uncontroversial, that is, among those who have a minimal commitment to human rights and international law. One can estimate the size of that category by determining how often these elementary matters are even mentioned. And from that exercise alone one can draw some grim conclusions about what lies ahead, if existing centres of power and ideology have their way.

The Nicaraguan case is far from the most extreme example. In the Reagan years alone, US-sponsored state terrorists in Central America left hundreds of thousands of tortured and mutilated corpses, millions of maimed and orphaned, and four countries in ruins in Central America. In the same years, Western-backed South African depredations killed 1.5 million people and caused $60 billion of damage. I need not speak of West and South-east Asia, South America, or much else. And that decade was not unusual.

It is a serious analytic error to describe terrorism as a 'weapon of the weak', as is often done. In practice, terrorism is the violence that *they* commit against *us* – whoever *we* happen to be. It would be hard to find a historical exception. And since the powerful determine what counts as History, what passes through the filters is the terrorism of the weak against the strong and their clients.

Excerpted from the Lakdawala Memorial Lecture 'Peering into the Abyss of the Future' sponsored by the Institute of Social Sciences, New Delhi and presented on November 3, 2001.

A QUESTION OF STATE CRIME?[1]
Penny Green

Are the United States and Great Britain guilty of crimes in Afghanistan? Can the bombing of Afghanistan be understood as a state crime? In retaliation for the terror attacks launched against it in September 2001, the world's most powerful nation launched its tremendous might against one of the poorest, most war ravaged and desperate countries in an act of vengeance. Aided by Britain, the US has bombed into further oblivion a people whose 'crime' was to be ruled by the wildly obscurantist Taliban – a regime which has given shelter and succour to September 11's prime suspect, Osama bin Laden.

The West argues that its crusade is a crusade against terror, an attempt to crush the forces that support international terror and a mission to capture and bring to justice (or eliminate) Saudi-born

Osama bin Laden, widely held to be responsible for the attacks on the World Trade Center and the Pentagon. Afghanistan has been the site of retaliation because its rulers, the Taliban pseudo-state, has knowingly harboured Osama bin Ladin and his terror network al-Qaida. But harbouring war criminals or terrorists has never been adduced as a reason for US attacks in the past. Quite the opposite if we consider Argentina, Chile, El Salvador, Panama and other Latin American countries, as well as some European states such as France, that have offered a haven to war criminals and terrorists. So why did the US attack Afghanistan? There are two obvious reasons. First, the attacks of September 11 took place not only on American soil, but, second, they were directed against one of the world's most important economic bases – the World Trade Center. These were very clearly attacks against Western capitalism. With the rise of the anti-capitalist movement in the past five years, the US has been on the back foot, struggling to defend the moral and economic value of world trade and strategies of globalisation. The attacks of September 11 provided a clear opportunity for the US to reassert the dominance and moral superiority of 'the free world' in countries that do readily subscribe to free market ideologies.

This war, trumpeted by Bush and Blair as a war waged in defence of 'civilisation' against the forces of irrationality and barbarism, is nothing of the sort. US allies in this war include some of the most undemocratic, repressive and violent regimes in the world: Saudi Arabia, a gross violator of human rights but, more importantly for the US, the conduit to the Middle East for multinational oil companies; Indonesia, responsible for the genocide of the East Timorese and the repression of internal dissidents; Russia, whose military has devastated the tiny Republic of Chechnya killing 50,000 since 1999; China, whose security forces massacred thousands of pro-democracy demonstrators in Tiananmen Square in 1989; and Turkey, whose war against its Kurdish population has brought fierce international condemnation. The argument about 'civilised nations' versus the rest simply does not hold up.

If the US was serious about tackling international terrorism it would first examine the causes which led to the attacks on its central institutions of finance and defence. It would recognise that in the Middle Eastern regimes that have spawned the anti-American terror networks (such as Saudi Arabia) all political opposition has been crushed. It would note the hypocrisy embodied in supporting those regimes. When there is no opportunity for the development of a liberal intelligentsia, when political dissidents are brutally suppressed where trade unionism is outlawed, then religion becomes the only means of dissent. And if religious dissent is all that is feasible then religious fanaticism becomes all the more possible. If the US is serious about defeating international terrorism it needs to confront these structural roots of terror in the same way that it must confront global poverty. But it is not really serious about defeating international terrorism because such a commitment would mean reforming the whole Middle East. It would mean encouraging democratic processes, a free press, multi-party rule and the development of a strong civil society – which would surely object to America's economic role in the region. Its absolute disregard for the plight of the Afghan population under the cruel and repressive rule of the Taliban since 1996 is legendary. The US would also need to withdraw its support for regimes like Israel, Saudi Arabia, Kuwait and Egypt. This it is not prepared to do while oil revenues remain so crucial to its international dominance. Its unrepentant support of one of the world's most notorious war criminals, Israel's Ariel Sharon ('personally responsible'[2] in 1982 for the Sabra and Chatila massacres carried out by Israel's proxy militia, the Christian Phalange) and its eleven-year campaign of bombing and economic sanctions against the people of Iraq are but two examples of what may be described as US 'criminal' Middle Eastern foreign policy.

The 'international war against terror' has provided a form of legitimation for states already engaged in human rights violations. Since September 11 Israel has increased the pace of its repression in the occupied territories, destroying Palestinian villages, sanctioning the theft of more Palestinian land by its right-wing settlers and carrying out political assassinations. The Russians too have revelled in the recent war finding in it a degree of international legitimation for their devastation of Chechnya.

On September 11 the US was introduced to a fraction (horrible as it was) of the daily terror and fear experienced by many of those living under regimes it not only funds and supports but also trains in the cruel and brutal methods of counter-insurgency. Yet even the horror of September 11 has not caused the US to stop and reflect on a foreign policy which has resulted in death and destruction on a far greater scale than Osama bin Laden (should he be found to have instigated the attacks) could ever hope to achieve. But the experiences of New Yorkers and, for example, Afghanis and Palestinians are not, in fact, comparable. Life under daily violence and routine state terror is a very different experience when compared with that of the isolated and anomalous attacks suffered by New York and Washington.

It is difficult to consider the actions of the US or Britain in relation to this dismal historical episode without reference to stunning hypocrisy. With astonishing ease the US, Britain and other Western allies deploy a double discourse around terror. The US, while publicly denouncing terror, has long provided extensive international assistance to regimes which engage in state terrorism. Israel, Nicaragua, Argentina, Chile, El Salvador, Guatamala, Angola and Mozambique have all been beneficiaries of American aid and/or training. 'Terror' is a politically flexible term.

British Prime Minister Tony Blair declared that the attacks on the World Trade Center required 'a fanaticism and wickedness that is beyond our normal contemplation'. Yet the carpet-bombing of Afghanistan was both contemplated and calculated, carrying no hallmarks of 'justice, humanity or mercy'. It suggested its own form of wickedness and fanaticism – resulting in the cold-blooded and calculated killing of ordinary innocent Afghans who could not have contemplated the events of September 11.

Hypocrisy has also taken a very specific form in this conflict. Just as the US was responsible for arming and developing the regime of Saddam Hussein prior to the Persian Gulf War, it was, in fact, the CIA with the support of the Saudi Arabian royal family and the Pakistani secret service which enlisted the support of Osama bin Laden in the early 1980s to strengthen US-backed forces for the war against the Russians. Just as the now renamed School of the Americas[3] trained the murderous generals of Latin America throughout the 1970s, bin Laden's knowledge of terror was taught to him by agents of the CIA. With the assistance of the Pakistani secret police, backed by the US, bin Laden built up a guerrilla force in the mountainous region of Eastern Afghanistan but turned against the US as its policy in the Middle East adopted an increasingly aggressive and imperialist edge. He had been central to the US-backed Saudi strategy to spread the Saudi version of Islam, Wahhabism, in Afghanistan in order to build a movement which would owe its allegiances to Western interests. Bin Laden was then persuaded by Prince Turki Al Faisal, head of the Saudi secret police, to lead a client guerrilla group inside Afghanistan for this purpose. Bin Laden's relationship with the Saudis and their friends, the US, however, broke down bitterly following Iraq's invasion of Kuwait and the Saudi invitation to the US and its allies to base themselves in Saudi Arabia to launch the 1991 Gulf War. Bin Laden, now marginalised by the powerful in the region, became an enemy of the US.

Following the attacks of September 11 George Bush spoke of 'punishment and justice' for the perpetrators but Osama bin Laden was not sought for trial. Rather, highly secret military courts designed to try, and then eliminate, 'terrorist murderers' have been legitimised in American law by a president who has a track record in state executions. There is little doubt that these secret military courts are, in fact, a legally sanctioned means by which the execution of certain terrorist suspects can take place away from public trials and scrutiny. Their secrecy indicates a recognition by the Bush administration that such courts would be challenged by civil society if they had a public face.

So, can it be argued that the US response to the attacks of September 11 was criminal? It has certainly been cloaked in breathtaking hypocrisy. But hypocrisy, itself, is not a crime. With Tony Ward, I have argued that state crime should be defined as state organisational deviance which involves violation of human rights. State organisational deviance is deviant activity in pursuit of the organisational goals of a state agency. From a criminological point of view, what is distinctive about the state is its claimed entitlement to do things which, if anyone else did them, would constitute violence and extortion.[4]

If we employ this definition of state crime then is it possible to argue that the US and its ally, Great Britain, have perpetrated crimes on a mass scale in Afghanistan? Certainly innocent human lives have been lost. But isn't that an inevitable product of war? The bombardment of Kabul, Kunduz, Khanabad, Kazikarez, Karem and Kandahar succeeded in bringing the Taliban to its knees but it also resulted in the untold murder of, possibly, thousands of Afghan men, women and children. In the 'coalition's' war against Osama bin Laden, al-Qaida and the Taliban (but in reality against the impoverished and war-ravaged people of Afghanistan), George W Bush and Tony Blair declared that they were 'reconciled to civilian deaths'. If this is so, and it has proven to be so, then Bush and Blair, with murderous intent, have blood on their hands. 'Collateral damage' is the ugliest of euphemisms – it equates to nothing less than murder. On any reckoning the revenge bombing of a country to punish one man, and a regime that protects him, is an act of unmitigated barbarity. It is even more barbarous when the country is already so devastated by 22 years of war that some 5 million of its inhabitants live on the edge of starvation.

The atrocities committed by the friends of the US and Britain, the Northern Alliance, in Mazar-I-Sharif and Kunduz are gross violations of human rights, for which America and Britain must take some responsibility. For the Northern Alliance warlords, said to be responsible for the murder of 50,000 people in Kabul between 1992 and 1996, the execution of Taliban soldiers and escaping prisoners in Mazar-I-Sharif, represented an expressive consolidation of their victory over the Taliban – an assertion of their power and brutal authority. US and British soldiers were involved in assisting the Alliance in suppressing the prison revolt while the US Secretary of State, Donald Rumsfeld, maintained that US bombing raids on Kunduz would only stop if the Alliance so requested. He acted in full military co-operation with the Northern Alliance militia.[5] As Robert Fisk argues, 'Mr Rumsfeld's incriminating remark places Washington in the witness box of any war-crimes trial over Kunduz.'[6] The US–British coalition, by its own actions and by the actions of its proxy militia, have violated human rights for very explicit organisational goals and have been condemned as 'deviant' by millions around the world. If a state's own actions depart from that state's own rules or is unjustifiable in terms of the values the rules purport to serve, then those actions objectively are illegitimate. The hypocrisy employed by the US and British states, discussed above, suggests just such a crisis of legitimacy – a disjunction between the rhetoric of justice, due process and the rule of law and the reality of retaliatory civilian bombing. In countries across the globe anti-war demonstrations have attracted hundreds of thousands of protesters. Muslims have reacted against what they see as a war against Islam. In London 100,000 people demonstrated their anger at New Labour's warmongering, and this was after the fall of Kabul. The organisational goals are clear – the US has exploited the attacks on New York and Washington in order to regain control, in Central Asia and Afghanistan, of access to the oil markets of Central Asia. As demonstrated above, its military actions are designed to reaffirm the dominance of Western capital in a region where the growth of Islamic fundamentalism has threatened that dominance.

The attacks against Afghanistan by America and Britain represent far more than gross hypocrisy and reasonable retaliation for the crimes committed on September 11. They represent the exercise of state terror by super-powerful states. The violations of human rights in pursuit of Western economic and military interests leave no doubt that the US and the UK governments are indeed guilty of state crimes in Afghanistan.

1. The author would like to thank Tony Ward and Bill Spence for their helpful and insightful comments.
2. The finding of the 1983 Kahan Commission Inquiry which was established in the wake of the Sabra and Chatila massacres in which at least 2,000 men, women and children were murdered by the right-wing Phalangist militia.
3. The School of the Americas was renamed 'the Western Hemisphere Institute for Security Cooperation' in 2001.
4. Green, P. and Ward, T. 'State Crime, Human Rights and the Limits of Criminology', in *Social Justice*, 2000.
5. Fisk, Robert, 'We are the war criminals now', *Independent*, November 29, 2001.
6. Ibid.

THIS WAR IS ILLEGAL AND IMMORAL, AND IT WON'T PREVENT TERRORISM
Michael Mandel

The US-led war on Afghanistan is a violation of international law and of the express words of the Charter of the United Nations. As such it is illegal. It is also immoral and it won't prevent terrorism.

The Charter of the United Nations, the most authoritative document in international law, seeks to ban war as a 'scourge'. Its very first words are 'We the Peoples of the United Nations, Determined to save succeeding generations from the scourge of war ...' War is permitted only when it is absolutely and demonstrably necessary. And the Charter does not leave that question to the individual states. Necessity is entirely a matter for the Security Council with only one exception: the strictly limited right of self-defence.

The Security Council passed two resolutions on terrorism between September 11 and America's attack on Afghanistan on October 7 (SR 1368 of September 12 and SR 1373 of September 28). No honest reading of these could possibly conclude that they authorise the use of force. They condemn the attacks of September 11 and take a whole host of measures to suppress terrorism, especially SR 1373 which has two dozen operative paragraphs outlining legislative, administrative and judicial measures for the suppression of terrorism and its financing, and for co-operation between states in security, intelligence, investigations and criminal proceedings. The resolution sets up a committee of all its members to monitor progress on the measures in the resolution and has given all states 90 days to report back to it. But not once does either of these resolutions mention military force or anything like it. They don't even mention Afghanistan by name. Nor do they use the accepted formula 'all necessary means' of Resolution 678 of November 29, 1990 by which the Security Council authorised the Gulf War of 1991.

Absent authorisation of the Security Council, the only even barely arguable legal basis for the war in Afghanistan, is the right of self-defence preserved by Article 51 of the Charter: 'Nothing in the present Charter shall impair the inherent right of individual or collective self-defense if an armed attack occurs against a Member of the United Nations, until the Security Council has taken measures necessary to maintain international peace and security.'

Much has been indeed made of the fact that the right of self-defence is mentioned in one of the paragraphs of the Preamble to both 2001 resolutions: '*Recognizing* the inherent right of individual or collective self-defense in accordance with the Charter.' But you'd really have to stretch that to turn it into an authorisation to attack Afghanistan. Once again, look at the difference in the way this was expressed in the Iraq-Kuwait case, in which the Security Council also affirmed the right of self-defence in Resolution 661 of August 6, 1990 in the following terms: '*Affirming* the inherent right of individual or collective self-defense, in response to the armed attack by Iraq against Kuwait, in accordance with Article 51 of the Charter.'

This was just the second of twelve resolutions by the Security Council in the crisis. Only the last one authorised the use of force. The others gradually upped the ante over a period of almost four months with a combination of diplomatic initiatives, sanctions and threats of prosecutions, with the final resolution 678 giving the Iraqis six weeks' notice as a 'pause of goodwill'. This just underlines the fact that an affirmation of the right of self-defence, even as specific as it was in the case of Kuwait, is in no way inconsistent with the Security Council's primary responsibility for the maintenance of international peace and security and its monopoly over the authorisation of the use of force.

In fact, the right of unilateral self-defence (viz. not authorised by the Security Council) in Article 51 is expressly stated as a *temporary* right. There is no getting around that word 'until'. It is limited to the right to repel an attack that is actually taking place or to dislodge an illegal occupier (in Kuwait's case Iraq remained in military occupation throughout). This temporary right of self-defence does not include the right to retaliate once an attack has stopped. Nor does it include the right to overthrow the government one holds in some way responsible for the attack, or to undertake long-term preventive measures. The idea is there for all to see in black and white in Article 51. A state is allowed to exercise self-help when there is no time for the Security Council to intervene and until it can intervene. The right of self-defence in international law is like the right of self-defence in our domestic law: it allows you to defend yourself when the law is not around, but it does not allow you to take the law into your own hands. It defies the imagination that one of the Permanent Members of the Security Council – one who has indeed voted for the extensive, non-violent anti-terrorism measures taken by the Security Council – could justify a long, open-ended 'war against terrorism' on the ground that the Security Council has not had time to intervene.

This rule is fundamental to the whole UN system. If it were otherwise, a superpower like the US would have a legal blank cheque to intervene wherever it likes for as long as it likes, even if there had been no attack whatever, because the self-defence it is claiming is not about past attacks but *future* ones. In fact a blank cheque is what President Bush wrote himself in his speech of September 20, 2001, when he declared that 'there are thousands of these terrorists in more than sixty countries ... Every nation in every region now has a decision to make. Either you are with us, or you are with the terrorists. From this day forward, any nation that continues to harbor or support terrorism will be regarded by the United States as a hostile regime.' In the words of the editors of the *Monthly Review*: 'Bush's speech thus establishes the basis for a series of military interventions without definite geographical boundaries or moral restraints on the weapons to be used; and without any limits on the numbers or types of enemies to be encountered.'[1]

If this were regarded as a valid exercise of the right of self-defence under Article 51, the job of the Security Council, as the (mostly) elected representative of the United Nations, to take primary and ultimate responsibility for the use of military force, that is to judge its necessity, set its objectives, impose limits and supervise those limits would have been completely displaced. This would be the end of the UN Charter.

The right of self-defence in domestic law does not allow you to take the law into your own hands when you have time to call the police. Nor does it allow you to go out and shoot the first person you see. The law of self-defence under international law is the same. The words 'in response to the *armed attack by Iraq* against Kuwait' (in Resolution 661/1990 quoted above) are also of enormous significance, not only because they specifically mention Iraq and Kuwait (unlike the lack of any mention of Afghanistan in SR 1368/2001 and 1373/2001), but because they illustrate one of the fundamental legal conditions for the invocation of the right of self-defence: the existence of an armed attack by the state against whom the right of self-defence is claimed. The US has alleged that the attack originated in Afghanistan with bin Laden and the al-Qaida network, though the evidence provided by Blair and 'accepted' by Pakistan (along with billions of dollars of loan forgiveness and the end of US sanctions) is so flimsy that it wouldn't stand up in traffic court. But nowhere is it alleged that the government of Afghanistan participated in the planning or execution of this attack, only that it has 'harboured' terrorists by allowing them to operate on the territory.

Precisely the same claim was made by the US against Nicaragua in the World Court – and flatly rejected in 1986.[2] Here the US was seeking to justify its bombing and mining of Nicaragua's harbours and its support of the counter-revolutionary Contras in a civil war that took tens of thousands of lives. The claim was that Nicaragua was allowing insurgents from neighbouring countries to operate from Nicaraguan territory and the US was acting in 'collective self-defence' of these countries. The claim was rejected by the court on the ground that allowing a group to operate on your territory is not the same as using it to attack another country. The court ruled that for the purpose of the law of self-defence an armed attack required either 'the sending *by or on behalf of a State* of armed bands, groups, irregulars or mercenaries, which carry out acts of armed force against another State … *or its substantial involvement therein*'. But the court does not believe that the concept of 'armed attack' includes 'assistance to rebels in the form of provision of weapons or logistical or other support'.[3]

The court held that while legal remedies exist for such an action, they do not include the right to attack the country in question. Indeed, the court held that the US funding and support for the Contras could not make the US responsible in law to Nicaragua, apart from acts performed by the US itself (like bombing and mining):

The court does not consider that the assistance given by the United States to the Contras warrants the conclusion that these forces are subject to the United states to such an extent that any acts they have committed are imputable to that State. It takes the view that the Contras remain responsible for their acts and that the United States is not responsible for the acts of the Contras, but for its own conduct vis-à-vis Nicaragua including conduct related to the acts of the Contras.[4]

It is true that the US, as a result of the Nicaragua decision, ceased to recognise the compulsory jurisdiction of the World Court. That is a big obstacle to enforcing the law against the US, but it doesn't make its actions any less illegal. In fact the US is a serial violator of the international law prohibitions on the use of force.[5] For all that has been said about how things have changed since September 11, one thing that has not is US disregard for international law. Its decade-long bombing campaign against Iraq and its spring 1999 bombing of Yugoslavia, complete with 'collateral damage' in the thousands, were both illegal (and remain so in the case of Iraq).

In the Nicaragua case, the World Court also decided that the US had not demonstrated the *necessity* of military force in self-defence:

Thus it was possible to eliminate the main danger to the Salvadorian government without the United States embarking on activities in and against Nicaragua. Accordingly, it cannot be held that these activities were undertaken in the light of necessity ... the court cannot regard the United States activities ... i.e. those relating to the mining of the Nicaraguan ports and the attacks on ports, oil installations, etc. as satisfying that criterion.[6]

Self-defence, in domestic and international law alike, is a branch of necessity. It is only justified when all other alternatives are demonstrably unavailable. Yet in the case of Afghanistan, none of the many realistic non-military alternatives, such as UN mediation or international judicial proceedings, were even explored. Negotiations offered by the Taliban were rejected out of hand by the US, which issued a series of ultimatums lasting just long enough to get its war machine in gear.

Furthermore, the US would have a tough time demonstrating that its military attack was even *useful* in the prevention of terrorism, let alone necessary. Israeli journalist and peace activist Uri Avnery knows something about terrorism. In November 2001 he wrote:

Since terrorism is always a political instrument, the right way to combat it is always political. Solve the problem that breeds terrorism and you get rid of terrorism. Solve the Israeli-Palestinian problem and the other flash-points in the Middle East, and you get rid of al-Qaida. It will wilt like a flower deprived of water. No one has yet devised another method.[7]

And here is another point of fundamental importance in assessing the 'necessity' of this military attack to counter terrorism, namely the huge responsibility borne by the Americans for the violence in the first place. Not only the 'blowback' of the fact that bin Laden himself was part of the US-supported Mujahideen opposition to the Soviet presence, and not only the subsequent total abandonment of Afghanistan to more than a decade of civil war. More important are the many deep and perfectly legitimate grievances that the Arab world has against the US and which undoubtedly played a major part in the motivation for the attacks of September 11, if only by the resonance they would have had in the communities from which the attackers came. These include: American support for corrupt and repressive Arab governments, for example in Saudi Arabia and Egypt, where American military aid is the only thing that keeps them in power; the US guarantee of Israel's brutal, indeed terrorist, occupation of the West Bank and Gaza that wouldn't have lasted 34 weeks, let alone 34 years, without American financing and the supply of its most sophisticated weaponry; the decade-long bombing of Iraq accompanied by a sanctions regime that is reputably estimated to have killed hundreds of thousands of Iraqi children. For many decades now, the US has spearheaded a Western war against the Middle East over oil; a war of the rich against the poor. American musician Quincy Jones recently put it like a rap lyric: 'That's why this fucking war is going on, that's why, because the gap between rich and poor is too large.'[8] On any definition of terrorism, the US has deployed it in this long war far more extensively than have its enemies.[9]

So this US-led attack cannot seriously be thought to be about 'preventing terrorism'. This attack, terrorist in itself on any fair definition, will be far more likely to provoke terrorism than prevent it, like previous retaliations by the US against Libya and Afghanistan itself, and Israel's military retaliations against the Palestinians. The attack on Afghanistan is about vengeance; about showing how tough the Americans are, or even occult geopolitical reasons that we can only guess at. It is being done on the backs of people who have far less control over their government than even the poor souls who died on September 11. It has already predictably resulted in many deaths of civilian men, women and children, both from the bombing itself and from the disruption of aid in a country where millions were already at risk. As I write this (November 14, 2001), the American-backed Northern Alliance has entered Kabul, and is reported to be taking bloody revenge on Taliban fighters and supporters with summary, and sometimes mass, executions. The Northern Alliance, representing ethnic groups that make up only a minority of Afghanistan's population, are considered to be no less violent and repressive and no less hostile to women than the Taliban,[10] who at least were drawn from the largest ethnic group in Afghanistan.

Already the law professors and journalists are talking of war crimes tribunals to punish atrocities on both sides.[11] But the boss of all the bosses in this one (like Yugoslavia and Rwanda) is Uncle Sam himself. The US government and the military and their allies are guilty of what Nuremberg called the supreme crime, the crime against peace. Every death and every maiming of every man woman and child is not just 'collateral damage' in Jamie Shea's unforgettable newspeak, but rather a *crime against humanity* because it is being caused knowingly and without lawful excuse.

Does legality matter in a case like this? I can think of at least two reasons why it does. In the first place, this attack is not wrong just because it is illegal. On the contrary, like murder itself, it is illegal because it is wrong. It is a deliberate taking of human life, not because this is absolutely necessary to save life, but rather to make some political point. In this it is the moral (and legal) equivalent of the attacks of September 11.

Furthermore, it is illegal because it has sidelined the real international community, as represented by the United Nations. If we allow the system of international legality as designed in the UN Charter to be overthrown, by the US or by a bunch of Pontius Pilates on the Security Council, there will be nothing left to limit international violence but the power, ruthlessness and cunning of the perpetrators. We are all at risk from what happens next, not just the US. Yet we know that even if the Taliban are completely vanquished and bin Laden handed over on a platter, our cities and skies won't be one bit safer. The best bet, based on experience, is that this is not the beginning of an end to violence, but rather an *escalation* of it. Violence begets violence. Look at it this way: the US is one of the few countries to think that the death penalty is an appropriate response to murder and they continue to have one of the highest murder rates in the world. Forget the Taliban; President Bush's Texas has the busiest execution chambers apart from China and Saudi Arabia. Letting the Americans 'handle it their way' means more tragedy for all of us, not just the Afghans.

We may come to remember September 11, not for its human tragedy, but for the beginning of a headlong plunge into a violent, lawless world.

1. 'After the Attack … The War on Terrorism', *Monthly Review*, Vol. 53, No. 6, November 2001: 1 at 2.
2. *Case Concerning the Military and Paramilitary Activities in and Against Nicaragua* (*Nicaragua* v. *United States of America*) (*MERITS*), Judgment of 27 June 1986, [1986] I.C.J. Rep.
3. *Ibid.*, paragraph 195.
4. *Ibid.* paragraphs 115 and 116.
5. See, for example, Hilaire, Max, *International Law and the United States Military Intervention in the Western Hemisphere*, The Hague: Kluwer Law International, 1997.
6. *Supra*, note 2 at paragraph 237.
7. Avnery, Uri, 'All Kinds of Terrorists', November 3, 2001 (available from avnery@actcom.co.il).
8. Saunders, Doug, 'The Pope, Picasso, Mandela and Q', *The Globe and Mail*, October 20, 2001: R8.
9. 'The United States is a Leading Terrorist State: An Interview with Noam Chomsky by David Barsamian', *Monthly Review*, Vol. 53, No. 6, November 2001: 10.
10. Saba, Sahar, a member of the Foreign Affairs Committee of the Revolutionary Association of Women of Afghanistan (RAWA) interviewed on 'As It Happens' *CBC Radio* November 13, 2001, http://radio.cbc.ca/insite/AS IT HAPPENS TORONTO/2001/11/13.HTML (visited November 14, 2001).
11. Makin, Kirk, 'Vengeance could imperil future', *The Globe and Mail*, November 14, 2001: A4.

EXPANDING THE CONCEPT OF TERRORISM?[1]

Thomas Mathiesen

The actions which took place in the United States on September 11 were terrible. So are many of the actions committed by the US against other states through the years. The latter actions have been part of the complex of factors causing the former ones. In the shadow of the September actions against the superpower, and at very short notice, plans have been proposed within the EU which imply a dramatic widening of what we usually understand by 'terrorism'.

The proposals contain two main characteristics. First, if implemented they will be of marginal importance when it comes to prevention of actions such as the ones we have seen in the US. Second, they may be of very considerable importance in preventing legitimate, but perhaps somewhat boisterous, protests, for example against international summit meetings such as those we saw earlier in 2001 in Gothenburg and Genova.

The first proposals were discussed at the meeting of the JHA [Justice and Home Affairs] Council on September 20, nine days after the events in the US. The EU Commission had presented two proposals for council framework decisions, partly drafted after September 11 – one on the issue of the European arrest warrant, and one on combating terrorism. The ministers agreed in principle on both of them, advocating rapid further handling. My focus of attention here will be the proposal on combating terrorism. The core provision in the Commission's proposal was its Article 3 (later renumbered as Article 1), where 'terrorist offences' were defined.

'Terrorism' is a complicated concept. As far as definition goes, it is in considerable measure dependent on political view: Palestinian actions in the Middle East are defined as 'terrorist' by Israel and many Western states, while they are defined as legitimate and necessary political actions by some or many Palestinians. Frequently, an important part of the political struggle consists of winning the battle over definition.

What is defined as 'terrorist' may also change through history. The demonstrations and actions of the Norwegian labour movement in the early 1900s were frequently defined as terrorist, while in retrospect they are seen as having been legitimate and necessary attempts to change Norwegian politics and social structure.

Despite variations such as these, some core activities are commonly understood as 'terrorist', at least by a large majority, more or less regardless of political view and historical phase. Violent and arbitrary actions consciously directed towards civilians, with a political or ideological goal more or less clearly in mind, constitute such a core (though admittedly, those who commit such acts may at the time not consider them 'terrorist'). I view the mass bombing of the city of Dresden during the closing months of the Second World War, followed by the shooting of civilians (from fighter planes) who tried to flee from the demolished city, as such acts. Though the professed aim was to shorten the war, the war was obviously coming to an end anyway, Dresden was of no military importance whatsoever, and it was a violent and arbitrary slaughter of tens of thousands of civilians. The carpet-bombing, the slaughter of civilians in My Lai and other attacks on civilians during the Vietnam War, the attacks on Somalia and the actions against the World Trade Center in New York and the Pentagon in Washington DC on September 11 constitute other cases in point.

Though this is one core activity, other types of action may also be included. For example, damage to or demolition of important institutions such as oil installations, symbolically important physical structures, or structures with important practical functions for civilian populations (Norwegian oil rigs, Buckingham Palace, WTC and Pentagon once more, electricity and water supplies, such as those in Serbia and Afghanistan, would be cases in point).

There is also an admittedly hazy 'outer parameter' of the concept, comprising activities which may or may not be included, depending on the circumstances. Even if consciously targeted against military goals, the incessant US bombing of Afghanistan in 2001, leaving craters as large as five football stadiums and killing an unknown number of civilians, would be included by many. In any event, and despite the unclarity, the concept as defined in Article 3 in the Commission's above-mentioned proposed framework decision *comprised activities which without doubt went far beyond any reasonable definition, and far beyond the concept of terrorism as commonly understood today.* The concept was greatly expanded and watered down compared with any of the core activities mentioned above.

A number of offences were listed, from murder to attacks through interference with information systems. Several of the offences, including theft and robbery, are not necessarily associated with anything particularly terroristic. More important is the fact that acts covering regular civil disobedience – Gandhi's time-honoured approach – were included. 'Unlawful seizure' of 'places of public use' arouses strong associations to environmental protests such as those in northern Norway in the early 1980s, where thousands of people participated in major sit-down demonstrations to prevent irreversible damage to nature in connection with the use of a particular river for electricity. Likewise, the demonstrations in Gothenburg and Genova are relevant. 'Unlawful seizure' of 'state or government facilities' covers protest against the erection of nuclear power plants in many countries.

'Damage' to such places of public use and facilities was also included. 'Damage' is in itself a highly subjective category, open to wide discretionary interpretation. Even in terms of crowns or pounds, the concept is open, as everyone who has a car knows. Earlier this year I accidentally bumped slightly into another car, leaving a small scratch in the other car's door. Repairs cost 10,000 crowns, an enormous price for such a damage. 'Damage' was performed in Gothenburg and Genova. However, there is wide disagreement on its extent and seriousness; the authorities and the courts argue that the events as a whole were two enormous 'damage occasions', while demonstrators and others argue that, despite some damage, the demonstrations on the whole were peaceful, the damage being partly provoked by police intimidation and brutality. This goes to show how much the concept is subject to interpretation. I will return to this below. Here, however, the point is that the significant word 'or' was injected between 'seizure' and 'damage', indicating that seizure alone was enough to qualify. Threats to commit offences of this kind were also included in the list.

But the offences in and of themselves, as listed by the Commission, were not enough. The *purpose* must be terroristic, and in the proposal a terroristic purpose was given a very broad definition indeed. If the offences which were listed 'are intentionally committed by an individual or a group against one or more countries, their institutions or people with the aim of intimidating them and seriously altering or destroying the political, economic, or social structures of those countries, [they] will be punishable as terrorist offences'. Note once more that there is an 'or' between seriously 'altering' and 'destroying'. Think of that – *with the aim of seriously altering political, economic or social structure*. The demonstrations mentioned above in northern Norway in the early 1980s as well as the Gothenburg or Genova demonstrations in 2001, had precisely this aim. So do environmental protests of various kinds. So does Attac. In northern Norway in the 1980s, the demonstrators were fined. The fines were nothing compared to the maximum prison sentences outlined in Article 5 of the Commission's proposal.

The first response of the JHA Council to the proposals of the Commission is interesting: the Council *widened* the definition of terrorism. Most significantly, in the definition of a terrorist purpose, the Council changed the word '*altering*' political, economic or social structure to '*affecting*' such structures. 'Affecting' includes almost anything. Also, in its response the Council did not wish to limit the issue to altering the political, economic or social structures of *countries*, but added *international organisations*. As *Statewatch* noted in a significant submission to the House of Lords Select Committee on the European Union, such 'a broad definition would clearly embrace protests such as those in Gothenburg and Genoa'. In addition, Ireland and the UK apparently proposed the deletion of the word *seriously* in the definition of a terroristic purpose, broadening the scope even more. In view of this, it was of little help that the Council in its reponse added the word 'serious' to the description of the offence called 'unlawful seizure of or damage to places of public use' (see above).

The EU Parliament was consulted – without introducing significant changes. In a draft report from the EU Parliament's Committee on Citizens' Freedoms and Rights, Justice and Home Affairs the Commission's definition of a terrorist purpose was not changed and the extremely broad definition of purpose was retained. In the final report it was somewhat altered, but not in a way that changed the content greatly. Among the offences, 'unlawful seizure' of 'places of public use' was only delimited in a vague and discretionary way in the draft report from the Committee 'unlawful seizure *of control* of, *thereby endangering persons ...*' (emphasis added by the Committee to indicate the changes). The word 'serious' was added to 'damage', and 'serious damage' would have to be performed 'by means of arms or dangerous acts'. The purpose of these formulations was, according to the Committee, not to confuse a terrorist offence 'with unlawful occupation, which may constitute a form of protest which is tolerated in the context of public demonstrations'. Well intentioned to be sure, but in actual practice hardly enough to limit the target area of the provision. What does 'endangering persons' mean? Resisting the police, such as in Gothenburg? What are 'dangerous acts'? Throwing cobblestones, such as some did in Gothenburg? The content of formulations such as these is dependent on the political climate of the time, and may under the circumstances be stretched far beyond intent and recognition. In times of panic over terrorist attacks, and in times when the authorities need to control demonstrations from the 'grass roots', as in Gothenburg and Genova, they may be stretched very far indeed.

What, in the end, became of all this? The JHA Council came to a 'political agreement' on December 6–7, 2001. It agreed on the following definition of a terrorist purpose:

i) serious intimidation of a population, *or* ii) unduly compelling governments or international organisations to perform or to abstain from performing any act whatsoever, *or* iii) seriously destabilising *or* destroying the fundamental political, constitutional, economic or social structures of a country or an international organisation. [My italics, translated from the French by the author]

The concept of 'destabilising' is perhaps slightly narrower than 'altering' (the Commission) and 'affecting' (the Council's first response). But the difference is small. What does 'serious intimidation of a population' mean? Were the demonstrators who probably intimidated people in Gothenburg, or for that matter Council members who were present there, terrorists? What does 'compelling governments ... to execute or to abstain from executing *any acts whatsoever*' (my italics) refer to? Certainly, the demonstrators in northern Norway in the early 1980s tried to compel the government to abstain from something, notably using a large river for electricity. What does 'destabilising' a structure mean? Certainly, and whether we like it or not, some demonstrators in Gothenburg and Genova had 'destabilisation' in mind. Were they for that reason terrorists? I can think of many legitimate groups and people who wish to 'destabilise' given economic or social structures, for example structures where some people at the top run the whole game, and the rest of society is characterised by destitution and poverty. Today, structures of this kind often develop and thrive on the basis of global capitalism, a major goal of attention of demonstrators at the summits. The definition of purpose is wide open.

If you search hard enough, you find some glimmers of light. Three, in fact, of varying strength. It is important to bring them out. First, the JHA Council apparently scrapped the concept of 'seizure ... of a public place' as an offence which, if coupled with the broad definition of terroristic purpose, would have made a person a 'terrorist'. The formulation was now limited to 'causing extensive destruction to ... a public place'. This could be viewed as a small victory on the part of the civil society groups (for example, *Statewatch*) and others (lawyers, independent writers) who had struggled ardently to narrow the EU concept. It goes to show that struggle pays. But we should not open champagne bottles, for the simple reason alluded to earlier: (i) 'damage' or 'destruction', even 'extensive destruction', is open to varying interpretations depending on the intepreter, on time and place; (ii) at almost any mass demonstration or protest of the kind we are discussing here (again with Gothenburg and Genova as examples), *a certain amount of 'destruction' will almost inevitably take place.* And not only destruction to 'a public place', but also to 'a government or public facility', to 'private property', and the like, mentioned in the formulation. An addition, 'likely to endanger human life' is a highly subjective category, keeping in mind how the police will interpret it. In short, the definition covers the political summit demonstrations which are our concern here, and it certainly covers the activities of various other protest movements and action groups which we normally do not view as terrorists.

Second, Recital 10 of the preamble stated that '[N]othing in this framework decision may be interpreted as being intended to reduce or restrict fundamental rights or freedoms such as the freedom of assembly or association or of expression, including the right of everyone to form and to join trade unions with others for the protection of his or her interests and the related right to demonstrate.' As an expression of generalised values this is fine but, at least to a Nordic ear, expression of such values sounds rather empty, and as something you put at the beginning of political statements without attaching too much significance to it. The reference to the 'right to demonstrate' refers to demonstrations related to ordinary trade union work, and not to demonstrations and protest movements such as those we are concerned with here. If protest actions such as Gothenburg or Genova were to be excluded, much clearer words would be necessary. Apparently, a small minority of governments wanted to ensure that 'trade union activities and anti-globalisation movements, under no circumstances could come within the scope of the Framework Decision'. Significantly, this was *not* included.

Third, the JHA Council agreed to add a Council statement to the Framework Decision. Such a statement does not have legal force. It is only a political statement. It stated: 'Nor can [the definition of terrorism] be construed so as to incriminate on terrorist grounds persons exercising their legitimate right to manifest their opinions, even if in the course of the exercise of such rights they commit offences.' The statement may be a recognition of the need to exclude regular illegal demonstrations from the concept of terrorism. But we should also note that the wording is vague, and that exclusion of a series of *other* kinds of acts from the concept is more crisply stated, even with reference to concrete historical examples which makes relatively precise comparisons possible: 'It ... cannot be construed so as to argue that the conduct of those who have acted in the interest of preserving or restoring these democratic values, as was notably the case in some member states during the Second World War, could now be considered as "terrorist" acts.' The authors were probably thinking first and foremost of the activities of liberation forces during the Second World War, but by the same token, essentially everything the Western alliance is or has been doing is excluded – the bombing of Dresden in 1945, My Lai and other atrocities during the Vietnam War, US bombing elsewhere after the Second World War. Those in power delimit what is 'terrorism'.

The glimmers of light show what can be gained in a struggle for civil rights against the powerful decision-making bodies in the EU. But they also show the limitations. In argument, the glimmers should be used for whatever they are worth. But the overarching point should not be lost from sight; throughout the 15 EU countries, almost the whole continent, a terroristic purpose, according to the political agreement of the JHA Council, should be understood as intimidation of a population, or unduly compelling governments or international organisations to perform or to abstain from performing *any act whatsoever*, or seriously destabilising or destroying given structures. In northern Norway in the early 1980s, in Gothenburg and Genova in 2001, one or more of these criteria were met, and actions were performed which could trigger the label of 'terrorist', with all its legal and social consequences.

As the editor of *Statewatch*, Tony Bunyan, recently put it in a piece on the web: 'How member states use this definition of terrorism in practice will be the acid test.' What has happened in terms of definition is potentially dangerous. Legal measures of the kind I have analysed will not be effective in preventing terrible and extraordinary events such as those we have seen in the US. Such actions are committed by very professional people, fully capable of acting outside the reach of the measures. But the measures may certainly enable state institutions and forces to stop legitimate protests against 'political, economic, or social structures'.

We should keep in mind that the JHA Council's definition is not entirely final. 'Political agreement' does not mean adoption, and at the time of writing the status is that the EU Parliament is to be re-consulted on the issue (although the Council decides). On the other hand, on the eve of 2002, notably on December 27 in the quiet week between Christmas and New Year, the Council of the European

Union by 'written procedure' adopted a common position on combating terrorism. The common position, made under Article 15 of the Treaty on European Union, does not have to be submitted to the EU Parliament (or any parliament) for scrutiny. Very briefly, the common position contains two vital points. First, in Article 4 it is stated that measures 'shall be taken to suppress any form of support, *active or passive*, to entities or persons involved in terrorist acts ...' (emphasis added). The implication is that no line is drawn between those who actively engage in terrorist support and those who agree with the political aims of terrorists, yet take no measures to help them. Suppression is on a wide scale, indeed. Second, in Article 16 it is stated that appropriate 'measures shall be taken ... before granting refugee status, for the purpose of ensuring that the asylum seeker has not planned, facilitated or participated in the commission of terrorist acts'. Keeping in mind the very broad definition of terrorism which is in the process of being adopted within the EU, asylum seekers throughout Europe will be subjected to extremely broad examinations of political beliefs, attitudes and activities (further details may be found on the *Statewatch* web site).

Methods of political protest available to ordinary people are under attack. Regardless of whether the attack is consciously planned and/or an unintended consequence of a major panic (it is probably a mixture of the two), it is politically dangerous. As far as the Commission's and the Council's definitions are concerned, they may possibly not be used in such a broad and generalised way at first. From long experience we know, however, that discretionary measures in this area will be employed less carefully, and more broadly, as time passes, when the time is ripe and when the need is there.

Postscript

As stated above, at the time of writing this article the EU Council's definition of terrorism was not entirely final; Parliament was to be re-consulted on the issue. On Wednesday February 6, 2002 the EU Parliament voted, by a large majority, to support the Framework Decision on combating terrorism, and with it accepting the broad definition of 'terrorism' discussed above. The definition had already been greatly extended by the common position, adopted on December 27, 2001, on which Parliament was not even consulted. Also by a large majority, the EU Parliament voted to support the Framework Decision on establishing a European arrest warrant, which suffers from a fundamental deficit as far as the protection of individual rights goes. The two far-reaching Framework Decisions are expected to come into force on January 1, 2003 and January 1, 2004 respectively.

1. This paper is a considerably expanded and revised version of an article published in the *Statewatch bulletin*, Vol. 11, No. 5, 2001. Warm thanks go to *Statewatch* editor Tony Bunyan for his great willingness to answer phones and e-mails at any and all hours, providing me with the latest updated information on the issues discussed here.

LEGISLATIVE RESPONSES TO TERRORISM
Philip A Thomas[1]

Introduction

Emergency legislation passed as a consequence of national catastrophe associated with terrorism has a predictable pattern. It involves an unseemly scramble amongst the legislature so that it is seen to be doing 'something'. The law is hastily tightened, with scant recourse to reasoned chamber debate or recognition of standard procedures, in order to respond to media and public outcry. Thus, the politicians' anxiety to be viewed as resolving the crisis overrides both established process and rational action. The result is predictably disturbing: enhanced powers to security agencies and the police; deviation from established principles of law; alienation of innocent, affected people; and disappointing results in controlling anti-terrorist activities. This is a formula that, once again, is evident both within the US and the UK as a consequence of the events of September 11.

The experience of history

In recent times the most striking examples of ill-considered legislation are to be found in the responses to terrorist activities. I show below that there is a strong and clear parallel between the current legislative processes in both the US and the UK. The Prevention of Terrorism (Temporary Provisions) Act 1974 was subject to a mere 17 hours of debate in the House of Commons before its 'draconian powers' were approved. Parliamentary debate was driven by the public outrage caused by the Birmingham pub bombings which resulted in the deaths of 21 people and the injury to a further 180. Brian Walden MP stated in the House of Commons: 'The justification for the Bill to my mind, is overwhelming, and I make no bones about the fact that I shall not listen with too much patience to any anxieties about whether this or that or the other civil right may temporarily be somewhat abridged ... Let us be frank. The overwhelming mood in my constituency, and I believe in my city, is one of vengeance.' The absence of thought and the presence of vengeance characterised the mood of both Parliament and the nation. Clare Short attended the debate on the Bill in her capacity as a Home Office civil servant. She whispered to her neighbour, the man who drafted the Bill, that it would do nothing to prevent terrorism. His reply was 'that is not what it is about'. Dafydd Elis Thomas MP told me at the time that despite his personal reservations it was more than a person's parliamentary seat was worth to vote against the Bill given the extreme level of public shock and outrage.

A similar legislative response pattern occurred both in Ireland and the UK over the Omagh bombings in Northern Ireland in August 1998. In Dublin the Offences Against the State (Amendment) Bill was published on August 31, debated in the Dail on September 2 between 10 a.m. and 11.30 a.m. and thereafter in the Seanad on September 3, followed by an immediate quasi-presidential signing (this was because the President of Ireland was overseas).

In Westminster a similar, complex Bill, which quickly became the Criminal Justice (Terrorism and Conspiracy) Act, was pushed through Parliament in 27 hours. It was published and made available to members for reading at 6 p.m. on the day before the House of Commons debate. Tony Benn, in debate, compared the procedure with that associated with the former USSR 'What a way to treat Parliament ... as though we were the Supreme Soviet, simply summoned to carry through the instructions of the Central Committee.' In addition, the Queen proved to be exceedingly obliging. Whilst on holiday in Scotland, she gave the Royal Assent to the Act some time before it had completed its Parliamentary passage.

US legislative responses

The principal legislative response to September 11 is the anti-terrorist legislation titled 'Uniting and Strengthening of America to Provide Appropriate Tools Required to Intercept and Obstruct Terrorism Act of 2001'. This creates the powerful acronym, the USA PATRIOT Act of 2001. It is a monster piece of legislation amounting to 342 pages, covering 350 subject areas, encompassing 40 federal agencies and carrying 21 legal amendments.

House Judiciary Committee chairman, F James Sensenbrenner, introduced the legislation on October 2. It became law on October 26. This was a record-breaking activity made possible only by forcing the pace to the point where serious debate and discussion was made impossible by the restricted timescale and the public demand for political action. In the Senate only Russell Feingold voted against the PATRIOT Act. With Congressional staff locked out of their offices due to the anthrax scare few members of Congress had time to read the summaries of the Bill let alone the fine print of the document that was passed in such haste. Indeed, what red-blooded American politician, with an eye on re-election, would vote against such legislation? Bush, whose sabre-rattling rhetoric demanded immediate political support, urged on the representatives. He declared that 'in order to win the war, we must make sure that the law enforcement men and women have got the tools necessary, within the Constitution, to defeat the enemy .... We're at war ... a war we're going to win.' The Act moulded by these warrior words and passed in furious and frustrated haste left federal prosecutors, defenders, regulators and administrators throughout the country scrambling to decipher what Congress and the Bush administration had packed into the legislation. The public responded in positive terms. In various public polls, roughly two-thirds say they support the actions of the administration: a quarter state that President George Bush and Attorney-General John Ashcroft have not acted in a sufficiently aggressive manner.

The US PATRIOT Act

In essence the Act creates, amongst other things, the following sweeping powers:

- Powers of detention and surveillance to the Executive and law enforcement agencies as well as depriving the courts of meaningful judicial oversight of the exercise of those powers.
- The Secretary of State is empowered to designate any group, foreign or domestic, as 'terrorist'. This power is not subject to review.
- A new crime, 'domestic terrorism', is created. It includes activities that involve acts dangerous to human life that are a violation of the criminal law, if it appears to be intended (i) to intimidate or coerce a civilian population; (ii) to influence the policy of government by intimidation or coercion; or (iii) to

affect the conduct of a government by mass destruction, assassination or kidnapping.

- It permits investigations based on lawful First Amendment activity if that activity can be tied to intelligence purposes.
- It undermines the privacy protection of the Fourth Amendment by eroding the line between intelligence gathering and gathering evidence for criminal proceedings. It expands the ability of the government to spy by wiretaps and computer surveillance. It provides access to medical, financial, business and educational records and allows secret searches of homes and offices.
- It undermines due process procedures by permitting the government to detain non-citizens indefinitely even if they have never been convicted of a crime.[2]

The possible uses and outcomes of this legislation have horrified many constitutional lawyers and civil rights groups. For example, domestic spying is given a renewed lease of life. Firewalls were erected after the Watergate scandal and the subsequent Senate investigation in 1975 chaired by Senator Frank Church. Church warned that domestic intelligence gathering was a 'new form of governmental abuse', unconstrained by law, which had been abused by Nixon and by the FBI which spied on over half a million Americans during and after the McCarthy era. One reform was the separation with the FBI of the bureau's criminal investigation function and its intelligence gathering against foreign spies and international terrorists. The Act foreshadows the end of that separation by making key changes to the underpinning law, the Foreign Intelligence Surveillance Act (FISA) 1978. FISA demanded that wiretaps and searches for intelligence purposes, as opposed to evidence, be undertaken only if the 'primary purpose' was to listen to a specific foreign spy or terrorist. The new Act lowers the level to a 'significant purpose'. Roving wiretaps throughout the US now operate on a single warrant. Americans engaged in civil disobedience or other forms of civil protest might be charged with 'domestic terrorism' if violence occurs. Senator Patrick Leahy, the Senate negotiator on the Bill, said on the day it was passed: 'The Bill enters new and uncharted territory by breaking down traditional barriers between law enforcement and foreign intelligence.'

Morton Halperin, a defence expert, stated that if a government intelligence agency 'thinks you're under the control of a foreign government, they can wiretap you and never tell you, search your house and never tell you, break into your home, copy your hard drive, and never tell you they have done it'. Some of the surveillance provisions expire, or 'sunset', after a period of four years, unless renewed. The experience of the UK with the 'temporary' nature of its anti-terrorist legislation would suggest that it is likely that the sun will never set on this Act.

For a modern nation created largely by immigrants the new laws covering non-citizens are ironically harsh. Section 412 of the Act permits indefinite detention of immigrants and other non-citizens. It requires that immigrants 'certified' by the Attorney-General be charged within seven days with a criminal offence or an immigration violation, which need not be on the grounds of terrorism. Those detained for non-terrorist offences face the possibility of life imprisonment if their country of origin refuses to accept them. Detention would be allowed on the Attorney-General's finding of 'reasonable grounds to believe' in the detainee's involvement in terrorism or an activity that poses a danger to national security, or the safety of the community or any person. A review of the detention takes place at six-monthly intervals, but what is striking is the absence of a trial in open court to test the state's case for prosecution.

The reality of declared war experienced by President Roosevelt, which resulted in the incarceration of more than 110,000 people of Japanese origin, 11,000 of German origin and 3,000 of Italian origin, is now being replicated through the rhetoric of undeclared war by President Bush. Should it be thought that these detention powers are merely precautionary and unlikely to be utilised, the actions of Attorney-General Ashcroft constitute a sobering reality. He began by authorising the detention of 1,100 non-citizens. Some have been held for months and through Section 412 may be held indefinitely. Legal advice is available but solely funded by the detainee. The government stopped updating the tally of those detained so firm figures became unavailable. After refusing to make any information public about the detainees – this included their names, location of detention, or nature of the charges – Ashcroft finally announced on November 27 that 548 detainees were being held on immigration charges and that federal criminal charges had been filed against 104 of them. The Justice Department also announced a plan for investigators to interview 5,000 people: Middle Eastern males between the ages of 18 to 33 who had arrived in the US after January 2000. In response to a claim that this is a racially based round-up Ashcroft declared that 'we are being as kind and as fair and as gentle as we can'. Of particular concern was the CNN poll which revealed that 45 per cent of those polled would not object to torturing someone if it provided information about terrorism. There was also media discussion about the possible need for the use of 'truth serums' or sending them to countries where harsher interrogation measures were common. In this context it is important to remember that the 'disappeared' and tortured people of South American countries in the 1970s and 1980s were killed and tortured by military personnel trained by the CIA.

The final illustration of the new wave of legislation is the Military Order signed by the president on November 13 which allows for non-US citizens suspected of involvement in 'international terrorism' to be tried by special military commissions. These commissions are not subject to the regular rules and safeguards that cover military court martials. The president claimed that it was 'not practicable' to try terrorists under 'the principles of law and the rules of evidence' applicable in the US domestic criminal courts. These commissions are empowered to act in secret, to pass the death penalty by a two-thirds majority, and their decisions cannot be appealed to other courts. Any such commission might be held offshore to minimise public awareness. For example, the US base in Cuba, Guantanamo Bay, was identified by General Tommy Franks, head of Central Command, as a suitable base to hold Taliban and al-Qaida terrorists. Subject to modification it could detain 2,000 prisoners. On January 12 the base received its first unlawful combatants and placed them in Camp X-Ray. Ninety men manacled, hooded, with shaved beards, and some sedated, were flown in from Afghanistan with more to follow. They were detained in wire 'cages', open to the elements. The conditions were described by Amnesty International as 'falling below the minimum standards for humane behaviour'. This is, perhaps, unsurprising given that Donald Rumsfeld, US Defense Secretary, described the men as 'the hardest of the hard core', adding, 'I do not feel the slightest concern over their treatment.'[3] The term 'unlawful combatant' was used because the US government did not define the Taliban as prisoners of war, thereby denying them their rights under the 1949 Geneva Conventions; nor were they defined as criminals, thereby denying them their rights under the US Constitution. Organising a defence from within this camp proved extremely difficult assuming that it was the intention to try the men in front of military commissions. The alternative was that the men were interrogated and detained at the pleasure of the president.

United Kingdom

The ink was hardly dry on the Terrorism Act 2000 that came into force in February 2001 before a fresh commitment to yet stronger anti-terrorist legislation was issued by the Labour government. The Terrorism Act extended the powers of the police to investigate, arrest and detain. It created new offences allowing our courts to deal with terrorist activities which occurred outside our national borders. The moral panic that consumes the US is reflected in its most constant ally, the UK, which considers itself a serious potential target because of its political and practical commitment to US policies and actions.

David Blunkett, Home Secretary, introduced the government's Anti-terrorism, Crime and Security Bill into the Commons on November 12. It was a big Bill, containing 118 pages, 126 clauses and 8 Schedules. After a protracted House of Lords savaging, it became law on December 15. While claiming the powers were measured, reasonable and necessary on the day of the Bill's Parliamentary presentation, Blunkett laid a Human Rights Derogation Order, thereby derogating from the European Convention on Human Rights because Article 5 guarantees the right to liberty and prohibits detention without trial.

The speed of the Bill's passage through the House of Commons was reminiscent of previous emergency legislation. The Bill was given its Second Reading on November 19. A timetable motion was passed which provided that the Committee Stage and the Third Reading should be completed in a further two days. The Derogation Order was debated for 90 minutes. The Committee Stage by the full House occurred on November 21 and November 26. It finished at 11.57 p.m. and was immediately followed by the Third Reading that was concluded at midnight. The Home Secretary spoke for three minutes and Oliver Letwin, the Shadow Home Secretary, responded by saying: 'I shall be brief ...' Indeed, he was. He was interrupted in mid-sentence for the vote that went 323 to 79. Royal Assent to the Act was granted on December 14.

It was in the House of Lords that opposition to the Bill occurred. The Lords made 70 amendments and although most were reversed in the Commons, several were maintained and constituted significant defeats for the government. It was the issue of indefinite detention without charge that raised major opposition. A person reasonably suspected of being an international terrorist could be detained indefinitely and without charge. It was to cover 'dozens of foreign' people, the Home Secretary claimed, who could not be prosecuted for insufficiency or inadmissibility of evidence, nor could they be deported if they faced either torture or death overseas. The detainee's appeal against detention is through the Special Immigration Appeal Commission [SIAC] that will sit in secret. A security-cleared special advocate appointed by the Commission will represent the detainee. The special advocate cannot take client's instructions without the express permission of the Commission. Evidence may be adduced without showing it to the detainee or special advocate. Although an appeal on a point of law could go to the Court of Appeal, there was no appeal against the Home Secretary's certificate of detention. The government amended the Bill, in the light of the Lords' opposition, by raising the status of SIAC to that of a superior court of record, thereby ensuring that its decision was not subject to judicial review!

In December and January 2002 several arrests were made in London and Leicester. Detainees, who were not charged, were incarcerated in the London high security prison, Belmarsh. They were locked up for 22 hours a day and did not see daylight. On detention they were given access neither to lawyers nor to their families. They were unable to speak to families without the presence of an approved translator visiting once a week. They were denied prayer facilities apart from 15 minutes on a Friday but in the absence of an iman. Gareth Peirce, a solicitor who represents several of them, stated that 'these men have been buried alive in concrete coffins and have been told the legislation provides for their detention for life without trial'.

Wide-scale trawling, retention and availability of data were other highly charged concerns. At the time of writing there were over 50 statutes allowing a number of public authorities to disclose information in the light of criminal proceedings. Oliver Letwin complained, 'The Home Secretary is saying that to catch terrorists, he has to allow 81 government agencies – from the BBC to the NHS – to reveal somebody's records, even if they are being investigated for a traffic offence in the US. I find that a difficult chain of logic to follow.' The Bill sought to extend 'criminal proceedings' to include general 'investigations', both within the UK and abroad. The Lords attempted to limit this power and succeeded in so far as the government finally agreed that the Act would carry an express requirement that any such disclosure would be limited by the Human

Rights Act. This requires that disclosure be proportionate to what was sought to be achieved by the disclosure. The human rights lawyer, Lord Lester, described this amendment as mere 'window dressing'.

Serious disagreements also arose over the retention of data. In addition, the adoption of criminal justice measures under Title V1 of the Treaty on European Union [known as the Third Pillar], including the proposed European arrest warrant, resulted in a defeat for the government. It agreed that such changes would be introduced through primary legislation and via the back door through negative resolution procedure. Nevertheless, the new anti-terrorism measures developed by the Justice and Home Affairs Council [JHAC] and the European Council after September 11 will be introduced through powers in the Act.[4]

Finally, the Lords successfully introduced expanded sunset clauses and reviews into the Bill. Thus, the provisions for detention without charge will lapse after five years unless renewed by primary legislation. In the meantime the provisions will be reviewed after 15 months and thereafter annually. The entire Act is to be reviewed by a body of Privy Councillors within two years of Royal Assent. However, the Home Secretary announced that the review body will have no access to the detailed cases that have gone through SIAC, nor to the evidence that was presented in private.

The Bill is a classic example of legislation drafted too quickly and too loosely and thereafter passed too hastily. Nevertheless, concerns voiced by legal experts over the scope and likely efficiency of the Act did little to cool the government's ardour. Michael Zander, a leading criminal law professor, noted that 'this was complex and controversial legislation rushed through Parliament at breakneck speed. We are unlikely to know whether it contributes to making this country a safer place.'

The Rule of Law, equality and fairness are challenged by terrorists as well as by ill-conceived terrorist legislation. The police and the security services cannot be allowed complete freedom through law to tackle terrorists. The European Court of Human Rights has laid down limits. 'The Court, being aware of the danger such a law poses of undermining or even destroying democracy on the ground of defending it, affirms that the Contracting States may not, in the name of the struggle against terrorism, adopt what measures they deem appropriate.' Thus, while terrorism is a threat to democracy, so the legislative responses of nation states, and the European Union, carry similar dangers. In the particularly sensitive area of terrorist control it is incumbent upon politicians that their decisions be considered, proportionate and appropriate and that both content and process accord with the principles of the Rule of Law. Neither the PATRIOT Act nor the Anti-Terrorism, Crime and Security Act meet these basic criteria.

In 1993 a senior Labour politician stated in Parliament: 'If we cravenly accept that any action by the government and entitled Prevention of Terrorism Act must be supported in its entirety without question we do not strengthen the fight against terrorism, we weaken it. I hope that no Honourable Member will say that we do not have the right to challenge powers, to make sure that they are in accordance with the civil liberties of our country.' The speaker? The Shadow Home Secretary, Tony Blair.

1. I wish to acknowledge the Research Committee, Cardiff Law School, for providing support for this paper.
2. My precis of the sections of the Act is based on the paper prepared by the ACLU of Michigan, www.aclumich.org
3. *Guardian*, January 17, 2002.
4. See the essay by Thomas Mathiesen in this volume.

ALL IN THE NAME OF SECURITY
Liz Fekete

On November 13, Home Secretary David Blunkett laid an order before Parliament declaring Britain to be in a state of public emergency due to the events of September 11. He was paving the way for new terrorism, crime and security legislation which, among other things, allows for the indefinite internment of foreign nationals, the incorporation into British law of an EU-wide definition of terrorism, and for wider powers to MI6 and GCHQ to carry out 'intelligence gathering' outside Britain.

Blunkett's internment proposal will be even harder for civil libertarians to oppose than similar measures adopted during the Gulf War (when scores of innocent Arabs were detained), given that the threat of terrorist actions against civilians is not an imagined one. Blair is Bush's top backer, Britain is a prime target for bin Laden's al-Qaida network. In this climate, the government's argument that it has to balance individual civil liberties against society's right to live free from terror seems reasonable. Yet the new legislation, particularly when set alongside other developments in asylum policy, is patently unreasonable. Just as the war in Afghanistan is not a limited and targeted intervention against a defined enemy, the domestic front of the 'war against terrorism' is similarly undefined. Heedless of 'collateral damage', the governments of the US and the UK trawl for suspects in 'foreign' communities.

In the US, 800 immigrants were rounded up immediately after the events of September 11 (one detainee died in custody in New Jersey). By mid-November, the figure had risen to 1,147, only four of whom were officially named as suspected members of al-Qaida. Such arbitrary detention without trial has been backed up by a raft of anti-terrorism measures; from the Mobilisation Against Terrorism Act (greater powers to detain suspected terrorists) to greater powers for the FBI, Immigration and Naturalisation Services and federal prosecutors (to spy, jail and interrogate); from the PATRIOT Act (sweeping powers granted to federal agents to break down the firewall between intelligence gathering and criminal justice) to the reversal of guaranteed protections of freedom of information (to suppress information on issues such as arbitrary detention on national security grounds).

Unlike the UK where Blair is attempting to delay the introduction of a Freedom of Information Act, the US has freedom of information legislation. Now the Attorney-General is reversing long-standing Freedom of Information Act provisions, to the extent that it is virtually impossible to breach the information blockade about the 1,147 people detained. Tracking them has proved difficult, as basic information, such as the names of the detainees and the reasons for their detention, has been labelled 'classified information'. But, according to US civil libertarians, the arrest of so many people, under such draconian measures, has failed to provide one scrap of new intelligence about the events of September 11 or, for that matter, other planned terrorist actions. So frustrated have the FBI become over the detainees' alleged unwillingness to talk that they have begun to demand the right to torture detainees, either by administering sodium pentothal or turning suspects over to a country where torture is not prohibited. Meanwhile, Bush has signed an Executive Order allowing special military tribunals to try non-citizens charged with terrorism in secret and to order their execution.

The UK's anti-terrorist legislation will pave the way for a similar information blockade on those detained. The government will not have to prove that 'foreign nationals' have been engaged in any criminal conspiracy to commit terrorist acts in the UK. Instead, foreign nationals would be detained indefinitely (subject to a six-monthly review by the Special Immigration Appeals Commission) on the information of the intelligence services alone. Suspects and their lawyers don't have the right to see all the evidence; an advocate to represent their interests, appointed by the Attorney-General, would deal with it in their absence. The Home Secretary, justifying these draconian measures, states that, in certain circumstances, foreign nationals cannot be deported (for instance if they are nationals of countries with which Britain has no extradition agreement, or if they might be tortured or executed in the country to which they are deported). He has no alternative, therefore, but to detain them until the suspects can find a safe residence in a third country or convince the Home Office that they pose no threat to public security. The writer and former Irish Republican prisoner, Ronan Bennett, compares this to the North of Ireland's notorious Diplock system of justice, where suspects were tried by a judge alone, acting as judge and jury, and where, owing to secret legal processes, evidence could not be fairly tested.

The Home Secretary has railed against the 'airy-fairy' fears of civil libertarians, but has failed to respond to criticisms of the government's airy-fairy definition of terrorism. The EU definition (which will be incorporated, without parliamentary debate, into the anti-terrorism, crime and security legislation) embraces anti-globalisation protesters and others involved in 'urban protest'. Blunkett says that society as a whole has nothing to fear from a proposal to detain foreign nationals, given that only a handful of people will probably be detained, but fails to indicate just what the quality – or the origin – of the evidence will be needed to detain someone indefinitely. During the Gulf War, scores of mainly Iraqi and Palestinian suspects were arrested and detained for deportation on suspicion of being supporters of Saddam Hussein, on intelligence which, it turned out, was almost 100 per cent inaccurate. Similarly, 97 per cent of those held under the Prevention of Terrorism Acts from 1974 to 2000 were not charged with any offence.

The new emergency legislation comes just a year after the Terrorism Act, 2000. This, the first emergency legislation in 25 years, contained the innovative Proscribed Organisations Order which outlawed membership or support of 21 foreign organisations. While, post-September 11, no responsible person could argue against proscribing al-Qaida and its associates, the Proscribed Organisations

Order also banned organisations fighting for self-determination of oppressed minorities in countries such as Sri Lanka and Turkey. This was tantamount to criminalising all Sri Lankan Tamils and all Turkish Kurds who would all sympathise, in one way or another, with the goals of the LTTE or the PKK.

Thus, even before the events of September 11, refugee communities in the UK were subjected to a special surveillance regime in the name of anti-terrorism. But in announcing the introduction of new asylum reception proposals (including a four-tier system of asylum centres and the introduction of identity cards), and in putting forward legislation plans for the internment of foreign nationals, Blunkett has gone even further than the Terrorism Act 2000, explicitly stating that as terrorists have, in the past, used the asylum system to gain entry to the UK, it justifies keeping all asylum seekers under a special surveillance regime.

A reasonable argument? Hardly. First, the few 'troublesome' Islamic fundamentalist refugees living in the UK could not be described as a terrorist threat; they are upfront and outspoken in their views (not the behaviour of surreptitious criminal conspirators). Second, should any criminal conspiracy be planned, the police have a panoply of existing powers to detain and question suspects (and numerous appropriate criminal offences already exist with which to charge those against whom there is any evidence of terrorist activity). Third, the facts about the September 11 conspirators (none of whom were refugees) go against Blunkett's arguments. All entered the US legally, criss-crossing the country by plane and rental cars quite openly. The Home Secretary cannot seriously expect us to believe that al-Qaida operatives would smuggle themselves into the First World (as Australian Prime Minister, Michael Howard, implies) on sinking boats controlled by mafiosi, or in lorry containers, or, indeed, apply to NASS as destitute asylum seekers.

Yet it is precisely destitute asylum seekers arriving in the UK who will, in future, be targeted as suspected terrorists. Blunkett argues that the new arrangements, accompanied by increased surveillance measures for the police and intelligence agencies, will allow the state to monitor more closely the 80,000 people who claim asylum annually. In future, the entire asylum procedure, from application to provision of welfare, to appeal, will be subjected to a 'terrorist check', as Ministry of Defence officials are drawn into advising the Home Secretary on every aspect of asylum and immigration procedure.

In terms of asylum applications, new anti-terrorist measures will specifically deny a safe haven to anyone suspected of being a terrorist or a danger to national security. While this power to exclude is not entirely new (the Refugee Convention itself provides that protection should not be given to those reasonably believed to be guilty of 'war crimes, crimes against humanity, acts contrary to the purposes and principles of the UN, or serious non-political crimes committed outside the country of origin'), its extent and scope are no longer clearly limited and defined. In future, all asylum seekers whose claims are based on their support for liberation struggles stand to be excluded from refugee status altogether.

The Home Secretary's November announcement of new welfare arrangements for asylum seekers also needs to be weighed against the Defence Ministry perspectives emanating from the 'war against terrorism'. In announcing the creation of a four-tier system of asylum centres and the introduction of identity cards, Blunkett explicitly stated that at the heart of his new proposals is the presumption that, from the moment someone applies for asylum, s/he should be tracked as well as supported. What is truly astonishing about this admission is its explicit linkage of a system of welfare to a system of surveillance. Blunkett has as good as announced the existence of a Soviet-style police state for asylum seekers.

Does the Home Secretary really believe that his approach is necessary to target terrorist asylum seekers, or is he just using the 'war against terrorism' to further his stated ambition of 30,000 deportations of rejected asylum seekers each year? By locking people up in institutions beyond the gaze of public scrutiny (the new Yarl's Wood Detention Centre, on Ministry of Defence land, is subject to the Official Secrets Act), and controlling their every movement; by forcing them to live in accommodation centres for the duration of their claim and appeal, it will be easier to deport them quickly, and without publicity, once their asylum applications are rejected.

Appeal procedures will also be streamlined and appeal rights curtailed. As appeals will probably be heard at 'reporting centres', it would be easy for rejected asylum seekers to be immediately arrested and detained for removal. No chance to integrate in the community, no chance of public support, they could just be bundled out of the country even before information could get out to those meddling supporters in refugee solidarity groups.

It is the government's use of the 'war against terrorism' to curb public scrutiny of the asylum system and to impose more detention, more camps and faster removals which is most worrying. By Blunkett's pronouncements, and by his proposal to introduce identity cards for one group in society only, he has further institutionalised xeno-racism against asylum seekers. Only, this time, foreign asylum seekers are not just economic scroungers and illegal immigrants but, more threateningly, criminal conspirators and terrorists: 'the enemy within'.

This article was published first in CARF 65. Information on the US is taken from *The Nation* (www.thenation.com). See in particular 'All in the name of security' by Bruce Shapiro, *The Nation*, vol. 273, No. 12, October 22, 2001.

IN DEFENCE OF CIVIL LIBERTIES
Paddy Hillyard

> We could live in a world which is airy-fairy, libertarian, where everyone does precisely what they like and we believe the best of everybody and then they destroy us.

> David Blunkett, UK Home Secretary
> *Guardian*, November 12, 2001

The Cave Hill, which resembles a person lying down with their nose pointing upwards, towers majestically over the City of Belfast, as I write. It is famous for two things. First, in 1795, following the failure of the government to support a bill to remove the ban on Catholics sitting in Parliament, a small group of Ulster Protestants climbed the hill, and in the words of their leader, Wolf Tone, 'took a solemn obligation ... never to desist in our efforts until we had subverted the authority of England over our country and asserted her independence'. Second, the Cave Hill's shape is believed to have been the inspiration for the giant in Jonathan Swift's *Gulliver's Travels* – a brilliant satire in which he excoriates the politics of the day and the closed-mind mentalities and fear-mongering of the little people. The first event, and what followed in its wake, illustrates the disastrous consequences of denying people political power in the country of their birth, while Swift's satire alerts us the dangers of small-minded politics: two lessons, which David Blunkett, the British Home Secretary, and his Labour colleagues should heed.

In December 2001 he successfully rushed another draconian piece of legislation through the UK Parliament – the Anti-Terrorism, Crime and Security Act, 2001[1] – which constitutes an unprecedented assault on civil liberties and human rights. Prior to its enactment it was pointed out by a UK parliamentary committee that 'this country has more anti-terrorist legislation on its statute book than almost any other developed democracy'. It went on to note that 'much of it, rushed through in the wake of previous atrocities, proved ineffective, and in some cases counterproductive and needed to be amended'.

Nearly 300 years earlier, in the same place, the government of the day introduced the infamous Black Act, which provided the death penalty for over 100 property offences. It was a product of unbridled political power, vested interest and disdain for argument in a pre-democratic society. It is now claimed that we live in a democracy, yet those who make up the government of today show the same disdain for the rights and liberties of individuals as their seventeenth-century predecessors. And what is more, they claim – just like those whose property was threatened by the dispossessed in the past – that the legislation is right and absolutely essential in the face of the threat posed.

Blunkett profoundly dislikes anyone who challenges his interpretation of what he thinks is right in fighting 'the enemy', however defined. He has little time for the civil liberties lobby and has consistently attacked it. He has accused his critics of indulging more in abuse than informed debate, adding, 'No one is going macho and no one is trying to do this to promote a vitriolic or anti-human rights approach.' The war in Afghanistan, he pointed out, has not, made the terrorist threat disappear. He continued, using an animal metaphor, 'A cornered tiger is more dangerous than ever.'[2] Blunkett likes hyperbole to attack his opponents. It is convenient and cuts out the necessity of producing valid arguments to support his position.

Blunkett made his 'airy-fairy' reference, which begins this piece, the day before he declared a state of emergency to bypass the awkward restrictions imposed by the European Convention on Human Rights. It is an extraordinary statement and requires a little textual deconstruction. It is first an appeal to the symbolism and imagination of childhood. This is the crazy world of Harry Potter – an exciting place where magic dominates over reason. It is very different from a Muggles' world of New Labour where rational men – and it is still mainly men – debate the affairs of state. Social and political problems haven't a chance in the Muggles' world. They are aggressively analysed, the causes explained and the blame apportioned selectively. At the global level, the boys are prepared to go to war to uphold human rights – 'muscular humanitarianism', as one commentator has described it.[3] Yet they are not prepared to do anything significant about the growing inequalities within or between nations. Human rights are certainly not about social and economic issues.

At the local level, the poor and dispossessed are attacked for their irresponsibility while there is no reference to the behaviour of the rich and powerful. We had yet another recent example of this prior to the publication of four reports on last summer's 'race' riots in a number of towns in the North of England. Blunkett cut through the careful and qualified analysis and announced that new immigrants and their children should do more to adopt 'British norms of acceptability', whatever they may be. Currently, the only official, widely available statement of Britishness is stated on the reverse of the cover page of the British passport. It notes: 'Her Britannic Majesty's Secretary of State requests and requires in the Name of Her Majesty all those whom it may concern to allow the bearer to pass freely without let or hindrance, and to afford the bearer such assistance and protection as may be necessary.'

While Blunkett rebukes millions of first, second and third generations of immigrants for their failure to live up to some essentialist, unstated, ingredient of Britishness, he further erodes the one element of Britishness which is articulated: the right to go about 'our' business 'without let or hindrance'.

Blunkett's crazy 'airy-fairy' world is also libertarian; 'where *everyone* (italics added) does precisely what they like and ... then they destroy us'. Civil libertarians are blamed for the annihilation of the civilised world. Of course, this is a caricature of the civil libertarian position, which has always recognised that rights are never absolute – one person's right has to be balanced against the rights of others – and a nonsense that violence stems from civil libertarians. These gross distortions, however, are unimportant to the Home Secretary's populist project. Spin is all that matters.

The most extraordinary feature of Blunkett's statement, however, is the use of prepositions. '*We* could live in a world ... where everyone does precisely what *they* like and *we* believe the best of everybody and then *they* destroy *us*.' This is a world of a frightened man where the enemy, or the cornered tiger, lies in dark places. It is heavily partitioned and binary divisions of good and bad can be imagined everywhere: the terrorist versus the law-abiding citizen, the civilised versus the uncivilised world, or Christian against

Muslim. It is a dangerous mindset, 'them' and 'us', a mindset which has dominated the Home Office since its formation. Far from accepting difference and diversity and an all-inclusive society, it is a society where the enemy is everywhere.

Pervading New Labour's thinking, and Blunkett's in particular, is the belief in rationality and the possibility of social engineering. Zygmunt Bauman, in his brilliant book *Modernity and the Holocaust*,[4] points out, however, some of the dangers of modernity. Science, he argues, is not an independent activity but is determined to improve on reality and to reshape the world. In a powerful juxtaposition of two ideas, Bauman notes that medicine and gardening 'are functionally distinct forms of the same activity of separating and setting apart useful elements destined to live and thrive from harmful and morbid ones, which ought to be exterminated'. Some of the key characteristics of modernity he highlights are: the detachment of any moral calculus from the use and deployment of violence or in bureaucratic decision making; the position of Jews as a 'non-nation'; racism; the hierarchical and functional divisions of labour; and the dehumanisation of bureaucratic subjects. Each of these characteristics is clear today. Bauman's conclusion is that the Holocaust cannot be reduced to something which happened to the Jews or something in the past which modernity has helped the developed world to move beyond. The Holocaust must be understood as a product of the nature of modernity. It is another lesson that New Labour has yet to learn.

The new anti-terror legislation includes: internment without trial; extended powers of arrest, stop and search, detention; interception of communications; access to computer databases; and proscription of selected organisations. A number of strong arguments can be marshalled against so-called anti-terror legislation. First, it is questionable whether any of the specific provisions contained in the legislation prevents terrorism while, on the other hand, there is ample evidence to suggest that certain provisions increase the level of political violence. Part of the problem is that those who propose this form of legislation make the assumption that it will prevent political violence yet fail to spell out precisely how it is likely to be more efficacious than existing powers in the ordinary criminal law.

To establish the argument that the legislation works, each of the separate provisions needs to be assessed. The evidence from Northern Ireland shows that few, if any, of the provisions prevented violence and that most exacerbated it. The introduction of internment was a disaster, as so many commentators have pointed out. The powers of stop and search alienated vast numbers of people and the extended powers of detention led to numerous allegations of people being abused while in custody. The proscription of organisations prevented any voice, principally to those whose protest had begun from the lack of any voice – Northern Irish nationalists.

The legislation created multiple 'suspect communities' within Northern Ireland and, more importantly, a 'suspect community' in Britain. Anyone who was Irish, or had a connection with Ireland or Irish people, became a suspect. Sometimes it was voice, appearance or the passport that gave rise to public or police suspicion. At ports and airports special procedures were put in place to separate Irish travellers from the rest of the travelling public – 'Northern Ireland and Republic of Ireland passengers this way'. They were subject to regular and systematic questioning from Special Branch. Bags were scrutinised, personal items examined and occasionally taken away for photocopying. A separate system of criminal justice was developed for suspects. While serial killers and rapists were dealt with through the ordinary criminal justice system, those arrested under the Prevention of Terrorism Act were dealt with under a system which gave the authorities far greater discretion and flexibility while denying suspects any rights. The detention process, for many, began with a form which was marked 'Irish suspect' or, as one suspect put it with an emphasis on Irish, a pause between the words and a question mark – 'Irish suspect?' In addition, political meetings were monitored, people prosecuted for collecting money on behalf of a banned organisation and spokespersons banned from the media.

The second argument against this type of legislation is that it erodes democracy by undermining the very principles on which this fragile form of social order is based. I have argued elsewhere that while political violence poses a threat to democracy the more important threat comes from the response to it by attacking the very principles on which it is based. A crucial element of any democratic system is the series of checks and balances to the exercise of power. Instead of these, we are expected to trust those who are exercising these extraordinary powers on our behalf.

We are asked to trust the Home Secretary who is now at the pinnacle of the new repressive order. So much will be left to his judgement. For example, he will decide who should be interned and who will be released. The last occasion any Home Affairs Minister had such powers was between 1922 and 1972 in Northern Ireland under the Special Powers Act. This unfettered discretion coupled with one-party rule were crucial factors in generating the political violence which continued for the next 30 years. We are also asked to trust the security personnel who act on our behalf. The botched intelligence over the introduction of internment, the numerous miscarriages of justice of those arrested under the Prevention of Terrorism Act in Britain and the widespread allegation of collusion between elements of the security forces and loyalist paramilitaries in Northern Ireland are three reasons why we should not trust those in authority and why any democracy needs robust systems of accountability and review. In their absence political expediency replaces the rule of law.

The previous Home Secretary, Jack Straw, shared this view, stating that we would hand those involved in terror a victory 'if, in combating their threats and violence, we descend to their level and undermine the essential freedoms and rule of law that are the bedrock of our democracy'.[5] In voting for this latest piece of legislation, however, he has shown the world, yet again, that Labour politicians are fickle when it comes to principles. He is not alone in this. Many current Labour MPs at one time in their careers were committed civil libertarians. Some worked for, or were on the Executive Committees of, organisations dedicated to protecting civil liberties. But they have jettisoned their earlier principled positions, either through fear of the Labour Party machine or because of political opportunism. Those of 'us' who were part of that movement, and travelled from far and wide to be part of the struggle for civil liberties, now have an intense feeling of betrayal.

The final argument against the legislation, together with numerous other developments within the EU, is that a new and more intensive form of surveillance has been put in place in which millions of people will be observed, listened to, classified, reported, recorded and monitored. With developments in computer technology and the sharing of data between countries, the detailed social administration of the concentration camps has been expanded to cover continents. Those involved in the detailed divisions of labour – secret service agents, police officers, customs officials, security specialists, immigration officials, the phone tappers, the database specialists, the computer analysts, and the prison warders – have, like the social administrators in the camps, only a technical responsibility for their work. Few, if any, are prepared to object to the specific tasks on moral grounds.

As the silhouette of the Cave Hill disappears into the darkness of another Belfast winter's night, the lessons of history and fairy tales are still to be learnt. As a witness to the solemn oath of the leader of the United Irishmen, the Cave Hill is a stark reminder that dispossession and powerlessness lead to resentment, rage and reaction. Exploitation and vast inequalities between and within nation-states will never produce a stable social order in which everyone is secure. The cries of dispossessed and exploited peoples around the world have to be listened to and taken seriously. While the threat is real, it is hypocritical to imply that tough laws and military intervention will increase everyone's security. Both will lead to greater anger and many more people will be prepared to use violence for political ends. When you have lost your father, mother, two brothers and two sisters in a bomb attack or have relatives and friends imprisoned for acts of terror for which they are innocent, your feelings are going to be little different from the thousands of Americans who lost loved ones on September 11. Violence begets violence.

At the same time, the Cave Hill, in its symbolic form as a sleeping giant, reminds us that narrow-minded mentalities, sanctimonious and selective moralising, unprincipled politics, greed, self-interest and fear-mongering need to be treated with ridicule and contempt. New and imaginative thinking and a commitment to all people everywhere is required to produce a very different social order for the twenty-first century.

1. Home Affairs Select Committee, *The Anti-Terrorism, Crime and Security Bill, First Report*, HMSO, 2001.
2. *Guardian*, November 19, 2001.
3. Orford, A, 'Muscular Humanitarianism: Reading the Narratives of the New Interventionism', *EJIL*, 1999, 10, p. 679.
4. Bauman, Z, *Modernity and the Holocaust*, Cambridge: Polity Press, 1989.
5. House of Commons Debates, *Hansard*, December 14, 1999.

POVERTY IS THE NEW BLACK[1]
A Sivanandan

Racism has always been an instrument of discrimination. And discrimination has always been a tool of exploitation. Racism, in that sense, has always been rooted in the economic compulsions of the capitalist system. But it manifests itself, first and foremost, as a cultural phenomenon, susceptible to cultural solutions such as multicultural education and the promotion of ethnic identities. Redressing the problem of cultural inequality, however, does not by itself redress the problem of economic inequality. Racism needs to be tackled at both levels – the cultural and the economic – at once, remembering that the one provides the rationale for the other. Racism, in sum, is conditioned by economic imperatives, but negotiated through cultural agency: religion, literature, art, science, the media and so on.

Which of these agencies, though, holds sway in a particular epoch is itself dependent on the economic system of that epoch. Thus, in the period of primitive accumulation, when the pillage and plunder of the new world by Spanish conquistadors was laying the foundations of capitalism, it was religion in the form of the Catholic Church that gave validity to the concept that the native Indians were 'sub-homines', the children of Ham, born to be slaves, and could therefore be enslaved and/or exterminated at will. In the period of merchant capital, when the monarch was no longer subordinate to the Church and the bourgeoisie was in its ascendancy, the racialist ideas of the earlier period became secularised in popular literature, political discourse and education and served to rationalise and justify the trade in black slaves.

With the development of industrial capitalism and its corollary, colonialism, the racialist ideas of the previous epochs congealed into a systemic racist ideology to condemn all 'coloured' peoples to racial and cultural inferiority. By the end of the nineteenth century, at the height of the imperial adventure, the ideology of racial superiority began to take on a pseudo-scientific validity in the Social Darwinism of Gobineau and Chamberlain – which in turn further popularised the view of racial hierarchies.

Today, under global capitalism which, in its ruthless pursuit of markets and its sanctification of wealth, has served to unleash ethnic wars, balkanise countries and displace their peoples, the racist tradition of demonisation and exclusion has become a tool in the hands of the state to keep out the refugees and asylum seekers so displaced – even if they are white – on the grounds that they are scroungers and aliens come to prey on the wealth of the West and confound its national identities. The rhetoric of demonisation, in other words, is racist, but the politics of exclusion is economic. Demonisation is a prelude to exclusion, social and therefore economic exclusion, to creating a peripatetic underclass, international *Untermenschen*.

Once, 'they' demonised the blacks to justify slavery. Then they demonised the 'coloureds' to justify colonialism. Today, they demonise asylum seekers to justify the ways of globalism. And, in the age of the media, of discourse, of spin, demonisation sets out the parameters of popular culture within which such exclusion finds its own rationale – usually under the guise of xenophobia, the (natural) fear of strangers. Such a term, it is thought, would include white refugees and asylum seekers streaming in from Eastern Europe, whereas the term racism strictly refers to people of a different race and colour. Xenophobia, besides, is innocent, racism culpable.

But the other side of the coin of 'the fear or hatred of strangers' is the defence and preservation of 'our people', our way of life, our standard of living, our 'race'. If it is xenophobia, it is – in the way it denigrates and reifies people before segregating and/or expelling them – a xenophobia that bears all the marks of the old racism, except that it is not colour-coded. It is a racism that is not just directed at those with darker skins, from the former colonial countries, but at the newer categories of the displaced and dispossessed whites, who are beating at Western Europe's doors, the Europe that displaced them in the first place. It is racism in substance but xeno in form – a racism that is meted out to impoverished strangers even if they are white. It is xeno-racism.

Xeno-racism is a feature of the Manichaean world of global capitalism, where there are only the rich and the poor – and poverty is the new Black. Where the national state works primarily in the interests of multinational corporations, where the national bourgeoisie collaborates with international capital, where the middle class is effete and self-serving and the working class, disaggregated and dispersed by technology, has lost its political clout. That is the context within which we have got to adjudge the changing nature of racism and from that, conversely, adjudge the nature of the society we live in.

In Britain, with its long tradition of racism over five centuries and three continents, racial prejudice has become an intrinsic part of popular culture, racial discrimination has come to inhere in the institutions of society and racist laws and policies have characterised state intervention at the point of economic need. But today, the state is much more regulatory and interventionist – in the interests, ironically, of an unregulated market – though wanting to appear open and democratic. Thus, in its avowedly liberal mode, it is prepared to go along with the Macpherson recommendations and dismantle institutional racism, especially in the public sector, but in its self-justifying regulatory mode, it brings institutional discrimination back into the system through the Immigration and Asylum Act, with its dispersal schemes, its voucher system and detention camps. And it is this demonisation of refugees and asylum seekers rather than the move to dismantle institutional racism that has caught the public's attention, resonating as it does with its misgivings about the 'alien invasion' – and so stoked the fires of popular racism, in the course of which, the fight against institutional racism itself has taken a beating.

There are other changes in the law, too, which, though affecting the population in general impact more harshly on black communities and further institutionalise racism in the criminal justice system. Thus the proposal to abolish the right of defendants to elect to be tried by a jury for offences such as minor theft, assault and criminal damage will affect black people more adversely because they are over-represented in those areas – not least because they are stopped and searched, arrested and charged more often than white people. To remove their right to request trial by jury, therefore, and put them up for summary trial before magistrates, who are perceived to be on the side of the police, is to deny them one of the few remaining legal safeguards against unfair treatment.

So too the Terrorism Act 2000, which gives the Home Secretary powers to proscribe any organisation which, according to him, threatens violence to advance 'a political, religious, or ideological cause', criminalises the liberation struggles of those who have fled the tyrannies of their own countries and, in the process, stigmatises them as terrorists. In sum, the laws, the administration, the criminal justice system – the whole state apparatus in Britain – is rife with racism and gives the lie to the government's pretensions to counter institutional racism and the culture which gives it a habitation and a name. At first glance, British racism would appear to have three faces – state, institutional, popular – but, in effect, it has one face with three expressions, the face of the state. To put it another way, institutional racism and popular racism are woven into state racism and it is only in unravelling that that you begin to unravel the fabric of racism.

Except that now there is another problem compounding racial conflict: poverty – the systemic poverty of a society which, at the dictates of a free market economy, is becoming increasingly polarised between the haves and the have-nothings. This has often been characterised as the North/South divide, with the North belonging to dead industries and the South to the modern economy. But there are pockets of poverty both in the North and the South, where mills and mines, docks and shipyards, steel and textiles have disappeared or been relocated by technology and the global factory. What is more to the point, however, is not so much the geography of decay as the composition of the working class in these industries and their subsequent disaggregation and segregation.

Some of these industries, such as mining, dock work and ship-building, had a workforce that was almost wholly white, whereas the steel and textile mills of Yorkshire and Lancashire, and textiles in particular, had also recruited labour from the Indian subcontinent. And it was these mill towns that the government, either by default or design, failed to bring into the modern economy, through investment or retraining, when the old industries had died. The white workers were able to move out to other jobs elsewhere, but racism and family ties (which was the only 'network' available to them) pointed Bangladeshis and Pakistanis towards restaurant work and mini-cabbing – and the sense of solidarity and comradeship between white and Asian workers that had been engendered on the factory floor was lost. Segregation in housing, resulting from local government policies, separated the communities further and led to the segregation in schooling of the next generation. Multicultural-ism, which was really a sop to white racism (people don't need to be given their cultures, only their rights) and its updated Scarman model, ethnicism, deepened the fissures between ethnic groups. And ethnic funding, instead of improving the local economy as a whole, helped only to improve the personal economy of a few – some of whom made it into the town halls and Tammany Hall style politics, where the currency of corruption was not money so much as com-munalism and religion.

All of which served to brand the Bangladeshis and Pakistanis as self-segregating and better served by local authorities than the local whites. That the former were mostly Muslim Asians, as distinct from other Asians, served to focus white hate on Islam. And it was that potent combination of racial and religious hatred that provided the breeding ground for the electoral politics of the British National Party, on the one hand, and the *goonda* politics of the National Front, on the other – and provoked the uprisings of young Asians in Oldham, Bradford, Burnley, Leeds and Stoke.

What were the youth to do? They had been born here, schooled here, grown up here, had been media-maddened by all the good things in life that could be, should be, available to them – and yet all around them were 'the rocks, moss, stonecrop, merds' of the industrial wastelands of derelict Britain. Whatever leadership there was had either retreated into the safety of religion or defected to the service of local and central government, from where they condemned the youth while feathering their own nests.

No economic infrastructures or hope of socialisation through work. No political parties, no ideology – no political culture – to unite the fragmented communities, to develop an alternative politics, to emerge as a political force – all that had died with New Labour. Locked into their degradation and defeat by a racist police force, vilified by a racist press and violated, finally, by the true fascists. What were the youth to do but break out in violence, self-destructive, reactive violence, the violence of choicelessness, the violence of the violated?

THE CHALLENGE OF SEPTEMBER 11[2]

An Interview with A Sivanandan

CARF: You have, for a long time, warned us against the growing anti-Muslim racism in this country. We remember a meeting in Camden town hall against the Gulf War when you ended your speech with 'We are all Muslims now'. Are you in favour of the new legislation in the UK to outlaw incitement to religious hatred?

A Sivanandan: No and Yes. First, we have to distinguish between our long-term goal – which is the creation of a broad-based secular society – and tackling the immediate problem – which is how to protect people on the ground who are being attacked because they are Muslims. Hence, at the same time as fighting fascism and racism in the specific (which means not opposing the incitement to religious hatred law in principle), we have to balance it with a wider recognition that, in the global age, the state has to become more secular, not less. State religion is an anachronism in a globalised society, and rights, not religion, should determine social conduct. So that any piecemeal reform we undertake now should not undermine the more wholesale reform to come. Besides, laws such as this are a two-edged sword. Don't forget that the first prosecutions under the incitement to racial hatred provisions were of blacks, although the law was supposed to protect them.

CARF: What about the fact that here in the UK, far from secularising society, the government is actually planning to expand the role of religion with an extension to the number of religious schools?

AS: Once again, we have to look at this in a twofold way. A democracy should not apportion rights on the basis of religion. It should, instead, de-institutionalise religion altogether, make it a private matter, not a matter for the state. Our problem is that ethnic race pundits have been pushing the government for equity within the given set-up, without wanting to change it altogether. Their argument goes: if you have Christian church schools and Jewish schools, then it is only fair to have Muslim schools. At that level, of course, it appears to be a reasonable request. But, at another level, it is saying that the answer to discrimination (allowing only certain children into a school) is more discrimination (allowing more groups to have exclusive schools). I believe that no school should be allowed to discriminate in its selection process on the basis of religion. In fact, we should do away with denominational schools altogether. Take religion out of state structures and institutions. Complete the Reformation by disestablishing the Church of England. Take religion out of the public domain, out of education, work, politics and Parliament. That, however, is the long-term goal. In the short term, we have to temper the ideal with the real. We should help communities which have been disadvantaged educationally (even if defined in religious terms) to improve standards of schooling irrespective of their religion. In that sense, we have to support the creation of more religious schools if that is the demand from those communities. But, perhaps, certain new conditions should be attached. Jewish, Catholic, Muslim schools should be told that they have to open their doors to everyone (as some Anglican schools do); that they have to teach the National Curriculum; that their primary purpose is not a religious one. In other words, Muslim schools, like Anglican schools, should be able to teach Muslim values but not enforce the observance of religious ritual in school time.

CARF: But isn't that a form of discrimination – when you don't allow people space or time off to perform rituals which, after all, are part of their religion?

AS: No, not if it discriminates against others in the process. Of course, everyone should be guaranteed his or her civil rights, including the right to freedom of religious expression. But each person's civil rights need to be weighed against the civil rights of others. Your freedom ends where mine begins. Hence, the freedom to express your religion ends at the point that it becomes anti-social or interferes with your work or puts others at risk. In the final analysis, we have to make a distinction between the right to a belief (a civil right) and the ritual of religion (which can affect the civil rights of others). Where rights clash with rites, rights must prevail. Else, we move the axis of religion itself from tolerance to intolerance, from an open system of thought to a closed circuit of dogma.

CARF: Are you going along, then, with Huntington's argument that there is a 'clash of civilisations' between the West and Islam?

AS: No. That's bullshit. It's ahistorical and superficial. What we are witnessing is not a clash of civilisations but the imposition of one civilisation on another, and the resistance that follows from that. The clash of civilisations theory also implies that the clash is between a superior civilisation and an inferior one. But it was Islamic civilisation that, through its achievements in mathematics, geography, medicine, literature, art and architecture, helped to advance European civilisation. Centuries of colonial oppression and imperialist exploitation, however, have forced certain sections of Islam to retreat into the safety of fundamentalist beliefs. And this has been further heightened by the mass poverty inflicted on Islamic countries by puppet dictatorships installed and/or maintained by Western powers for their own interests – principally oil.

Where then can the oppressed find succour, except in religion, 'the sigh of the oppressed'? But what begins as the sigh of the oppressed is transformed, in the hands of the religionists, into the 'opiate of the masses' and gives fundamentalism its impetus. And the West, in turn, has tried to counter nationalist aspirations and communist influence by financing and promoting fundamentalist movements and reactionary regimes. Is it any wonder that, as

Malcolm X said in another context, the chickens have come home to roost?

To get back to Huntington, the clash of civilisations theory distracts us from locating the epicentre of the conflict: Israel, which is not only a vivid example of the West's double standards and the humbug of Western 'democracy', but also a constant, in-your-face reminder that terror can work if it is properly organised in the guise of a state, under the pretext of survival.

CARF: Moving on to the war, Blair is trying to sell it to us as some kind of humanitarian-bearing, democracy-building initiative. Do you see any truth in that?

AS: Blair, unlike Bush, has been quick to realise that global capitalism has to be reformed to be acceptable. But you don't do that with a bomb in one hand and bread in the other. Certainly what September 11 signalled to me was the fact that unless global capitalism – which is in effect a new mode of production – begins to embrace the poor and corrects the injustices that it breeds, it cannot work. The immediate assault may have been upon 'Western civilisation', whatever that means, but the long-term assault is on the global economy. So first we need an economic solution to poverty (till such time as we abolish capitalism and therefore poverty altogether) and, second, we need to find an international political organisation (the UN has a built-in American bias) which can represent all countries and give weightage to the poorer countries over the more powerful ones.

Nation-states, which are subject to the imperatives of multinational corporations, cannot look after their poor. We need a world government that redresses the imbalances of globalisation, which acts as a countervailing force to multinationals, which upholds the universal values of the Enlightenment and allows them to develop in poorer countries and not be destroyed by dictatorships. The Third World is facing economic genocide in which its own governments are collaborators. Debt has forced these countries into a cycle of ever-increasing poverty. What they produce is barely sufficient to pay back the interest on their debt, let alone feed themselves; so the people are starved yet further. Debt kills off the present generation and the imposition of structural adjustment programmes that accompany IMF loans kills off the future generation. It's a choice

between starving to death in the short term or in the long term –
economic genocide by stealth.

CARF: But why the rise of fundamentalism?

AS: Since the Communist Parties died, since the post-independence
nationalist projects of autonomous development foundered, people
have had no alternative value system to turn to, no political agency
to organise them. Against the ideology of global capitalism is only
the ideology of religion – Mammon versus Mohammed. But religion
comes with a price tag: ritual. And when ritual begins to define
religion, it corrupts it. Ritual is based on customs and habit, religion
is based on rights and values. Rites separate; rights unify. Rites
contribute to superstition and ceremony; rights contribute to
universal values. There are no essential differences in the value
systems of religions, only in their rituals, social habits and customs.
And that is why, for me, the most significant thing about September
11 is the challenge it poses to Islam itself: to live up to its own values
and principles of universality, which are not only the values and
principles of all religions, but also of modernity. What I am saying,
in effect, is that the modernist revolution is not over, only re-
charged. It is postmodernism that is dead – at birth.

CARF: You almost sound optimistic!

AS: If we are not to wallow in the sadness of that terrible day and
the miseries of its aftermath, we've got to learn to turn defeat into
victory. A number of 'hopeful' things came out of it. Most importantly, it dealt a blow to the arrogance of power and showed how
the technology produced by global capitalism is also the technology
that can strike at its heart. It therefore made it objectively necessary
to see that globalisation benefits all the people of the world and not
just the West. And America and the rest of the West, that had been
so smug and conceited, can now feel the pains of the Third World.
For so long it was America's standard of living, America's morality,
America's culture that dominated the world. All this has been
challenged; the Western world is in shock. People have been woken
from the deep sleep of individualism and are taking conscience of
society, their society and others'. We have had a whole generation
that was rendered so apolitical that it didn't even bother to vote; it
thought helping the Third World was wearing a comic nose for one

day in the year. Now the Third World is every day. Now the Third World is on the breakfast table every morning.

1. This paper was written just before September 11 and published in a special edition of *Race and Class* entitled *Three Faces of British Racism: A Special Report*, vol. 43, No. 2, October–December 2001.
2. This interview was conducted by CARF, Campaign Against Racism and Fascism, and was published in the CARF Newsletter No. 65.

THE POLICING OF IMMIGRATION IN THE NEW WORLD DISORDER

Leanne Weber and Ben Bowling

While attempts to control unwanted migration into Britain stem back four centuries or more, in an era of globalisation, mass migration, shifting modes of regulation and a moral panic about 'globally mobile' terrorists and criminals, the role of the immigration enforcer is taking on a new significance. This paper assesses recent developments within the agencies most involved in the operation of internal and external immigration controls, and considers the implications for the policing of immigration in the new world disorder.

The social construction of undesirable aliens

Migrants have been seen as 'trouble' for England and its rulers since the time of Queen Elizabeth's famous declaration that 'all black-amores' should be 'sent forth of the realme' at the end of the sixteenth century.[1] In the emerging globalised world, developed states have once again assessed the spectre of uncontrolled migration from the less developed world as a threat to their way of life, and have responded by erecting a system of 'global apartheid' aimed at shoring up the unequal distribution of risk.[2] The aircraft suicide bombings that caused such shocking loss of life at the World Trade Center and the Pentagon and terror among the populations of North America and Europe have emulated within the developed world the conditions of life-threatening insecurity that have been the product of 'global apartheid' for much of the world's population. This has led governments to another deep re-evaluation of the issues of security, migration, policing and its linkages with military action. As well as killing many thousands of people, destroying the most powerful symbol of American world trade dominance and sparking war on Afghanistan, the events of September 11 have generated a worldwide moral panic about terrorists, Islamic fundamentalists and, more generally, the migration of populations whose origins lie in the Middle East, Africa and the Indian subcontinent.

In many contexts, including those with which we are most familiar – the UK, the USA and Australia – legislation is being hastily assembled relating to terrorism, security and migration. Much of this new law – driven by fear, a desire to act decisively and in favour of security rather than liberty – is concerned with tightening controls against 'undesirable aliens'. These measures are likely to accelerate trends that have emerged over the past two or three decades which have shifted immigration controls both inwards and outwards from physical borders, while at the same time seeking to reassert the symbolic importance of strong border protection as an expression of national sovereignty.

Immigration policing (the role of the police)

The arrival and settlement in Britain of African, Caribbean and Asian people in the 1950s and 1960s triggered a 'moral panic' about uncontrolled immigration. The 1971 Immigration Act gave the police and immigration authorities considerable powers to detain and question those people who were suspected of being in breach of immigration law, such as entering illegally or overstaying terms of entry. The Act introduced border controls against groups which had not been subject to controls hitherto and also prompted a major recruitment drive for new immigration officers to work at ports. At the same time the Act stimulated the creation of 'internal' immigration controls, or 'pass laws' for people of African, Caribbean and Asian descent resident in Britain.

Studies during this period uncovered evidence that ordinary policing often involved checking immigration status such as asking for passports, for instance, when people from ethnic minorities reported crimes of which they had been victim. These tactics could be understood as opportunistic – as police using the new and highly flexible provisions of the Immigration Act as a resource to achieve other policing aims. But more systematic operations were also documented, for example major passport raids amounting to a 'witch-hunt' of African, Caribbean and Asian communities, and the activities of the covert Illegal Immigration Intelligence Unit in London the purpose of which was to 'receive, collate, evaluate and disseminate information relating to known or *suspected* offenders'.[3] Consequently, immigration policing became a major source of suspicion and mistrust between the police and minority communities, labelled 'Sus 2' by the Institute of Race Relations.

Despite the waning of the moral panic associated with the immigration of the 1950s and 1960s, immigration policing remained contentious throughout the 1990s. A renewed panic about 'bogus asylum seekers' led to a further wave of immigration legislation – the 1993 Asylum and Immigration (Appeals) Act, 1996 Asylum and Immigration Act and 1999 Immigration and Asylum Act – which, among other measures, increased the range of immigration offences, particularly in relation to those who employed or facilitated the arrival of illegal entrants. Commentators tended to view the new criminal provisions against individual immigrants as largely symbolic, since the sweeping administrative powers to detain and expel – exercised largely by the Immigration Service, or by the police working in concert with immigration authorities – remained considerably more flexible. However, much criticism was directed towards the employer sanctions in particular, which were expected to have a detrimental effect on race relations and to impact adversely on established residents from ethnic minorities.[4]

It was predicted that the signalling of a 'tough' stance on immigration would prompt a wave of vigorous immigration policing. The Joint Council for the Welfare of Immigrants reported that the police increasingly asked for identification documents and evidence of immigration status from black and 'foreign-looking' people they stopped during routine traffic stops or as witnesses to an accident or crime. Joint enforcement operations with the Immigration Service where police powers of search and arrest are needed were also stepped up. These activities included large-scale employer raids and forced deportation actions, some of which have resulted in deaths and attracted national and international criticism. In light of this, the Metropolitan Police have expressed anxieties about the impact that their role in enforcing deportation orders will have on policing ethnic minorities and attempts to tackle racist violence.[5]

The proliferation of internal immigration controls has also drawn the police into more routine enforcement activities which are viewed as 'rubbish' from a police perspective – draining police resources, and unlikely to lead to any result in terms of prosecution or crime control. The Metropolitan Police have declined to continue their role in monitoring asylum applicants who are required by the Immigration Service to report regularly to a police station, and various regional forces have indicated their displeasure at dealing with clandestine entrants found emerging from lorries on major arterial roads. When several asylum seekers escaped from the Oakington Detention Centre soon after it was opened, Cambridgeshire Police announced that they would not pursue the escapees unless they committed a criminal offence.

The police appear to have been drawn more willingly into specific aspects of border control which involve the application of criminal sanctions. The creation of a market for people smuggling in response to restrictive visa regimes has inevitably attracted organised criminal networks that were previously engaged in less lucrative smuggling enterprises. This has been met by intelligence-driven policing tactics originally designed to deal with other forms of cross-border crime. Special Branch officers are routinely deployed at major ports of entry, charged with the detection and prosecution of the facilitators of illegal immigration. The convergence of concern about immigration control, national security and transnational crime has therefore been apparent long before the events of September 11.

Policing immigration (the role of the immigration service)

Unlike police officers, immigration officers are specialists in the operation of immigration controls. For traditionally minded officers, the 'removal' of individuals who are considered not to meet UK entry requirements is seen as a 'result'. Many of today's senior officers were recruited in the 1970s to work at ports, putting into effect the provisions of the 1971 Act which made many categories of arriving passengers subject to immigration control for the first time. Since then, resources and policy emphasis has gradually enlarged after-entry controls, resulting in the establishment of separate Enforcement and Ports Directorates and the proliferation of specialist units to oversee the increasingly complex legal and administrative system and manage the burgeoning detention estate.

In-country enforcement work appears to be popular among immigration officers bored with the routine stamping of passports, demoralised by significantly increased workloads at ports, and frustrated by the perceived abandonment of political commitment to border controls. The processing of asylum seekers is particularly likely to be seen by these control-minded officers as 'rubbish' – having no likelihood of an immigration 'result' since international law prohibits their summary expulsion, pending determination of their claims. In contrast, in-country operations aimed at the removal of failed asylum applicants or the detection and deportation of 'immigration offenders' are directed towards a clear, if not always attainable, outcome.

The number of people subject to enforcement action under the 1971 Immigration Act has increased sharply in recent years – from 3,200 in 1986 to 22,890 in 1999. Still, critics of Britain as a 'soft touch' have demanded more efficient removal of those deemed to be 'undesirable aliens', prompting a more than doubling of the level of enforcement action to over 50,000 in the year 2000.[6] Not satisfied with this, in the summer of 2001 the government stated another massive increase in immigration enforcement – through arrest, detention and forced removal. Much of this activity has been carried out by so-called immigration 'snatch squads' consisting of both police and immigration officers. The opening of two new immigration detention centres during that year at Dungavel and Yarls Wood, and the expansion of the existing facility at Harmondsworth provided 1,500 new detention spaces to facilitate this programme of expulsion.

Immigration officers were also granted increased powers of search and arrest in the 1999 Immigration and Asylum Act, presumably with the aim of reducing their dependence on police during in-country enforcement operations. Critics expressed concern about the expansion of the already considerable powers of immigration officers and the lack of clarity over the extent to which their actions are limited by the Police and Criminal Evidence Act – which governs the detention and questioning of criminal suspects – and the Race Relations (Amendment) Act – which seeks to prevent ethnic and racial discrimination by police and other officials.

It was suggested earlier that, alongside the increased emphasis on internal controls, affluent states have also sought to reinforce the protection of their borders by extending controls beyond their national territory. This shifting frontier has been most obvious in Australia, with the highly publicised diversion of unwelcome 'boat people' to tiny Pacific nations such as Nauru and the Cocos Islands. However these tactics, including the controversial involvement of the Australian navy, are not without precedent, having been well rehearsed in the 1980s with the forcible 'interdiction' of Haitian boat people by the US coast guard.

In Britain, the notional extension of national boundaries has been less visible but has followed the same rationale. In the face of increasingly porous internal borders, the nations of Western Europe have exhorted countries at the perimeter to exercise greater control over entry to 'Fortress Europe'. The prospect of EU expansion has created further opportunities to extend this *cordon sanitaire* by exerting pressure on hopeful new members to stem the flow at points even further to the east. In addition, a targeted system of offshore visa controls operated by immigration officers stationed at British overseas missions has been selectively introduced, giving rise to large numbers of asylum applicants. These pre-emptive measures have been supported by Carrier's Liability legislation which transfers partial responsibility for border control on to airlines and, more recently, on to other transport companies.

This deterrence-based programme has failed to produce the lasting reduction in asylum applications which policy makers have sought. Faced with relentlessly rising workloads – due to increased business and tourism traffic, the opening of internal EU borders, and the time consuming processing of asylum applications – legal changes were introduced in 1999 aimed at further streamlining the processing of 'desirable' passengers at ports. These changes effectively shift the granting of leave to enter the UK from the time of arrival at the border to the moment a visa is granted at an overseas mission, creating the legal fiction that an individual is lawfully present in the UK before they have even left their country of origin.

At the same time, on-entry and pre-entry controls have been selectively targeted against less welcome visitors. A controversial exemption to the Race Relations (Amendment) Act 2000 allows immigration officers to discriminate against groups identified in 'authorisations' promulgated by the Home Secretary. These categories of 'undesirable aliens' are identified through intelligence information that links certain nationalities or ethnic groups to 'systematic abuse' of asylum procedures. Czech Roma, prevented by UK immigration officials from boarding flights at Prague airport, were among the first reported targets of these highly selective, offshore controls. These moves towards more targeted, supposedly 'intelligence-led' controls, although motivated in large part by a desire to improve efficiency at ports and make more effective use of resources, have clearly discriminatory outcomes. These established practices also pave the way for further targeting of groups who may be broadly identified as threats in the light of the September 11 events.

Implications of the September 11 attacks

The events of September 11 and their aftermath were, in many ways, world-changing, unprecedented and unique. However, our analysis suggests that the implications for the policing of immigration are likely to be an acceleration and crystallisation of trends that have been in evidence for some time. In the long term, the anxiety of the populations of affluent states in relation both to large-scale migration and terrorist threats will only be allayed by the establishment of a fairer and more stable world order. In the short term the threat of further attacks being launched on the US from within its own borders gives rise to legitimate and pressing security concerns which should be met with a response that is proportionate, well grounded in evidence and constrained by international law. However, the lesson of history is that the heightened and undifferentiated perception of threat prevailing in the aftermath of the attacks will give rise to reactive and defensive policies which will further marginalise groups perceived as 'trouble'.

We have already seen the US Congress taking the extraordinary step of writing a blank cheque for virtually any measure which can be justified in the name of 'homeland security', and a president who has resorted to war rather than law in his overseas response to the September attacks; an Australian electorate sweeping back into power a conservative prime minister who exploited and conflated the issues of asylum seeking and national security in an election campaign soon after those events; and a British prime minister, faced with Continental criticism about lax internal controls against terrorists and domestic pressure about the failure to prevent the arrival of asylum seekers through the Channel Tunnel, announcing sweeping changes to the asylum system via the fourth piece of immigration legislation within a decade.

As recently as July 2001, an article in the Amnesty International newsletter noted a positive shift in government rhetoric about immigration, spoke with cautious optimism of a possible 'brighter outlook', and called on the UK government to stop treating asylum seekers as a 'problem'. Just a short time later, that hope seems to have collapsed along with the twin towers in New York. We are now faced with a renewed moral panic about global terrorism that threatens to further undermine the rights of immigrants, asylum seekers and refugees, and to promote hostility towards established minority communities. Policy makers, researchers and activists need the courage to resist the drift towards authoritarian exclusionism but also to engage with the question of how best to ensure the peace and safety of all communities in what seems to be a more fractious and disorderly world.

1. Quoted in Fryer, P, *Staying Power: The History of Black People in Britain*, London: Pluto Press, 1984, pp. 10–12.
2. This highly descriptive term is attributable to Richmond, A H, *Global Apartheid: Refugees, Racism and the New World Order*, Oxford: Oxford University Press, 1994.
3. From Gordon, P, *White Law: Racism in the Police, Courts and Prisons*, London: Pluto Press, 1983, p. 35 – emphasis added.
4. See *The Asylum and Immigration Bill 1995. The report of the Glidewell Panel*, London: April 16, 1996 for documentation of a range of concerns surrounding the 1996 legislation.
5. 'Met Frets over Drive Against Migrants', *Guardian*, October 19, 2001; 'Met Warns Blunkett of Deportation Risks', *Guardian*, August 30, 2001.
6. The source for these statistics is *Control of Immigration Statistics: United Kingdom, 2000*, Home Office Statistical Bulletin 14/01, August 2001.

SEPTEMBER 11 AND ALL THAT: AN AFRICAN PERSPECTIVE

Tunde Zack-Williams

On the eve of writing this paper, I spent a week in Lumley, some ten miles outside Freetown, the capital of the troubled land of Sierra Leone, with a relation of Hilda E Taylor, a passenger on American Airlines Flight 77 that crashed into the Pentagon. Ms Taylor, a Sierra Leonean, was on a National Geographical field trip to California with four of her best pupils. Like thousands of her compatriots she had voted with her feet by moving to the United States in search of security and a better life. The news of September 11 shook the citizens of this war-wearied country, themselves the victims of some of the most brutal acts of violence the African continent has witnessed since the end of colonialism. Here, there was no rejoicing in the streets, as in the Middle East. People were shocked that such a devastating act of wanton destruction could befall the most powerful nation on earth.

Ms Taylor's country had been laid waste by revenge violence unleashed on the citizens of Sierra Leone by Liberian warlord and current president, Charles Taylor, for their country's participation in the ECOMOG peacekeeping force despatched to Liberia by the

Economic Community of West African States to bring peace to that country. In the event it prevented Charles Taylor from capturing the capital, Monrovia. For this act of 'treachery', he promised retribution. Taylor, who had mysteriously escaped from a Boston penitentiary in the United States, turned up in Liberia to start a bloody civil war. It soon spilled over to engulf Sierra Leone, posing a major security threat to the nations of the sub-region. Taylor was instrumental in setting off the rebel leader, ex-military Corporal Foday Sankoh, in his war of amputation and murder against the civilian population of Sierra Leone. Many people in the region questioned America's inability to bring order to what was its former colony, and long-term sphere of influence. In particular, it was pointed out that American multinationals such as Firestone played a major role in feeding Taylor's war machine, by providing 'communications facilities and a supply base for "Operation Octopus", of the National Patriotic Front of Liberia (NPFL)[1] October 1992 attack on Monrovia'.[2] In the view of many observers of the African political scene, America's nonchalance towards the region's problems is exemplified in the thesis of the much read travelogue of Robert D Kaplan.[3]

Kaplan's caricature of the new African wars has been characterised as the 'New Barbarism' thesis, or 'Malthus-with-Guns'[4] since its central premise is to warn against the effects of such wars which he saw as the product of social breakdown, demographic pressure and environmental crisis, epitomised in the HIV/AIDS crisis. Kaplan was at pains to warn against laissez-faire immigration, which he felt would pose a threat not only to the health service delivery systems of the West, but their populations.

The end of the Cold War did not bring many peace dividends to the people of Africa. In Southern Africa, despite losing the internationally supervised elections, former Western protégé, Junas Savimbi, and UNITA continued their cruel war against the people of Angola with impunity. Like Charles Taylor's sponsored Revolutionary United Front (RUF) in Sierra Leone, blood diamonds fuelled these wars. Indeed, recent reports from the *Washington Post* indicate that Osama bin Laden's al-Qaida network had cashed in on Sierra Leone's diamonds by purchasing gemstones worth millions of dollars from the leadership of the RUF, which were sold in the market just before the September 11 events.[5] It is also common knowledge that Sierra Leone diamonds have been used to finance Hamas's War in the Middle East.[6] The question most frequently asked by African people is: 'Where were our friends?' This question is particularly relevant in the area of human rights in Africa. Western complacency and, specifically, French duplicity in human rights abuses in Rwanda, culminating in the genocide of almost a million Tutsi, is strong in the African memory.

Similarly, Britain and the United States rewarded Foday Sankoh, 'the butcher of Sierra Leone', with the penultimate political office, that of vice-president, for killing, raping, amputating limbs and abducting thousands of innocent young children and socialising them into an ogre of grotesque violence. This was done by imposing 'a peace settlement' on the democratically elected president, insisting he signed a carte blanche agreement with Sankoh. The latter and his henchmen were granted immunity from prosecution for gross human rights abuses. As a further sweetener, Sankoh was offered the chair of the Commission for Mineral Resources Reconstruction and Development. As a Sierra Leonean official observed, 'It is like putting the cat in charge of a basket of fish.' The Lome injustice imposed on the government and people of Sierra Leone is second only to Jesse Jackson's (US presidential ambassador to Africa) malapropism of equating Foday Sankoh with Nelson Mandela.

For most African people, the New World Order, which President George Bush heralded in 1990, was a myth as dictators and warlords continued their 'business as usual'. The average African is economically worse off today than s/he was on the eve of independence. Africa's problems have been caused not just by wars, bad government, economic mismanagement and kleptocracy, but by Africa's structural position within the international capitalist order. As Africa's share of world trade continued to decline under the aegis of globalisation (imperialism?), it hastened marginalisation from the global market, thus forcing Africans to seek desperate measures for their survival. The fillip to this process of marginalisation was the neo-Liberal-designed, and International Financial Institutions-sponsored, structural adjustment programmes. The conditionalities imposed on African nations have created widespread unemployment, poverty and a much weakened state. Structural adjustment programmes, by pauperising the nascent bourgeois class, put paid to any notion of a transition to capitalism. Africa's share of world trade continued to decline as African leaders were continuously advised and coerced into pursuing the policy of promoting traditional exports. Consequently a glut soon emerged, reducing the price for Africa's exports in the international market. In Africa, the neo-Liberal project has succeeded in de-legitimising the state, not only as a locus of nationalist aspirations and resistance,[7] but also as the cradle of post-colonial developmental efforts. Even branded goods, which carry better prices in the world market, have been reduced in value thanks to the privatisation of state-controlled marketing boards.[8]

The functions of the state have been usurped by Northern non-governmental organisations, thus posing a threat to any notion of social citizenship. The weakened state and the absence of social welfare have tended to impel citizens into the ranks of either social movements challenging the state for hegemony, or have forced them into the hands of millenarian groups such as The Lords Resistance Movement of Uganda, the Maitatsine Movement of Nigeria and the RUF of Sierra Leone. In a hypocritical way, and in spite of their efforts at undermining the African state, neo-Liberals continue to point to 'state collapse' and 'state decay' as examples of the vampire nature of a 'Lame African Leviathan'. The fundamentalism endemic in these counter-revolutionary movements has tended to pitch one community against another in the emerging project of vertical consciousness. Many of these movements take their cue from beliefs and practices external to Africa. Thus one Nigerian bishop has warned that the Islamophobia holding sway in the West has often resulted in Nigerian Christians being singled out for religious violence by home-grown fundamentalists.

The new discourse on terrorism demands the full co-operation and support of all African states. States like Sudan and Somalia have been identified as providing sanctuary for al-Qaida cadres. Both countries are among the poorest in Africa with collapsed and decayed states, and both have experienced bloody civil wars in the 1990s. Indeed, the failure of US-mounted humanitarian peace enforcement in Somalia, resulting in the death of 18 US Army Rangers in October 1993, led to the US retreat from humanitarian intervention in Africa and the call by the Clinton administration for an African Crisis Response Force to be equipped and trained by the US and its West European allies.[9] This retreat from Africa gave a fillip to reactionary elements, such as warlords and dictators, to threaten the emerging democratic project in Africa. Also, the retreat created space for private security agencies such as Executive Outcomes and Sandline International to assume the mantle of state security. Many of these security outfits were adjuncts to mining concerns in the continent. Thus Tony Buckingham, a Director of Sandline International (which helped the Sierra Leone government to deflect the rebels from the diamond fields), was instrumental in setting up Branch Energy, which later merged with Carson Gold to form Diamond Works of Canada.[10] The latter has been able to obtain a mining concession in Sierra Leone.

In short, Africa's history is littered with incidences of terrorism: the slave trade, the colonial project, the post-colonial violence triggered off by super-power rivalry, which saw the spread of low-intensity conflicts throughout the continent (from Algeria in the north to South Africa in the south, and from Ethiopia in the east to Guinea Bissau in the west). The anti-colonial struggle instructed Africans in the ability to recognise the relativity of the term 'terrorist'; not only is one group's terrorist another group's freedom fighter, but yesterday's terrorist is tomorrow's statesman. To draw attention to these points is not to excuse the dastardly act of September 11, but to emphasise that the African experience of terrorism is not a recent phenomenon; that the lived experience of African people has been punctuated by institutional and individual acts of terror. Thus the denial of cheap retroactive drugs to HIV/AIDS sufferers in Africa by Western multinational corporations can be seen as a form of passive institutional violence against these unfortunate people.

Ms Taylor, the passenger on American Airline Flight 77 (like the other victims of the wicked act of September 11), can rest in peace, with the knowledge that the US government has now lifted immigration restrictions to enable members of her immediate family to move to the US with help from a generous federal government.

1. The National Patriotic Front of Liberia was the name of Taylor's movement which helped to create the Revolutionary United Front (RUF) of Sierra Leone, which unleashed mayhem, amputation, raping, looting and the death of over 3,000 Sierra Leoneans.
2. Reno, W, 'Reinvention of an African Patrimonial State: Charles Taylor's Liberia', *Third World Quarterly*, Vol. 16, No. 1, 1995, p. 114.
3. Kaplan, R D, 'The Coming Anarchy: How Scarcity, Crime, Overpopulation, and Disease Are Rapidly Destroying the Social Fabric of Our Planet', *Atlantic Monthly*, February 1994, pp. 44–76.
4. Richards, P, *Fighting for the Rain Forest: War, Youth and Resources in Sierra Leone*, Heinemann/James Currey, 1996.
5. Farah, D, 'Al Qaeda Cash Tied to Diamonds Trade: Sale of Gems From Sierra Leone Rebels Raised Millions, Sources Say', *Washington Post*, Friday, November 2, 2001.
6. Fithen, C, 'Diamonds and War in Sierra Leone: Cultural Strategies for Commercial Adaptation to Endemic Low-intensity Conflict', unpublished PhD thesis, University College London, 1999.

7. Beckman, B, 'The Liberation of Civil Society: Neo-Liberal Ideology and Political Theory', *Review of African Political Economy*, No. 58, 1993, pp. 20–33

8. Van der Laan, H L, 'Misconception About The "World Market": Implications for African Export Policies' in T Zack-Williams, D Frost and A Thomson (eds) *Africa in Crisis*, Pluto Press, 2002, forthcoming.

9. Zack-Williams, A, 'Peacekeeping and an "African High Command": C'est Ca Plus, C'est La Même Chose', *Review of Africa Political Economy*, No. 71, Vol. 24, 1997, pp. 131–7.

10. 'Kayode Fayemi, J, 'African Search of Security: Mercenaries and Conflicts: An Overview', in A F Musah and J 'Kayode Fayemi (eds) *Mercenaries: An African Security Dilemma*, Pluto Press, 2000, p. 24.

THE KHAKI ELECTION
Russell Hogg

I don't want a mosque in my backyard.
Elector expressing her intention to vote for the incumbent Australian prime minister, John Howard, Election Day, 2001

Three days before the national Australian election on November 10 the Conservative prime minister, John Howard, made his most overt personal foray into the public debate about links between terrorism and asylum seekers arriving by boat in Australia.

In late August a Norwegian container ship, the *Tampa*, had rescued a boatload of more than 430 Afghani asylum seekers in the Indian Ocean off the north-west of Australia at the request of Australian Search and Rescue. When the *Tampa* – licensed to carry less than 30 people – sought to deliver its desperate human cargo on Christmas Island, an Australian territory, the government refused it entry to Australian waters. When it disobeyed this order armed members of the SAS boarded and took control of the ship. 'That boat will never land in Australia, never!' stormed the prime minister. New Zealand agreed to take some of the asylum seekers and the balance were packed off to the small and very poor Pacific island state of Nauru (population 10,000) in a 'petrol for people' deal with the Australian government. The policy was wildly popular in Australia.

The events of September 11 did not so much succeed the local ferment over the *Tampa* as add to it new layers of meaning. The asylum seeker issue had already shaped the context in which news of the US attacks and US retaliation was received and interpreted in

Australia. This was clear from the attacks on mosques and other Muslim targets occurring in Australia, as elsewhere, in the aftermath of September 11. Many people clearly shared the views of Osama bin Laden and Samuel P Huntington that this was a 'clash of civilisations'.

This shaped answers to questions like: who was responsible? Where should retribution be sought? And (the more pressing local issue in Australia) how should we understand the plight of those fleeing the lands of Osama bin Laden, the Taliban and (that other erstwhile friend, now enemy and likely – next target – of the 'war on terror') Saddam Hussein? Were they refugees from terror, its victims, or were they the bearers of terror, 'sleepers' awaiting the opportunity to mount their own attacks on the citadels of Australian civilisation?

As election day approached the prime minister made his position clear. In a pitch to voters in one key state, he claimed that Australia could not be certain that terrorists or people with terrorist links were not amongst those, primarily Afghani and Middle Eastern, arriving in Australia on decrepit and overcrowded fishing boats. This despite the uncertain and perilous sea journey involved, the evidence that the asylum seekers included increasing numbers of women and children and that the overwhelming majority were accepted after arrival in Australia as refugees. Most picked up by the *Tampa*, for example, were Hazara Afghanis, a persecuted minority who had been victims of several massacres carried out by Taliban and al-Qaida militia in the late 1990s.

Just two weeks before the election another boat heading for Australia had sunk in the Indonesian Sea with the loss of over 350 lives, mostly women and children. Howard and his immigration minister publicly refused an Iraqi father of three drowned children permission to travel from Australia (where he was already resident on a temporary protection visa) to Indonesia to join his grieving wife. If he went, they said, he would not be allowed to return to Australia. The growing trend for women and young children to risk their lives in the people smugglers' boats was a response to the increasingly draconian and discriminatory apparatus for managing asylum seekers who arrive in Australia by boat.

Under laws originally introduced by a Labour government it is mandatory for all such arrivals (men, women and children) to be incarcerated in detention centres pending determination of their refugee status. There is no requirement for a court order.

Management of most detention centres is contracted out to Australasian Correctional Management, a subsidiary of the US-based Wackenhut Corporation. Australia's little gulags are mostly located in remote outback places isolated from public and media scrutiny, from access to lawyers and other support services and from contact with the detainees' family members who, in some cases, do not know they are alive and have made it to Australia. Detention for many is not a short-term experience but can last for one or two years or, in some cases, longer. Currently there are over 50 unaccompanied children detained in the centres. For many detainees the experience of isolation and uncertainty about their fate, and that of other family members, comes in addition to torture or other trauma suffered in their countries of origin. The incidence of mental breakdown and suicide attempts is high. In the last two years there have been many escapes, riots, hunger strikes, and other protests. Protests have frequently been suppressed with tear gas and water cannon. Inquiries have found instances of brutality and persecution by staff in centres. Some asylum seekers found that they had more rights and better treatment when transferred to prisons than in the detention centres.

In 1999 there were further refinements to the system of discriminatory controls exercised over asylum seekers. Those unauthorised arrivals by boat given refugee status were only released into the community on temporary protection visas. This disentitled them to apply for their families to join them in Australia, to leave the country and to access English lessons. This status lasted three years, after which they could apply to be permanent residents. Stooping to yet grosser levels of callousness, in September 2001 the government rushed through regulations that removed the prospect of boat arrivals ever gaining permanent status and hence ever applying to bring their families to Australia. These measures fed the growing tendency for women and children to seek to make the journey themselves. When the immigration minister was asked whether these new provisions in effect created a system of second-class citizenship he cheerily replied, 'That's right.'

The government's response to the *Tampa* represented yet another new chapter in asylum seeker policies. In a move which echoes Australia's history as a place of penal transportation for the social detritus of Britain's industrial revolution, the government entered the business of forced people movements by spreading its network of detention centres throughout a number of small Pacific island states. Asylum seekers heading for Australia are now diverted to camps on these islands by Australia's armed forces. These arrangements reflect relationships between Australia and its weaker neighbours that are colonial in all but name. For example, 700 asylum seekers are now being held on Nauru (the first Pacific country to receive them), overnight representing a 7 per cent increase in its population, or the per capita equivalent of Australia receiving one and a quarter million asylum seekers.

Howard's intervention in the closing stages of the election campaign, making an explicit link between terrorism and asylum seekers was merely the culmination of a sustained political strategy to manufacture a national crisis and to demonise Middle Eastern and Asian asylum seekers. The *Tampa*, the September 11 attacks in the US and other local issues – like 'ethnic gangs' in Australia's suburbs – presented an exquisite confluence of events and opportunities for Australia's self-declared most conservative prime minister facing likely defeat in the election. He played them to brilliant electoral, and awful social, effect.

From the time the *Tampa* anchored off Christmas Island, his government pursued a relentless strategy linking refugee and immigration policy directly to national defence. The move tapped the deep reservoirs of sentiment in favour of a founding condition and principle of Australian nationhood. It was, in large part, the ingrained fear of Asian 'invasion' and the concern to preserve a 'white Australia' that at the end of the nineteenth century led six small British colonies occupying a huge continent to unite as one nation – an outpost of European civilisation at the foot of South-east Asia – and thereafter hitch itself to the apron strings of others, first Britain and then the United States.

By the 1970s Australia had formally abandoned the 'white Australia' policy and was making halting steps towards a new independence and acceptance of its geopolitical position in the world. But after more than 20 years of bipartisan political support for multiculturalism at home and engagement with Asia abroad John Howard signalled on a number of occasions his preference for 'one-nation' nationalism and the role of US deputy sheriff in the region. By conviction a moral and cultural conservative, Howard's social agenda coincided neatly with what was politically opportune among a growing number of electors suffering the insecurities and adverse effects of global economic change. To assuage their fears Howard offered them the illusion at least of a return to some older cultural certainties. He thereby cut the ground from under the emergent populist, xenophobic right rapidly rising to electoral success under the leadership of Pauline Hanson. As a hitherto political unknown she rode into the national parliament at the 1996 election as an independent on the back of a 20 per cent swing in a Labour stronghold deemed unwinnable by the Conservatives. They had dumped her as their local candidate after she had made overtly racist comments to a local newspaper. Taking Hanson's ensuing electoral success to heart, Howard's Conservatives set about appealing to her supporters on race and immigration issues; not in her overtly xenophobic voice but with what the Americans call 'dog whistling'. Attacks on Aboriginal 'handouts', on the multicultural 'industry' and, ultimately, on boat people were conducted *sotto voce,* in coded words whose meaning was clear to their audience but whose overt intent to denigrate and demonise was open to plausible denial. Oftentimes Howard's supporters at either end of the talkback line did not mess with such subtleties, but this never earned them a rebuke from the prime minister.

Unlike the economic nationalist Hanson, though, Howard has also always been an enthusiastic champion of free markets, small government and economic globalisation. Inevitably such policies breed the growing inequality, uncertainty and insecurity that find an outlet in intolerance towards refugees and other minorities. Because Howard's economic policies are the source of, rather than the solution to, these reactions he has no choice but to ride them, to deflect attention on to external threats to security, nurturing the hardening of attitudes and identities that accompanies it. The increasing role of deception, scapegoating and repressive measures in domestic political life has shown that Howard is a wily grim reaper to the disorders sown by the unregulated global market forces whose cause he also espouses.

Border protection became the instant catch cry and agenda of the election campaign. Australia's armed forces were pushed into the front line; not to protect the country from an armed invading force, but from desperately poor and persecuted people in leaky old fishing boats. Insofar as it affected Australia, a global humanitarian crisis was redefined as a threat to national security. The government added the tactic of 'military repulsion' to the apparatus of mandatory detention without court order in a regime that Robert Manne has called 'exclusionary nationalism'.

The official election campaign began with a claim by the minister of defence, Peter Reith, that an Australian navy boat had a video of Iraqi asylum seekers throwing their children into the sea. It was filmed when the navy intercepted the asylum seekers close to Australian waters. 'I certainly don't want people of that type in Australia. I really don't', opined the 'family values' prime minister in an indignant tone. Others in the government and the media depicted it as a cynical and inhuman attempt to emotionally blackmail Australian authorities into taking families. For weeks the government refused to release the video and sought to ban all armed forces personnel from speaking out. When finally forced to make it public in the last week of the campaign it showed the claims were a pack of lies. Navy personnel confirmed that no children had been thrown overboard. Descending ever further into 'the quicksand of lying statements', Howard claimed on the day before the election that he had just received notification that asylum seekers on another boat had deliberately set fire to it, leading to the death by drowning of two women. The following day, tucked away in the election day press coverage, the immigration minister acknowledged that the fire may have been an accident.

But it was the events of September 11 in the US that allowed the Australian government to add 'terrorist' to the lexicon of vilification they had been developing against asylum seekers, solidifying the link between refugee policy and national defence. It was commonplace for politicians, shock jocks and the tabloids to refer to asylum seekers as 'illegals' and 'queue jumpers'. Government ministers, especially the immigration minister, had long ceased to open their mouths on the refugee issue, other than to allege some scam or other deviance on their part. At one stage the immigration minister claimed that asylum seekers were taking first-class flights to Indonesia before boarding on fishing boats to enter Australia illegally. In response to recent calls for an inquiry into the detention of children he alleged that parents conspired to send unaccompanied young children as a tactic to gain entry for themselves. And then there was the nonsense about Iraqi children being thrown overboard by their parents. Amid this catalogue of demonising myths and labels it was rarely, if ever, conceded that people fleeing countries like Afghanistan and Iraq might have legitimate claims to refugee status, although this is the conclusion of tribunals in the overwhelming majority of cases. Rarely, if ever, did the politicians acknowledge the human suffering behind these desperate attempts to seek a new life on the other side of the world.

Within two days of the attacks on the US the Australian defence minister suggested publicly that boat people might include terrorists. Soon after, one of his colleagues claimed, 'There is an undeniable linkage between illegals and terrorists.' This idea was promoted widely in sections of the media and used by many government members in local election campaigns to condemn opponents who opposed or were equivocal about the government's asylum seeker policies. Such a position, they argued, was now tantamount to inviting terrorists into the country.

It is the 'fragility' of 'the whole texture of facts in which we spend our daily life' that, according to Hannah Arendt, makes deception so 'easy' and 'so tempting'. As she notes: 'Facts need testimony to be remembered and trustworthy witnesses to be established in order to find a secure dwelling place in the domain of human affairs.' Isolation, denigration and dehumanisation of those who might provide such testimony are, of course, familiar tools in the apparatus of denial and have been refined in the Australian government's asylum seeker policies. They lay the groundwork for the systematic mistreatment of other human beings. In one remote detention centre in north-western Australia some men sewed their lips together with a needle and thread as a protest. What might have been seen as an eloquent commentary on the abject silence to which they had been reduced was reported in the press (insofar as it was reported at all) as 'bizarre', 'gruesome' and 'grisly', yet further evidence that these were people of alien habits and sensibilities. In what might stand as a fitting commentary on the Howard re-election strategy Arendt points out that 'lies are often much more plausible, more appealing to reason, than reality, since the liar has the great advantage of knowing beforehand what the audience wishes or expects to hear. He has prepared his story for public consumption with a careful eye to making it credible ...'

Arendt's comments appeared in the course of her analysis of the sorry trail of US government deception during the Vietnam War recorded in the Pentagon Papers. Alexis de Tocqueville also made salutary observations of a more general kind about the impact of war in democratic societies. 'War,' he argued, 'does not always give democratic societies over to military government, but it must invariably and immeasurably increase the powers of civil government; it must almost automatically concentrate the direction of all men and the control of all things in the hands of the government. If that does not lead to despotism by sudden violence, it leads men gently in that direction by their habits.' This is hardly less true of a 'war on terror'. Indeed the striking thing about the concept of 'terrorism' is how it can encourage a blurring and a convergence of civil and military powers and roles, of national defence and domestic law enforcement.

Even in the absence of credible evidence that there were significant 'terrorist' threats to Australia, the apparatus of counter-terrorist measures has been slowly and silently erected over the years. The watershed event often referred to is the 1978 Sydney Hilton Hotel bombing when a police officer and two garbage collectors were killed by a bomb that exploded outside the hotel during a Commonwealth Heads of Government conference. No organisation claimed responsibility and the jury remains out on whether it was actually the work of the security agencies themselves. In 2000 legislation passed through the Australian parliament largely unnoticed empowering the Prime Minister, the Attorney-General and the defence minister to utilise the armed forces in aid (or substitution) of civilian authorities where Commonwealth interests are threatened by 'domestic violence'. Late amendments were added, prohibiting the use of such powers to 'stop or restrict any protest, assembly or industrial action, except where there is a reasonable likelihood of death or serious injury or serious damage to property'. The threat of terrorism at the Sydney Olympics was the stated pretext for the legislation but there may have been more concern at the time over expected protests at the imminent World Economic Forum.

Critics of the legislation also alluded to the bitter wharf dispute from a few years before. In 1997–98, in a highly proactive effort to bring about waterfront reform, the Howard government entered into a clandestine arrangement with a stevedoring company to facilitate the training of serving and former members of the armed forces in Dubai as an industrial 'mercenary' force who, after a dispute was engineered, were to take over the docks enabling the entire workforce of the company to be sacked and the union's power to be broken. When this plan was exposed prematurely the strategy shifted onshore, culminating in a lockout of the union workforce after private security personnel conducted a carefully planned dawn takeover of the docks. Ultimately it was frustrated when the union initiated a conspiracy action against the company, government ministers and others. The key actors, including members of the government, publicly lied throughout about their knowledge of, and involvement in, the alleged conspiracy. A major political scandal was averted when the case was settled out of court. There is little doubt as to the potential application of the 2000 legislation in industrial disputes of this kind, especially where, as in the maritime dispute, police in parts of the country refused to be drawn into the partisan role of suppressing the union and community pickets, thereby earning the ire of the national government, the stevedore and other participants in the conspiracy.

There is ample scope for laws, and other measures deemed necessary to fight 'terrorism', to find their real application in the control and suppression of peaceful protest, political dissent, industrial conflict and scapegoated minorities like asylum seekers. Polls indicated overwhelming popular support for the military repulsion of asylum seekers. Public attitudes to Australia's participation in the 'war' in Afghanistan, however, were more lukewarm. Australia had a khaki election of sorts on November 10 but its outcome was dictated less by the 'war' abroad than the national emergency at home, an emergency manufactured out of the confluence of the *Tampa* and the September 11 attacks. The dangers of a 'war on terror' can be seen in the peculiar fact that in Australia this produced an assault on those who were manifestly the victims of terror. People fleeing and seeking refuge from the state terror of the Taliban and Saddam Hussein were themselves made out to be a terrorist threat to Australia for no other reason than that they were Muslims. Does their treatment not show that there is an element of terror of which all states and peoples are capable however much they might congratulate themselves on their civilised values?

SIGNS OF THE TIMES
Naomi Klein

As shocking as this must be to New Yorkers, in Toronto, the city where I live, lamp-posts and mailboxes are plastered with posters advertising a plan by anti-poverty activists to 'shut down' the business district on October 16. Some of the posters (those put up before September 11) even have a picture of skyscrapers outlined in red – the perimeters of the designated direct-action zone. Many have argued that O16 should be cancelled, as other protests and demonstrations have been, in deference to the mood of mourning – and out of fear of stepped up police violence.

But the shutdown is going ahead. In the end, the events of September 11 don't change the fact that the nights are getting colder and the recession is looming. They don't change the fact that in a city that used to be described as 'safe' and, well, 'maybe a little boring', many will die on the streets this winter, as they did last winter, and the one before that, unless more beds are found immediately. And yet there is no disputing that the event, its militant tone and its choice of target will provoke terrible memories and associations. Many political campaigns face a similar, and sudden, shift. Post-September 11, tactics that rely on attacking – even peacefully – powerful symbols of capitalism find themselves in an utterly transformed semiotic landscape. After all, the attacks were acts of very real and horrifying terror, but they were also acts of symbolic warfare, and instantly understood as such. As Tom Brokaw and so many others put it, the towers were not just any buildings, they were 'symbols of American capitalism'.

As someone whose life is thoroughly entwined with what some people call 'the anti-globalisation movement,' others call 'anti-capitalism' (and I tend to just sloppily call 'the movement'), I find it difficult to avoid discussions about symbolism these days. About all the anti-corporate signs and signifiers – the culture-jammed logos, the guerrilla-warfare stylings, the choices of brand name and political targets – that make up the movement's dominant metaphors. Many political opponents of anti-corporate activism are using the symbolism of the World Trade Center and Pentagon attacks to argue that young activists, playing at guerrilla war, have now been caught out by a real war. The obituaries are already appearing in newspapers around the world: 'Anti-Globalisation Is So Yesterday', reads a typical headline. It is, according to the *Boston Globe*, 'in tatters'. Is it true? Our activism has been declared dead before. Indeed, it is declared dead with ritualistic regularity before and after every mass demonstration: our strategies apparently discredited, our coalitions divided, our arguments misguided. And yet those demonstrations have kept growing larger, from 50,000 in Seattle to 300,000, by some estimates, in Genoa.

At the same time, it would be foolish to pretend that nothing has changed since September 11. This struck me recently, looking at a slide show I had been pulling together before the attacks. It is about how anti-corporate imagery is increasingly being absorbed by corporate marketing. One slide shows a group of activists spray-painting the window of a Gap outlet during the anti-WTO protests in Seattle. The next shows The Gap's recent window displays featuring its own prefab graffiti – words like 'Independence' sprayed in black. And the next is a frame from Sony PlayStation's 'State of Emergency' game featuring cool-haired anarchists throwing rocks at evil riot cops protecting the fictitious American Trade Organisation. When I first looked at these images beside each other, I was amazed by the speed of corporate co-optation. Now all I can see is how these snapshots from the corporate versus anti-corporate image wars have been instantly overshadowed, blown away by September 11 like so many toy cars and action figures on a disaster movie set.

Despite the altered landscape – or because of it – it bears remembering why this movement chose to wage symbolic struggles in the first place. The Ontario Coalition Against Poverty's decision to 'shut down' the business district came from a set of very specific and still relevant circumstances. Like so many others trying to get issues of economic inequality on the political agenda, the people the group represents felt that they had been discarded, left outside the paradigm, disappeared and reconstituted as a panhandling or squeegee problem requiring tough new legislation. They realised that what they had to confront was just not a local political enemy or even a particular trade law but an economic system – the broken promise of deregulated, trickle-down capitalism. Thus the modern activist challenge: how do you organise against an ideology so vast, it has no edges; so everywhere, it seems nowhere? Where is the site of resistance for those with no workplaces to shut down, whose communities are constantly being uprooted? What do we hold on to when so much that is powerful is virtual – currency trades, stock prices, intellectual property and arcane trade agreements?

The short answer, at least before September 11, was that you grab anything you can get your hands on: the brand image of a famous multinational, a stock exchange, a meeting of world leaders, a single trade agreement or, in the case of the Toronto group, the banks and corporate headquarters that are the engines that power this agenda. Anything that, even fleetingly, makes the intangible actual, the vastness somehow human-scale. In short, you find symbols and you hope they become metaphors for change. For instance, when the United States launched a trade war against France for daring to ban hormone-laced beef, José Bové and the French Farmers' Confederation didn't get the world's attention by screaming about import duties on Roquefort cheese. They did it by 'strategically dismantling' a McDonald's. Nike, ExxonMobil, Monsanto, Shell, Chevron, Pfizer, Sodexho Marriott, Kellogg's, Starbucks, The Gap, Rio Tinto, British Petroleum, General Electric, Wal-Mart, Home Depot, Citigroup, Taco Bell – all have found their gleaming brands used to shine light on everything from bovine growth hormone in milk to human rights in the Niger Delta; from labour abuses of Mexican tomato farm workers in Florida to war-financing of oil pipelines in Chad and Cameroon; from global warming to sweatshops.

In the weeks since September 11, we have been reminded many times that Americans aren't particularly informed about the world outside their borders. That may be true, but many activists have learned over the past decade that this blind spot for international affairs can be overcome by linking campaigns to famous brands; an effective, if often problematic, weapon against parochialism. These corporate campaigns have, in turn, opened back doors into the arcane world of international trade and finance, to the World Trade Organisation, the World Bank and, for some, to a questioning of capitalism itself. But these tactics have also proven to be an easy target in turn. After September 11, politicians and pundits around the world instantly began spinning the terrorist attacks as part of a continuum of anti-American and anti-corporate violence: first the Starbucks' window, then, presumably, the WTC. *New Republic* editor Peter Beinart seized on an obscure post to an anti-corporate Internet chat room that asked if the attacks were committed by 'one of us'. Beinart concluded that 'the anti-globalization movement ... is, in part, a movement motivated by hatred of the United States' – immoral, with the United States under attack.

In a sane world, rather than fuelling such a backlash the terrorist attacks would raise questions about why US intelligence agencies were spending so much time spying on environmentalists and Independent Media Centres instead of on the terrorist networks plotting mass murder. Unfortunately, it seems clear that the crackdown on activism that predated September 11 will only intensify, with heightened surveillance, infiltration and police violence. It's also likely that the anonymity that has been a hallmark of anti-capitalism – masks, bandannas and pseudonyms – will become more suspect in a culture searching for clandestine operatives in its midst. But the attacks will cost us more than our civil liberties. They could well, I fear, cost us our few political victories. Funds committed to the AIDS crisis in Africa are disappearing, and commitments to expand debt cancellation will likely follow. Defending the rights of immigrants and refugees was becoming a major focus for the direct-action crowd in Australia, Europe and, slowly, the United States. This too is threatened by the rising tide of racism and xenophobia.

And free trade, long facing a public relations crisis, is fast being rebranded, like shopping and baseball, as a patriotic duty. According to US Trade Representative Robert Zoellick (who is frantically trying to get fast-track negotiating power pushed through in this moment of jingoistic groupthink), trade 'promotes the values at the heart of this protracted struggle'. Michael Lewis makes a similar conflation between freedom fighting and free trading when he explains, in an essay in the *New York Times Magazine*, that the traders who died were targeted as 'not merely symbols but also practitioners of liberty... They work hard, if unintentionally, to free others from constraints. This makes them, almost by default, the spiritual antithesis of the religious fundamentalist, whose business depends on a denial of personal liberty in the name of some putatively higher power.' The battle lines leading up to next month's WTO negotiations in Qatar are: trade equals freedom, anti-trade equals fascism. Never mind that Osama bin Laden is a multimillionaire with a rather impressive global export network stretching from cash-crop agriculture to oil pipelines. And never mind that this fight will take place in Qatar, that bastion of liberty, which is refusing foreign visas for demonstrators but where bin Laden practically has his own TV show on the state-subsidised network Al-Jazeera.

Our civil liberties, our modest victories, our usual strategies – all are now in question. But this crisis also opens up new possibilities. As many have pointed out, the challenge for social justice movements is to connect economic inequality with the security concerns that now grip us all – insisting that justice and equality are the most sustainable strategies against violence and fundamentalism. But we cannot be naive, as if the very real and ongoing threat of more slaughtering of innocents will disappear through political reform alone. There needs to be social justice, but there also needs to be justice for the victims of these attacks and immediate, practical prevention of future ones. Terrorism is indeed an international threat, and it did not begin with the attacks in the United States. As Bush invites the world to join America's war, sidelining the United Nations and the international courts, we need to become passionate defenders of true multilateralism, rejecting once and for all the label 'anti-globalisation'. Bush's 'coalition' does not represent a genuinely global response to terrorism but the internationalisation of one country's foreign policy objectives – the trademark of US international relations, from the WTO negotiating table to Kyoto: you are free to play by our rules or get shut out completely. We can make these connections not as 'anti-Americans' but as true internationalists.

We can also refuse to engage in a calculus of suffering. Some on the left have implied that the outpouring of compassion and grief post-September 11 is disproportionate, even vaguely racist, compared with responses to greater atrocities. Surely the job of those who claim to abhor injustice and suffering is not to stingily parcel out compassion as if it were a finite commodity. Surely the challenge is to attempt to increase the global reserves of compassion rather than parsimoniously police them. Besides, is the outpouring of mutual aid and support that this tragedy has elicited so different from the humanitarian goals to which this movement aspires? The street slogans – PEOPLE BEFORE PROFIT, THE WORLD IS NOT FOR SALE – have become self-evident and viscerally felt truths for many in the wake of the attacks. There is outrage in the face of profiteering. There are questions being raised about the wisdom of leaving crucial services like airport security to private companies, about why there are bailouts for airlines but not for the workers losing their jobs. There is a groundswell of appreciation for public sector workers of all kinds. In short, 'the commons' – the public sphere, the public good, the non-corporate, what we have been defending, what is on the negotiating table in Qatar – is undergoing something of a rediscovery in the United States.

Instead of assuming that Americans can care about each other only when they are getting ready to kill a common enemy, those concerned with changing minds (and not simply winning arguments) should seize this moment to connect these humane reactions to the many other arenas in which human needs must take precedence over corporate profits, from AIDS treatment to homelessness. As Paul Loeb, author of *Soul of a Citizen*, puts it, despite the warmongering and coexisting with the xenophobia, 'People seem careful, vulnerable, and extraordinarily kind to each other. These events just might be able to break us away from our gated communities of the heart.' This would require a dramatic change in activist strategy, one based much more on substance than on symbols. Then again, for more than a year, the largely symbolic activism outside summits and against individual corporations has already been challenged within movement circles. There is much that is unsatisfying about fighting a war of symbols: the glass shatters in the McDonald's window, the meetings are driven to ever more remote locations – but so what? It's still only symbols, façades, representations.

Before September 11, a new mood of impatience was already taking hold, an insistence on putting forward social and economic alternatives that address the roots of injustice as well as its symptoms, from land reform to slavery reparations. Now seems like a good time to challenge the forces of both nihilism and nostalgia within our own ranks, while making more room for the voices – coming from Chiapas, Porto Alegre, Kerala – showing that it is indeed possible to challenge imperialism while embracing plurality, progress and deep democracy. Our task, never more pressing, is to point out that there are more than two worlds available, to expose all the invisible worlds between the economic fundamentalism of 'McWorld' and the religious fundamentalism of 'Jihad'. Maybe the image wars are coming to a close. A year ago, I visited the University of Oregon to do a story on anti-sweatshop activism at the campus that is nicknamed Nike U. There I met student activist Sarah Jacobson. Nike, she told me, was not the target of her activism, but a tool, a way to access a vast and often amorphous economic system. 'It's a gateway drug', she said cheerfully.

For years, we in this movement have fed off our opponents' symbols – their brands, their office towers, their photo opportunity summits. We have used them as rallying cries, as focal points, as popular education tools. But these symbols were never the real targets; they were the levers, the handles. They were what allowed us, as British writer Katharine Ainger recently put it, 'to open a crack in history'. The symbols were only ever doorways. It's time to walk through them.

This essay was first published in *The Nation*, October 22, 2001, pp. 15–20.

BUSINESS AS USUAL?
CORPORATE MORALISM AND THE 'WAR
AGAINST TERRORISM'

Dave Whyte

> Thanks to America, and only thanks to America, the world has
> enjoyed these past decades an age of hitherto unimagined
> freedom and opportunity. Those who would deflect from its path
> must not, and surely will not, succeed.[1]

> There have never been as many business opportunities around as
> now![2]

Since the World Trade Center and Pentagon attacks, we have been
instructed by people with more knowledge and experience of world
affairs than the rest of us that the free market is set to play a growing
role in the war against terrorism. As the latest round of World Trade
Organisation talks approached in November 2001, US Federal
Reserve chief Alan Greenspan argued that a successful round of WTO
talks 'would not only significantly enhance world economic growth,
but would also answer terrorism with a firm reaffirmation of our
commitment to open and free societies'. Similarly, UK Chancellor
of the Exchequer Gordon Brown argued for an immediate
resumption of meetings of the IMF and the World Bank in order to
'show that the work of the international financial community would
not be disrupted by terrorism'.

These statements have a familiar ring to them. One of the most
widely acclaimed, if eccentric, popular theories of market globalisation in recent years, 'The Golden Arches Theory of Conflict
Management', was disseminated by the *New York Times*. The theory,
concocted by columnist Thomas Friedman in the late 1990s, argued
that no two nation states with McDonald's restaurants in their
capital cities had ever gone to war. His contention was that when a
country reached the level of economic development required to
sustain a middle class and a McDonald's network 'it became a
McDonald's country'. People in McDonald's countries have,
according to Friedman, a greater desire to wait in line for burgers
than to fight wars. Simplicity in a bun.

Market populism and the war against terrorism

It may seem like half-baked political science, but Friedman's crackpot Big Mac thesis fits broadly into a growing tide of thought which sustains the defenders of a neo-liberal world order. Echoing their intellectual heirs (the liberal economic theorists of the nineteenth century) neo-liberals explicitly associate free markets with ideas of economic democracy, human freedom and development. Critic Thomas Frank calls it market populism; a set of ideas that allow the apostles of neo-liberalism to preach: 'Markets are where we are most fully human; markets are where we show that we have a soul. To protest against markets is to surrender one's very personhood, to put oneself outside the family of mankind.'

They have not noticed that humanity is being ripped apart by 'free' markets. Between 1990 and 1997, a period of consolidation for neo-liberalism, the income ratio between the richest 20 per cent and the poorest 20 per cent in the world rose from 60:1 to 74:1. The top three billionaires in the world now own the same combined wealth as the poorest 48 countries. Meanwhile, 19,000 children die each day for want of basic nutrition or through preventable diseases. Despite the flaws, the chinks and the gaping chasms in neo-liberalism's intellectual armour, the core message of market populism (capitalist economy = freedom and democracy) enables even the most extreme versions of market exploitation to claim a 'civilising' influence throughout the world. It is in this role that capitalist markets have been cast in the new war against terrorism.

The remarkable scenes at the reopening of the New York Stock Market (six days after the World Trade Center attacks) displayed a unique blend of market triumphalism and military ceremony. A US Marines major, from a rostrum high above the market floor, led the traders in a rendering of 'God Bless America'. At the moment the market opened, cheers resounded, ticker tape went up, and the officials on the podium punched the air. The opening of the market was, for some, a symbolic moment. Failure to open, according to the *Financial Times*, 'would not only have handed the terrorists a victory, it would have been an unprecedented blow against the heart of capitalism'.[3] The moral fibre demonstrated by the stock and bond traders of Wall Street, for this brief moment, elevated their public esteem to the cultural commanding heights deservedly enjoyed by the brave firefighters and police officers of New York City.

Beyond the market floor, consumers were being asked to play their part to offset crisis. In the UK, the prime minister launched a plea for people to 'carry on shopping and travelling as usual in order to maintain patriotic normality and help avoid recession'. Bill Clinton was pictured on a downtown shopping spree for ties in order to remind citizens of their 'patriotic duty to spend money'. Overnight, consumerism had become part of the strategy to defeat the new terrorist threat. As the bombs began to fall on Afghanistan, signs in the windows of Manhattan jewellers urged potential custom to 'buy to defeat the Taliban'.

Corporate moralism

Neo-liberal market populism is increasingly embellished with an explicitly *moral* rationale. Market populism relies upon a creeping popular acceptance of representations of private businesses as morally responsible. Corporations, we are told, are better placed than ever to promote a wider range of 'stakeholder interests' than simply those of their profit-hungry shareholders. This corporate moralism has rarely been as prevalent or widely promoted as it has in the period following September 11. It is a period in which the moral currency of doing business has been greatly inflated by the war against terrorism.

In the immediate aftermath of the Manhattan and Pentagon attacks, volumes of newsprint column inches on both sides of the Atlantic were devoted to revelations of a truer, 'human' side to Wall Street, one that bore little resemblance to Gordon Gecko's avaricious yuppie gluttony. Up to a point, this was accurate, as businesses large and small chipped in to the rescue effort, from the street vendors giving away free water to the millions of dollars worth of free fuel and hamburgers donated by the multinationals. Normally bitter rivals were seen to co-operate in unprecedented ways. The usual secrecy and backstabbing was suspended in several trading markets to agree temporary 'fair prices' for stocks and the Bank of England even agreed not to trade dollars 'unnecessarily'. One senior banker in London observed: 'People almost feel guilty to want to trade for profit in circumstances like these ... we are not encouraging people to speculate.'

But beyond the high-profile amnesties, the reality was that markets continued to trade wherever they could. The International Petroleum Exchange in London, for example, experienced its most frenetic activity since the 1990 Gulf War as traders rushed to cover their backs and others came in to make a quick profit on the sharp rise in oil stocks. In fact, the exchange was forced to close for an hour, not out of respect for the dead, but in order to catch up on the backlog of transactions.

We heard little of this type of amoral trading. Instead reports of the al-Qaida network profiting from 'terrorist insider trading' mushroomed in the international press as the French, Belgian and German governments launched inquiries into unusual movements of gold and oil markets. In the US, inquiries were launched into the levels of short trading[4] by terrorists. Banks considered to be operating outside the Western financial system were closed down. US institutions, on the other hand, were allowed to present themselves as operating on a higher moral plane: above the shady world of alien financiers and mysterious Eastern accounting systems.[5] It is widely recognised that US banks have in the past provided financial services for the enemies of their government. If this was the case in relation to the US's newly emergent enemies, the public will never know; commercial confidentiality rules ensure that bankers secrets are kept secret. No such luck for the Third World. In Somalia, the US closure of Barakat, the country's largest remittance company, with little warning, brought financial chaos to tens of thousands of people and effectively cut off NGO aid programmes.

Neo-colonialism and the war on terrorism

In stark contrast to the confusion that has since been visited upon some of the world's most vulnerable populations, Western governments acted to shore up their money markets before the dust had time to settle on the rubble of the World Trade Center. In the US, banks promised as much liquidity as the markets required to stay buoyant, and effectively imposed a global cut in interest rates. A joint statement by the European Union finance ministers, the European Central Bank, other EU banks and the European Commission had promised 'all necessary measures to ensure the proper functioning of markets and the stability of the financial system'. The level of co-operation between Europe and the US was unprecedented.

Contrary to what we have been told by 'globalisation' intellectuals for two decades – that there is little that the state can do to influence the economy – since September 11 it has become obvious to even the most fervent neo-liberal evangelist that governments can and do intervene to prop up their markets. But this is a rule which has always been applied with extreme prejudice. It is only the poorer countries which must refrain from protecting their economies or the well-being of their populations. This is precisely what has been going on in the struggle to stop countries such as Brazil and South Africa from generically manufacturing and distributing cheap drugs. It seems, however, that those distinctly unfree market principles do not apply when North America needs drugs. The supposedly sacred patent rules that prevent the treatment of millions of people in poorer countries were swept aside at the first whiff of the threat of biological warfare. The US and Canada (both heavily involved in the campaign to defend drug patents) threatened to override Bayer's patent for Cipro, an antibiotic for the treatment of anthrax, if they did not drop their prices. Knowing which side the bread was buttered on, Bayer promptly did.

In the air industry, US and UK governments intervened to gift the airlines huge subsidies, underwrite insurance premiums and suspend anti-monopoly laws. The $15b channelled by US Congress to the US airlines outstrips even the most exaggerated estimates of their post-September loss. In calamitous contrast to Western economic protectionism and handouts for big business, the rest of the world can expect a backlash. Oxfam has warned that the collapse of some commodity prices since September 11 is causing turmoil in the poorest countries. The sharp fall in coffee prices for example has exacerbated hunger and forced migration in some parts of Africa and South America.

Shoulder to shoulder

It is no secret that the US administration has sought to construct an all-out war against terrorism since the Reagan era. A generalised, 'common sense' war on terrorism is useful because it depoliticises and therefore masks the motives of US involvement in conflict. Generalised 'wars' also hold premium potential for exploiting a growing parade of global folk devils. For Western corporations there are considerable gains to be made, as an ever-wider range of 'security' discourses are reproduced in order to legitimise the global march of neo-liberalism.

There is a truism that seems to materialise before our eyes – and just as quickly disappears behind the newscasts and the newsstands – every time there is a war in a far-off land. It is that corporate muscle always stands shoulder to shoulder with military coercion. It is a truism that most social and political commentators choose to ignore or dismiss. In Afghanistan, the big prize is, of course, the possibility of a more stable political environment for building a pipeline linking the huge oilfields in the central Asian republics to the US-friendly Pakistan. Some have speculated that Afghanistan could be strategically significant for developing new markets in the region. On the night that the Taliban were driven from Kabul, one US senator could not contain his excitement: 'We must move quickly to give the people of Afghanistan what they need...' which is, just in case you haven't guessed yet, '...democracy and privatisation.' Several international forums, including one in Pakistan, hosted by the World Bank, had, by November 2001, already met to discuss how to bring 'market freedom' to Afghanistan.

Where Western companies operate overseas, corporate moralism obscures the direct role that foreign capital plays in sustaining conflicts in developing countries. It is for this purpose that human rights discourses are increasingly hijacked by corporate moral entrepreneurs. According to fashionable management double-speak, it is operating in corrupt and brutal regimes that guarantees that human rights will be kept on the political agendas of rogue states. It is a perverse rhetoric that does not stand up to any scrutiny. The most obvious examples here are the oil majors. BP in Columbia, Shell in Nigeria and Premier Oil in Burma have each been implicated in collusion with the violent suppression of local communities.

Neither can the harms caused by corporate activity be glibly dismissed with the assurance that private corporations have our common interests at heart. Across the globe, more than 50 times the number of people killed in the World Trade Center will have died at the hands of their employer between September 11 and the end of the year. Every year, more people are killed at work for profit than are killed in wars. We can expect the carnage to worsen as September 11 continues to provide the justification for less red tape, and fewer legal controls on corporate activity. This is the next offensive that looms in the war on terrorism. Already business organisations are arguing for a bonfire of controls to ensure 'economic stability'. Those demands are once more peppered with reference to uncertainties of the post-September 11 business environment. In the UK, the CBI may have some success on this front in 2002 as Prime Minister Blair launches a trawl through every government department for 'unnecessary regulations'.

Unreported scandals

The great unreported scandal of the West is that business is reaping unprecedented cash benefits from the war on terrorism. Of course, the defence industry is always a major benefactor from wars of whatever hue.[6] But thanks to Bush's 'recovery' package – ostensibly in aid of 'stimulating the post-September 11 economy' – every major corporation stands to gain.[7] Of the $100 billion spending package rolled out in November, a massive three-quarters went straight to tax handouts for business, mostly for the largest corporations.

There is no doubt that capital has made some significant material gains under the guise of the war on terrorism. But at the same time, capital remains vulnerable to counter-struggle, especially when it fights on a moral terrain. In 1998 US oil giant Unocal's attempt to secure government support for the Afghanistan pipeline was thwarted ultimately through a tenacious campaign by the international women's movement which forced Clinton to sever links with the Taliban. Unocal had insisted the pipeline would bring peace and human rights. The counter-campaign was successful because it effectively exposed the reality of women's rights under the Taliban.

There are currently few locations in the world where British or US capital operates unhindered by worker or community resistance. The recent success of campaigners to force Balfour Beatty's withdrawal from the Ilisu Dam project in Kurdish Turkey signifies a key moment. Here was a victory for an international struggle against international capital. No matter how big business cloaks its motives – whether allied to the war on terrorism or not – corporations are certain to face many more of their own battles in the post-September 11 world.

1. Leader, *The Economist*, September 15, 2001.
2. Jack Welch, former chair of General Electric, October 2001.
3. *Financial Times*, September 22/23, 2001.
4. In the US, investigations centred around this type of trading. Short trading is based on the agreement that shares will be sold at a specified price on a specified future date. Investors 'shorting' stocks in United Airlines and American Airlines (the two companies whose aircraft were hijacked) made over $25m on the New York Stock Exchange and over $5m in Chicago. The later figure represents 90 times the normal trading activity.
5. In particular, the Hawala system of banking, a traditional Asian system of accounting which often operates outside international financial rules, was singled out for enforcement by US regulatory authorities.
6. The soaring share prices of companies such as Lockheed Martin, Northop Grumman and Raytheon in September and October 2001 indicates that

the war against terrorism has also provided a shot in the arm for the weapons business. It could not have come at a more opportune time, since the industry has for some time been in the midst of a restructuring process to produce exactly the highly sophisticated weaponry and surveillance equipment required for a more generalised war against multiple, mobile targets. Congress's hastily rewritten defence plans reflect the realignment of those priorities. British and American manufacturers of internal security equipment and torture equipment also stand to make unexpected gains, not only from the Western clampdown on suspected terrorists, but also from aid packages offered to the developing world. The £4 billion IMF loan deal with Pakistan may yet prove to be an important signpost of the shape of international finance deals to come. In the small print, the Pakistan deal includes a large slice of revenue to be spent on military and police equipment to control (anti-US and anti-government) public protest. Most of this equipment is likely to be supplied by US and UK manufacturers.

7. At the time of writing, President Bush's business stimulus package was due to be ratified by Congress.

MARKETS, REGULATION AND RISK: THE US AIRLINES INDUSTRY AND SOME FALLOUT FROM SEPTEMBER 11

Steve Tombs

In a typically polemical piece, the radical American satirist Mike Moore recounted some of his recent experiences with airport security:

At Newark Airport, the plane is late at boarding everyone. The counter can't find my seat. So I am told to just 'go ahead and get on' – without a ticket! At Detroit Metro Airport, I don't want to put the lunch I just bought at the deli through the x-ray machine so, as I pass through the metal detector, I hand the sack to the guard through the space between the detector and the x-ray machine. I tell him, 'It's just a sandwich.' He believes me and doesn't bother to check. The sack has gone through neither security device. La Guardia in New York, I check a piece of luggage, but decide to catch a later plane. The first plane leaves without me, but with my bag – no one knowing what is in it. Back in Detroit, I take my time getting off the commuter plane. By the time I have come down its stairs, the bus that takes the passengers to the terminal has left – without me. I am alone on the tarmac, free to wander wherever I want. So I do. Eventually, I flag down a pick-up truck and an airplane mechanic gives me a ride the rest of the way to the terminal. I have brought knives, razors; and once, my traveling companion brought a hammer and chisel. No one stopped us.[1]

For those used to taking domestic flights in the US, such tales are hardly revelatory. But how has this situation arisen? How is it that American airlines and their 'regulators', the FAA, have colluded to produce a level of 'security' that presented an opportunity for the actions that took place on September 11? How could teams of three to five people penetrate airport security at three different airports on the same day to commence their bombing of New York and Washington? These questions need asking since they have been buried in the torrent of posturing and comment that followed these bombings. Further, if they are not asked, and answered, the prospects for further such atrocities remains.

The starting point in a search for some of the answers is the de-regulation of the US airline industry. The process formally began with the 1978 Airline Deregulation Act – though this had little immediate effect until the election of Reagan in 1980, a president who came to power committed to widespread deregulation as part of his neo-liberal assault on economy and state. In his first term, a key obstacle to real deregulation – namely 1,800 striking air traffic controllers – was removed, through their being sacked, and replaced by non-union labour. By this time the National Labour Relations Board was dominated by Reagan appointees and proved to be no effective body of appeal. This action was crucial in setting the tone for union-busting in the Reagan period; and airline deregulation set the stage for subsequent efforts to deregulate other industries.

What did deregulation actually produce? For a start, intensified competition, the emergence of 'lo-cost', 'no-frill' airlines, and a wave of price-cutting. Now some – especially neo-Chicagoan economists – may say that greater competition and lower prices are good for the general consumer. There are at least two reasons why this is not the case here. First, because in respect of domestic air travel in the US, the typical customer is not exactly a general consumer; the most recent American Travel Survey (1995) showed that 43 per cent of domestic airline travel is business travel. In other words, much of the cost savings of cheaper travel are passed on to corporations not individual passengers, so that cheaper fares are hardly a demand of the 'ordinary' consumer. Second, because the consumer cannot in this area make an informed choice. If it is possible to make some comparative checks of airline safety prior to booking a ticket (as some sites on the Internet allow), most people simply do not do this. Even if they do, it is by definition impossible to make comparative checks on the level of airport and airline *security* prior to making a flight booking. This is one industry in which imperfect information for the consumer 'sovereign' is virtually inherent.

Back to the fallout from deregulation. As competition heightened, some operators were forced to insolvency, and profit rates declined significantly. The airline industry sought to drive down costs, with the target (as usual) being 'labour' costs. For example, while wages in the industry rose by some 8 per cent in the four years prior to 1980, between 1980 and 1984 the increase was just 1 per cent, a decline in real terms. Subsequently wage costs were further controlled through casualisation throughout the industry, one element of which was the contracting out of a range of functions, not least of which was gate and flight security. At the time of the bombings, many security staff at US airports earned the minimum wage of $5.60 an hour. More generally, turnaround times have become increasingly important within the context of decreasing profit margins. In this context, it is hardly surprising to find security compromised as passengers are whisked through airports to preserve crucial turnaround times and thus numbers of flights. In such compromises of security, the FAA has colluded, private business in and beyond the airline industry is a key benefactor, and ordinary people have paid the ultimate price.

Safety fears about the deregulated industry were raised, not least by the National Transportation Safety Board, from the late 1980s onwards, largely as a result of a series of crashes, mostly in the low-cost sector. Although speculation, it is at least plausible to suggest that as increased safety costs were forced on airlines, these extra costs meant that security was either not improved or was further compromised through cost savings. Increased costs put operators out of business. By end of the 1990s, the number of operators had fallen so that the industry was much smaller than at the start of the decade, while prices had increased. In 1996 a White House Commission on Safety and Security in the US Aviation Industry made a series of recommendations to bring security on domestic flights to the levels which obtained on international flights. Few were acted upon.

Warnings about lax, profit-driven airport security continued to be raised up to the time of the bombings. Even the most basic precautions, such as criminal background checks for some airport workers, were resisted by the airlines. Indeed, this proposal continues to be resisted, even in the wake of September 11 and eleven years after being first proposed in the Presidential Commission following the Lockerbie bombing. Unsurprisingly, during the 1990s, the FAA uncovered thousands of breaches of security and issued millions of dollars in fines to the airline industry – though most of these were greatly reduced through negotiation, while others were simply never paid.[2]

And what do we also find after September 11? Working men and women cast aside under the euphemism of 'layoffs' as routes are cut, plane orders cancelled, and shareholders soothed as profits warnings abound. Yet even mainstream commentators have noted that airlines have begun to do with gusto what they wanted to do anyway, prior to September 11. Namely, to restructure an industry characterised by over-capacity. Their timing – and that of companies in related and not so related industries – is a telling reminder of the fundamental amorality of the capitalist corporation and the unrelenting, persuasive whip of the stock market.

Where airline business continues, security is now receiving the attention, if not the dollars, of the companies. Fifteen billion dollars in short-term subsidy was agreed within ten days of the attack, on the basis that this subsidy was needed for 'special circumstances' which were the 'need to find money for extra security'. Congress agreed on November 15 for the federal government to take over traveller and baggage screening – with the cost of hiring the 28,000 workers passed on to passengers in the form of a $2.50 levy on each flight. Federal employment of air marshalls is currently being negotiated. At the same time, the US Business Travel lobby – such as the National Business Travel Association and the Business Travel Coalition – are urged to establish a reasonable balance between security and convenience. What we are witnessing, then, is the unseemly if hardly surprising spectacle of the airlines lobbying to protect their rights to compete on price at a risk to security and safety. While, at the same time, they argue that the need for extra (read 'adequate') security means extra costs, which should be borne by the general taxpayer. A quite simple, if common, privatisation of profit, accompanied by a socialisation of risk or the costs needed to mitigate that risk.

In this context, one positive consequence of the bombings might be greater critical scrutiny of the industry – this could result in practical changes anywhere on a continuum from tighter regulation (possible) to the consolidation of a global industry consisting of state-owned national carriers (extremely unlikely). At a more general level, fallout from such scrutiny might also place the issue of the regulation of corporate activity back on national and international political agendas, from which it has been systematically removed during a quarter of a century of free-market neo-liberal dogma. This may occur in very specific areas, as well as in a generalised fashion. For example, the regulation of the banking industry and in particular offshore banking centres has gathered political momentum since the bombings, not least through renewed interest in the issue of money laundering. As the journalist Larry Elliot noted recently,

> Everywhere, those responsible for security are asking finance ministries how terrorists can move money around the globe to finance their activities without being detected. The answer they are getting is that it is ludicrously easy when there are no controls on the movement of capital and when tax havens operate with the frontier mentality of the wild west. As a result, we now have frantic attempts by governments to strengthen the rules against money laundering, which will involve far stricter regulation and enhanced powers for those fighting financial crimes to uncover the details of suspicious transactions.[3]

About time too. In 1989, G7 nations established the Financial Action Task Force, which produced a series of recommendations aimed at combating money laundering. By 2001, only a minority of FATF member states were in full compliance. Of the 28 recommendations, the US failed to comply with more than a third, putting it third from bottom, ahead of Canada and Mexico, its key NAFTA trading partners, in a survey of 29 industrialised nations.

At a more general level, and albeit in still rather muted fashion, there have been some attempts to understand why the US is so hated and, indeed, why the Twin Towers were selected key targets of the bombers. Answers to each question require that some attention is given to the international economic experiences of the past quarter of a century: general deregulation in the international economy, trends towards economic globalisation, the international hegemony of neo-liberalism, each accompanied by clear trends of growing inequality within and between nations. If precise causal linkages remain unproven, this is in a sense irrelevant. Most important is the increasingly widespread perception that US-driven globalisation, as neo-liberalism on an international scale, is causing extreme poverty amongst marginalised peoples, with the World Bank, the WTO, the IMF, and so on, popularly seen as instruments of the US and the richer, more powerful nation-states of the West. Indeed, such perceptions had already been forced on to political agendas by the so-called anti-globalisation protests that have developed such international momentum and profile since Seattle. The scrutiny of international economic policy and international activity that will follow the September 11 bombings may have an effect in furthering the case for greater regulation of corporate activity precisely because it will be undertaken in a context in which the untrammelled free market is seriously under question. At the most general level, and to quote from Larry Elliott again, the crisis generated by the bombings could mark the moment when 'the free market tide ... turned'.

1. Moore, M, 'Death Downtown', http://www.corpwatch.org, posted September 13, 2001.
2. Moss, M, and Eaton, L, 'Federation Interest Varies, but Cost-Cutting is Constant for Security Firms', *New York Times*, November 15, 2001.
3. Elliott, L, 'The free market tide has turned. This crisis is fuelling economic activism and a Keynesian revival', *Guardian*, September 20, 2001.

DANGERS OF THE ARMED RESPONSE AT HOME
Mick North

In 1999 the Violence Policy Center (VPC), a US non-profit educational foundation, produced a report on what it described as 'a serious threat to American National Security'.[1] Although the report did not anticipate the attacks on the World Trade Center and Pentagon, the danger was linked with terrorism and remains as serious today as it was before the events of September 11. Yet it is doubtful whether this is receiving much attention from a nation at war with terrorism because the source of the problem is not an 'evil' foreign force. It lies within US domestic policy, the threat is a consequence of the US attitude towards the private ownership of firearms.

The VPC report was concerned with the unfettered sale to civilians of military 50-calibre heavy sniper rifles, but terror can be created with guns of every type. Making firearms available to almost anybody and everybody who wants them has implications for the well-being of civilians within and beyond America's borders. In the aftermath of September 11 it is not apparent that American attitudes to guns have changed.

It is a sobering fact, though not one the US government will highlight, that in spite of the horrendous scale of the slaughter in New York and Washington, the number of people who have been killed in America by terrorism is dwarfed by the annual toll from gun violence. Since 1965 about 1 million Americans have died of gunshot wounds. In 2000, a total of 28,117 people died, more than 10,000 of whom were murdered. The permissive attitude to gun ownership, seen by some to be a fundamental part of the American way of life, helps fuel a level of gun violence that equates with terrorism.

The price of the 'freedom' to bear arms in the US is gun death on a scale that most civil societies would never tolerate. Comparisons of data collected from around the globe reveal a clear correlation between the frequency of gun death and a country's level of civilian gun ownership. This fact fails to get through to many Americans, a significant number of whom have reacted to the terrorist attacks by buying even more guns. From Oklahoma to Colorado, from Texas to Washington, more US citizens have sought permits to carry concealed handguns. The Professional Gun Retailers Association estimates a 10 per cent rise in sales of guns and ammunition during the two months after September 11 compared with the same period in 2000. The National Rifle Association (NRA) reports membership enquiries up from an average of 300 per day to 700 to 900 per day and its firearms training classes are booked solid. At a time of uncertainty too many are persuaded that gun ownership provides increased protection.

'They're buying a gun because they're saying, "I don't know what's going to happen. I don't know that there's not going to be civil unrest"', one gun range owner was quoted as saying. Wayne La Pierre, executive director of the NRA considers that 'People fear some type of threat, they don't know what form it will take or what the consequences will be. They don't know if the attacks will be in their backyard or their neighbourhood, and they'd rather face that threat with a firearm than without one.'[2] The NRA will be the last to admit it, but having more armed citizens will inevitably increase the risk of those attacks taking place. But they won't come from terrorists, the perpetrators will be fellow citizens. In America a gun is 22 times more likely to be used against a family or friend than against an intruder, the suffocating outcome to society offered by this false security blanket of gun ownership.

There is a view that the public aren't protected by the police and should take the law into their own hands. A pro-gun message frequently aired since September 11 is that 'what many Americans have taken from this experience is that we should each take more responsibility for our own safety'.[3] However, it is difficult to envisage many situations in which the private possession of firearms could offer adequate defence against highly trained terrorists. More likely the twitchiness of worried and armed citizens will lead to increased rates of gun deaths involving innocent people. There are those who want to arm air passengers to increase the chances of stopping a terrorist incident. Presumably they are in favour of gun control when it comes to disarming potential terrorists before they board a plane, but how do you recognise the potential terrorist? As a Canadian journalist recently speculated, what does a security guard ask as passengers proceed through the airport screening system: 'Will you be using this gun to hijack the plane, sir, or to defend us from hijackers?'[4]

Sadly, a more typical story is that of a Virginia father who shortly after September 11 brought a handgun into his house for protection. Within days his three-year-old son died after shooting himself in the neck. The abiding myth that, without a gun, American citizens are insufficiently protected is sustained at an awful cost. Gun violence in the US must be regarded as a national catastrophe. Afflicted communities should question why measures to counter it fail to gain financial support on a scale equivalent to that immediately allocated to anti-terrorism efforts ($11 billion). A modest $10 million, sought by the Center for Disease Control to support a National Violent Injury Statistics System, has not been provided. Although an overwhelming majority of Americans believe that laws making it easier for regular citizens to carry concealed firearms undermine public safety,[5] the influence of the powerful and well-funded gun lobby on state and federal legislatures allows the over-arming of the US to continue.

Those of us who observe the situation from abroad might be tempted to dismiss all of this as America's problem and one in which, as we are constantly told by the American gun lobby, we should not interfere. However, it does impact on the rest of today's global village. US gun culture makes it all too easy for would-be owners of any description to purchase guns, including the powerful 50-calibre heavy sniper rifles described in the VPC report. These are weapons which can 'knock down aircraft, including helicopters, and punch holes through concrete block, armoured vehicles, and other materials that may be relied upon for executive protection'. In the US they are only as regulated as hunting rifles and can be easier to obtain than handguns. The civilian market has 'exploded'.[6] Ronnie

G Barrett, founder and owner of Barrett Firearms Manufacturing, has described his company's sniper rifle as 'a toy for big boys' and 'a fun toy, a nice collectible'. Among those who have obtained these toys are criminals, insurrectionists and terrorists. Osama bin Laden's al-Qaida has acquired at least 25. Attempts to outlaw civilian sales of these rifles have been killed by Congress at the behest of the gun lobby. Representative Rod Blagojevich, a politician who is pressing for a ban, says, 'We should not be held hostage to a legislative process that is dominated by the National Rifle Association.'

The fact that the US offers unique opportunities for acquiring firearms has not gone unnoticed. A jihad training pamphlet posted on a web site informs trainees: 'In some countries of the world, especially the USA, firearms training is available to the general public. It is perfectly legal to obtain weapons such as AK-47 assault rifles.' The pamphlet advises that when buying guns the laws of a country should be respected, dealing in illegal firearms should be avoided. Thus weak US gun laws aid a potential wrongdoer like Ali Boumelhem, a convicted felon with links to Hezbollah, who was able to buy guns and ammunition at gun shows in Michigan.[7] Gun shows offer opportunities for the purchase of firearms without the background checks required by licensed gun dealers, but attempts to close gun show loopholes are described by the gun lobby as restrictions on the rights of gun owners.

The selfish influence of American shooters extends to regions outside the US. In 1999 the Economic Community of Western African States (ECOWAS) announced a three-year moratorium throughout its 16 member nations on the export, import and manufacture of small arms.[8] Most of the guns came from outside the region, and ECOWAS needed financial support and technical expertise to implement the ban. The international community was asked to help, and a number of governments, including the US, agreed to pledge $1.2 million towards the moratorium and conflict resolution. The US funding was blocked by Senator Jesse Helms, the chairman of the Senate Foreign Relations Committee. His reason was that 'the moratorium project proposes using US taxpayer's money to lobby or promote policies in foreign countries that may very well be a violation of the second amendment to the US Constitution'. It was, Helms added, 'nothing less than a brazen international expansion of the President [Clinton] and Vice-President's [Gore] domestic gun control agenda'. Helms is a long time ally of the NRA, and there is little doubt that one immediate goal of his remarks was to frighten American gun owners, thereby raising money and membership. The big-game hunters' group Safari Club International, an NRA ally, actively attacked the moratorium because it might interfere with its members' sport. No thoughts for the victims of terrorism and gun violence in West Africa (civil wars had left more than 250,000 dead, mostly killed by rifles, machine guns and semi-automatics), the entertainment of a few big spending sportsmen was more important.

The Second Amendment of the American Constitution, cited by Helms, states that 'A well regulated Militia, being necessary to the security of a free State, the right of the people to keep and bear Arms, shall not be infringed.' On the basis of these late eighteenth-century words the US gun lobby has argued that there is a constitutional right to own guns. When the words were written the threat came from the British army of King George III, and the idea of a well-regulated citizen militia may then have had merit. But in an age of sophisticated military and security forces and highly trained terrorists the situation is entirely different, and rather than enhance security, the prevalence of gun-toting citizens represents a destabil-ising force. Notwithstanding its suspect value in the twenty-first century, exactly how well regulated is a militia made up of self-selected gun owners who select their own personal arsenals? While the world staggers from one crisis to the next, the Second Amendment of the US Constitution remains unchanged, its anachronistic message aiding arms dealers and terrorists.

For the gun lobby it is anathema to raise questions about possible links between gun rights and terrorism. According to them, groups and individuals who believe that a sane re-examination of domestic gun policy is essential after September 11 are *capitalising on a national tragedy*. At a time when there is much soul-searching about many other aspects of the American way of life, why should gun ownership be sacrosanct? Americans, including the gun owners, would surely not want everyone to own weapons. Guns, they would say, are for the law-abiding and the good. Yet US permissive laws can't guarantee this. The law-abiding and the good cannot be identified in the simplistic way the gun lobbyists believe. The naive pigeonholing mentality, which suggests that 'People are either law-abiding or criminals', 'They are either good or evil', 'You are either with us or against us', runs through gun lobby logic and goes right up to the top. It denies the complexity of human nature, never registering the real possibility that a gun-owning upright citizen might have a crisis and turn on his family or neighbours, that a quiet employee might react to redundancy by gunning down his fellow workers or, on a different but parallel level, that a freedom fighter might one day become a terrorist.

If the US cares about creating a more secure world it must think more about preventative measures. It is all very well for the most powerful nation to react to gun violence by handing down the most severe sentences to culprits, or dealing with terrorist atrocities by bombing a nation that harboured the perpetrators, but this type of retributive action is always too late for the victims. There are ways of trying to reduce the risk of violence besides meeting out punishment. One of these is to place more limits on the availability of lethal weapons. What does George Bush mean when he said to the UN in his November 10 speech, 'We have a responsibility to deny weapons to terrorists – and to actively prevent private citizens from providing them'? Will Bush stand up to the NRA and prohibit the sale of military weapons to citizens? Will he support the move by Senators John McCain and Joe Lieberman, among others, to plug loopholes that allow terrorists to obtain firearms at gun shows? I have my doubts.

Americans arm themselves and others too easily, but seem bewildered when the consequences impact on their own lives, whether after school massacres at home or through experiencing blow-back (the phenomenon of the use of a country's exported weapons against its own soldiers) in conflicts abroad. More widespread gun ownership is not the solution to the present fears of the American public, it will not protect them from the threats posed by terrorism. If the war against terrorism is to be fought on all possible fronts then the US must take a long hard look at itself and question the notion that civilian ownership of guns is a good thing. It failed to stop the attacks on September 11, and if left unchallenged is likely to bring more deaths, not less.

1. *One Shot, One Kill. Civilian Sales of Military Sniper Rifles*, Violence Policy Center, May 1999.
2. Spencer, Jane, *Newsweek*, November 8, 2001.
3. Brown, Michael S, *Cybercast News Service*, October 19, 2001.
4. Delacourt, Susan, *Ottawa Citizen*, October 18, 2001.
5. Rostler, Suzanne, *Reuters Health*, November 29, 2001.
6. Violence Policy Center, *Voting from the Rooftops*, October 2001.
7. Barnes, Michael, *Washington Post*, November 11, 2001.
8. Austin, Kathi and Bondi, Loretta, *California Peace Action*, Summer 2000.

TERRORISM, NEIGHBOURS AND NUREMBERG
Herman Schwendinger and Julia Schwendinger

On November 11, millions of Americans were astonished by telecasts of two hijacked passenger jets smashing into the twin World Trade Center skyscrapers that collapsed into an immense pile of toxic rubble. People remained glued to the reruns of this disaster until President G W Bush returned from his safe haven in the SAC bunkers in Nebraska, appeared on television, and grimly declared: 'This is war!'

Immediately, our neighbours joined millions of other flag-waving patriots and flew Old Glory from flagstaffs on their lawns or on standards clamped to car doors or pickup-truck bumpers. People in local supermarkets walked proudly with red, white and blue ribbons pinned to their lapels. Walking proudly is well and good, but look at another side of this sentiment. Consider those who sported T-shirts imprinted with patriotic sentiments: *You're Gonna Get Yours bin Laden! Death to Terrorists!* In accord with the president's declaration of war, journalists, officials and policy pundits confronted critics with the classic one liner from the president's speech to Congress: 'If you aren't with *us*, you're with *them*.' Wherever we went, we heard, 'Bomb the shit out of the Taliban!' 'Nuke 'em!' A red-blooded neighbor snapped, 'Who gives a rat's ass about their civilians? *They* killed 6,000 *American* civilians!'

How does an informed person deal with these gut reactions? Not by resorting to obtuse academic discourse. After all, our next-door neighbour never graduated from high school and would nod off before the boring lecture was done. But he certainly knew that we had our heads screwed on right when we agreed that the terrorists had murdered 6,000 people and that those still alive should be hunted down and punished.

Still, fetching credible 'talking points' that will get people to back off and think for a moment about the whole picture is not easy. The president and mass media have underplayed America's role in helping the Taliban and other fundamentalists to crush their secular opposition and institute one of the most politically repressive and sexist regimes in the world. They have said little or nothing about the financial support given by the CIA to Osama bin Laden and his cronies. And even those who know about this support cynically write it off as just another stupid mistake made by our incredibly imperfect government.

Nonetheless, the historical events leading to the atrocity in New York City might at least provide answers for one woman who complained, 'Why did these Muslims do it? We didn't hurt them.' Recall US policies in the Middle East supporting the Israeli hardliners against the Palestinians, the CIA's overthrow of Mossadegh's democratic regime in Iran, the sanctions that have killed half a million in Iraq and the dictatorships propped up by the US in Saudi Arabia, Kuwait and Pakistan, where immensely wealthy families oppress millions of impoverished people. Mentioning these policies does provide some idea of why the terrorists despise the US – and why they depict it as *The Great Satan*, the angel who defied God Almighty and fell from grace.

On top of this everybody is going crazy about anthrax, where to buy rubber gloves to open their mail and whether to go to Disneyland in Orlando by plane. Why not relieve your neighbour's anxiety by injecting a quick comment into a conversation about the global economic forces that have been slowly grinding Middle Eastern small farmers and shopkeepers into the dirt? This will not work for most but, surprisingly, if you know someone well enough to talk about politics as well as everybody's health, sales at the mall or sailing on the Gulf of Mexico, bearing global capitalism in mind is possible. US corporations have helped destroy the hopes and dreams of secular movements and democratic forces in oil-rich countries, leaving small farmers and shopkeepers with their utopian images about a past where tribal elders and religion kept order and where one did not have to serve Satan by working in oilfields or growing opium for overseas trade.

Our president attributes the World Trade Center atrocity to forces of evil and religious fanatics. In a moment of candour, however, he himself sounded the call for a Christian jihad, calling upon Americans to resurrect the Crusade. But, before all our might is completely unleashed against the modern Saracens, and the 60 nations that may house them, he should heed international recoil from civilian killings.

Unfortunately, as we seek worldwide co-operation by promising not to target non-combatants it should be noted that neither the Nuremberg Tribunal nor the Geneva Conventions provided unequivocal standards for condemning civilian deaths in war. As the chief prosecutor at Nuremberg, General Telford Taylor noted in *Vietnam an American Tragedy* (1970), Nuremberg (and Tokyo) precedents would not have prohibited the aerial bombardment of

North Vietnam. Ignoring the distinction between civilians and combatants, American planes dropped countless anti-personnel bombs that each released several hundred pellets to kill or wound all living creatures within two-thirds of a square mile – even in the most densely populated parts of North Vietnam cities. In 1966, 25 provincial cities were bombed – six of which were completely razed. The city of Dong Hoi – covering an area of 3.2 square kilometres, and with 16,000 inhabitants – was bombed 396 times, including 160 night attacks. Of the 110 district centres, 72 were bombed, leaving 12 of them in ruins and 25 completely destroyed.

Furthermore, such bombing was not restricted to the North. In the South, residential areas, schools, hospitals, clinics and churches were bombed. High explosive bombs, fragmentation bombs, napalm bombs and anti-personnel bombs pounded regions occupied by the National Liberation Front (NLF). US forces also dropped herbicides and so-called 'defoliants' that destroyed hundreds of thousands of farming acres, causing massive civilian casualties due to malnutrition, starvation and ingestion of toxic chemicals. On returning from a session with President Johnson and his advisers in 1967, John Naughton, an Assistant Secretary of Defense, admitted: 'We seem to be proceeding on the assumption that the way to eradicate the Vietcong [i.e., NLF] is to destroy all the village structures, defoliate all the jungles, and then cover the entire surface of South Vietnam with asphalt.'

Nonetheless, the Nuremberg precedents, as General Taylor pointed out, did not portray this kind of warfare as a crime. The Allies who administered the Nuremberg trials and their victor's justice, relying on the mitigating standard of 'military necessity', had never considered as war crimes the bombing of Dresden, Tokyo, Hiroshima and Nagasaki. How then could Nuremberg be justifiably used to condemn the bombardment of Hue or Hanoi, for instance? Of course, Taylor granted that military necessity could hardly be invoked for Dresden when the Russians were poised to seize the city or Nagasaki when surrender negotiations were virtually over. (Both of these were 'open cities' and, because they lacked military targets, were only lightly defended; moreover, the railroad yard and Shell Oil tanks in Dresden, which might have been considered military targets, were not bombed.) But Arthur 'Bomber' Harris, who ordered Allied bombers to drop 650,000 incendiary bombs and high explosives on Dresden (producing a firestorm that immolated or asphyxiated more than 35,000 civilians), or the American politicians and generals who ordered the atom bomb that killed more than 100,000 civilians in Nagasaki, were never put on trial at Nuremberg.

So, how can we trust the US government's promises today? It whitewashes civilian deaths in warfare as 'collateral damage'. It has terrorised or backed terrorists in Nicaragua, Brazil, Uruguay, Cuba, Guatemala, Indonesia, East Timor, Zaire, Angola and South Africa. It provides sanctuary for the Miami Cuban 'refugee' terror network and it has given safe havens to terrorists fleeing from Vietnam, El Salvador, Haiti and even Nazi Germany. Unquestionably, the slaughter of 3,000 people in New York was a heinous crime. Nevertheless, given Nuremberg, Vietnam and the thousands who died from bombing the only pharmaceutical plant in Somalia, the probity of the US hunt for the murderers cannot be taken for granted.

Now, one month after the towers collapsed and the dreadful stench of rubble and bodies at Ground Zero remains unbearable, the name of the game is *Grab! Grab! While you can!* or *Bastard Keynesianism*. Despite gainful employment millions of Americans cannot afford health care and unemployment is increasing; nevertheless, billions are being poured into corporate troughs in order to insulate the military-industrial complex from the recession. Meanwhile, the FBI and CIA finally may be getting their star chamber proscriptions, unlimited electronic eavesdropping, open-ended detention of immigrants without charges, dumping the statute of limitations on certain crimes, enhancing forfeiture laws where property of a suspect can be seized prior to trial or conviction, and so on.

Although judges have rejected only three federal or state criminal wiretap requests in the last decade, these new laws would reduce or eliminate the role of judges in ensuring that law enforcement wire-tapping is conducted legally and with proper justification. The laws would also erode the long-standing distinction between domestic law enforcement and foreign intelligence collection, which protects Americans from being spied upon by their own intelligence agencies, as happened during the Cold War. The definition of 'terrorism' is too broad, permitting surveillance powers to be applied far beyond what is commonly considered by the term. Even acts of simple civil disobedience conducted against the war or World Trade and International Monetary Fund conferences could make protesters become targets of 'terrorist' investigations.

Yesterday, while the US Special Forces parachuted into a remote Kandahar airport in Afghanistan, we spent the evening with old friends at a 'dinner-theatre' that served up good food and an old play, *Guys and Dolls*. The actors were delightful even if their rendering of Sky Masterson, Sister Sarah, Nathan Detroit and Miss Adelaide weren't as good as the cinematic performances by Marlon Brando, Vivian Leigh, Frank Sinatra and Carol Channing. However, before the play began, a loud chord abruptly interrupted our friendly argument about the war against Afghanistan. The curtain opened and suddenly the stage lights illuminated Old Glory. The audience rose spontaneously and belted out a patriotic song. While everyone rose, some remained silent during the singing.

It is hard to tell how things will turn out this time. It's a new war yet an old war. As a new war, it requires thinking about going beyond Nuremberg and defining as unjust a war of aggression that does not seek genuine political alternatives and is conducted against terrorists without the auspices of the United Nations. Impartial war crimes tribunals should conduct investigations and adjudicate terrorists. These should not be the tools of an aggrieved nation.

As in old wars, civil liberties will be tested again. Americans will have to be reminded that airport security must be shored up but the inevitable objections to the wiretapping, infiltration of political groups and assassinations abroad should not be blamed on an irresponsible desire for liberty at the expense of security. Our civil liberties were responses to real abuses of power, and their fate must not be left to jingoists who are ready to dismiss them as 'handcuffs' on law enforcement.

The Vietnam struggle taught us that, even though most Americans backed our government, it didn't take a majority to change things around. The people who know the score will know what has to be done. They also will realise that opposition to that war has made our government awfully reluctant to risk massive protests and political turmoil by waging war with unacceptable American casualties. Still, they must also keep the other side of this strategic concern in mind. When a high-tech country like the US is forced to minimise casualties while fighting a guerrilla war waged by a low-tech country, the main victims will not be combatants. Inevitably, they will be civilians.

PLEDGING ALLEGIANCE:
THE REVIVAL OF PRESCRIPTIVE PATRIOTISM

Cecilia O'Leary and Tony Platt

In a matter of a few months, we have witnessed far-reaching changes in American global doctrines, the domestic economy and politics of government, and national security and criminal justice. Our focus in this essay is on shifts in the cultural politics of nationalism. During the flush years of an exuberant dot.com economy, being an American meant little more than the freedom to consume or visit Disneyland. But since the September 11 attacks, a resurgent patriotism is omnipresent and nowhere is it more on display than in our schools.[1]

In October 2001, the Bush administration launched a series of initiatives aimed at prescribing patriotism among the nation's 52 million schoolchildren. Government officials urged students to take part in a mass recitation of the Pledge of Allegiance, and called upon veterans to teach 'Lessons for Liberty'.[2] The House of Representatives voted 444–0 for the display of signs proclaiming 'God Bless America' in the public schools. On the local level, the New York City Board of Education unanimously passed a resolution requiring all public schools to lead a daily pledge in the morning and at all school assemblies. 'It's a small way to thank the heroes of 9/11', explained the board's president.[3] In Madison, Wisconsin, the school board reversed its previous position and voted to allow schools to recite a daily Pledge of Allegiance and sing 'The Star-Spangled Banner'.[4] Nebraska dusted off a 1949 state law requiring schools to devise curriculums aimed at instilling a 'love of liberty, justice, democracy and America ... in the hearts and minds of the youth'. And after years of futile attempts, a conservative, fringe organisation in Orange County – Celebration USA Inc. – succeeded in synchronising a nationwide recitation of the pledge at 2 p.m. eastern time on October 12.[5]

In the aftermath of September 11, people are hungry for social rituals and eager to communicate a deeper sense of national belonging. But this new wave of orchestrated patriotism is aimed at closing down debate and dissent through the imposition of a prescribed allegiance. Rituals of patriotism were first institutionalised in the United States between the Civil War and the First World War. At the end of the bloodiest civil war of the nineteenth century the combatants left the battlefields for political, economic, and cultural arenas, where the struggle to make a nation continued with renewed intensity. In fact, many of the patriotic symbols and rituals that we now take for granted or think of as timeless were created during this period and emerged not from a harmonious, national consensus, but out of fiercely contested debates, even over the wording of the pledge. Confronted by the dilemma that Americans are made, not born, educators and organisations, such as the Grand Army of the Republic, Women's Relief Corps and Daughters of the American Republic, campaigned to transform schools, in George Balch's words, into a 'mighty engine for the inculcation of patriotism'.

Balch, a New York City teacher and Civil War veteran, wrote what is thought to be the first pledge to the flag in which students promised to 'give our heads and our hearts to God and our Country! One nation! One language! One flag!' Balch intended the pledge to teach discipline and loyalty to the 'human scum, cast on our shores by the tidal wave of a vast migration'. In 1890, Balch published a primer for educators on *Methods for Teaching Patriotism in the Public Schools*, which called for the use of devotional rites of patriotism modelled along the lines of a catechism. 'There is nothing which more impresses the youthful mind and excites its emotions', noted the West Point graduate, than the 'observance of form'.

To commemorate the first celebration of Columbus Day in 1892, and in preparation for the grand opening of the Columbian Exposition in Chicago, the *Youth's Companion* magazine charged Francis Bellamy with writing a new pledge. Bellamy, a Christian socialist with a commitment to social reform, dismissed Balch's formula as a 'pretty childish form of words, invented by an ex-military officer'. He wanted a pledge that would resonate with American history and make students into active participants in a 'social citizenry'. For Bellamy the notion of 'allegiance' evoked the great call to union during the Civil War' and 'one nation indivisible' recalled a phrase used by Lincoln. Bellamy was tempted to add the historic slogan of the French Revolution – 'Liberty, Equality, Fraternity' – to the language of his pledge, but in the end he decided that this would be too much for people to accept. Instead, he settled for the final phrase, 'with liberty and justice for all'. This way, he reasoned, the pledge could be ideologically 'applicable to either an individualistic or a socialistic state', a matter for future generations to decide.

Bellamy's words – 'I pledge allegiance to my flag and to the Republic for which it stands, one Nation indivisible, with liberty and justice for all' – were gradually adopted throughout the country. But the pledge, once imagined as a living principle of justice and liberty, perhaps even equality, quickly became suffused with militarism and obedience to authority. On Columbus Day, 1892, according to newspaper reports, children marched with 'drilled precision' as 'one army under the sacred flag'.

In the wake of the Spanish-American War, state-sanctioned rituals of patriotism became more common. In New York, the day after war was declared on April 29, 1898, the legislature instructed the state superintendent of public instruction to prepare 'a program providing for a salute to the flag at the opening of each day of school'. Daily rituals aimed at reaching children's hearts were backed up with new civics curricula to secure their minds with heroic images of virile soldiers and the honour of dying for one's country. A typical children's primer published in 1903 taught that 'B stood for battles' and Z for the 'zeal that has carried us through/When fighting for justice/With the Red, White and Blue'.

During the First World War, Americanisers worried about dual allegiances and feared that Bellamy's pledge allowed cunning fifth columnist immigrants to swear a secret loyalty to another country. To close this loophole, the words 'my flag' were extended into 'the flag of the United States'. Many states now required students to salute the flag every day. In Chicago in 1916, an eleven-year-old African American student was arrested because he refused to respect a symbol that represented Jim Crow and lynching. 'I am willing to salute the flag', Hubert Eaves explained, 'as the flag salutes me.'

Meanwhile, Boy Scout troops across the country staged massive operettas in celebration of 'America First', while vigilantes forced German Americans suspected of insufficient loyalty to kiss the flag. A judge, unable to reverse a lower court's decision to sentence a man to 20 years' hard labour for abusive language toward the flag, believed that the man was 'more sinned against than sinning'. The mob, he wrote in his opinion, had descended into the kind of 'fanaticism' that fuelled the 'tortures of the Inquisition'.

Between the World Wars, campaigns for '100 per cent Americanism' led to the persecution of thousands of Jehovah's Witnesses and the expulsion of their children from school when they refused to salute the flag.[6] What began as a movement to encourage loyalty to a nation 'with liberty and justice for all' had deviated into the suppression of dissent and unquestioning homage to the flag. In 1943, the US Supreme Court ruled in *West Virginia State Board of*

Education v. *Barnette* that an obligatory loyalty oath was unconstitutional, thus putting law on the side of any student who refuses to participate in patriotic or religious rituals. But even after the ruling, refusal to say the pledge took both courage and conviction. The pledge remained unchanged until Flag Day, 1954, when President Eisenhower approved the addition of the constitutionally questionable phrase 'under God' to differentiate this country from its godless Cold War antagonist.

In the wake of public opposition to the Vietnam War, educators were not inclined to impose rote patriotic drills on their students or to resurrect the slogan of 'One country, one language, one flag', which guided the teaching of civics earlier in the century.[7] Since the 1980s, many schools have slowly begun to adopt textbooks and develop curriculums that speak to the needs of a multi-ethnic, polyglot population living in an increasingly interrelated world. This is not the time to reverse this trend by reverting to form over substance and rote memorisation over democratic participation.

'What of our purpose as a Nation?' pondered Francis Bellamy more than a century ago when he crafted his pledge. Our students today can better use their time debating this question than marching in lockstep loyalty. 'At times of crisis,' writes historian Eric Foner, 'the most patriotic act of all is the unyielding defense of civil liberties, the right to dissent and equality before the law for all Americans.'[8]

1. Unless otherwise referenced, information and quotes in this essay are taken from Cecilia O'Leary's *To Die For: The Paradox of American Patriotism*, Princetown University Press, 1999.
2. Milbank, Dana, 'Bush makes a pitch for teaching patriotism', *Washington Post*, November 2, 2001, p. 2.
3. Wyatt, Edward, 'New York schools to require recitation of pledge of allegiance', *New York Times*, October 18, 2001, p. 20.
4. Associated Press, 'In shift, schools can use pledge to flag', *New York Times*, October 17, 2001, p. 12.
5. Sack, Kevin, 'School colors become red, white and blue', *New York Times*, September 28, 2001, p. 1.
6. Goldstein, Robert Justin, *Saving 'Old Glory': The History of the Flag Desecration Controversy*, Boulder, USA: Westview, 1995, pp. 93–4.
7. Hartocollis, Anemona, 'Pledge, indivisible, with meaning for all', *New York Times*, October 23, 2001, p. 19.
8. Foner, Eric, 'The most patriotic act', *The Nation*, October 8, 2001, p. 13.

MY FELLOW AMERICANS:
LOOKING BLACK ON RED TUESDAY
Jonathan David Farley

When I walked into the meeting chamber, Oxford's ornately decorated Town Hall was brimming with people, all of them there to protest against the war in Afghanistan. Well, almost all of them.

On my way to the meeting, I had seen a group of students standing outside the hall, one of them draped in an American flag. I didn't think much of them until they came in and sat behind me. There were several men and a few women in their group – Americans, judging by their accents. At the centre of attention was a smiling girl with curly brown locks. She looks a lot like Chelsea Clinton, I thought, but I wasn't sure. Then the meeting began.

The 600-person crowd sat in rapt attention. But at one point, some of the Americans went to the front of the room with their flag, in an apparent protest against peace, and one of the others tried to drown out the speakers by shouting. Embarrassed, I got up to move away from them. The heckling Americans, who were few in number, failed to derail the meeting, however; and their jibes were deftly countered by the speakers.

Chelsea, to her credit, remained silent throughout. But, according to recent interviews with CNN and *Talk Magazine*, she has now broken her silence. Chelsea has said that, because of anti-American and anti-war sentiment in England, she no longer wants to 'seek out non-Americans as friends'. Instead, she wants to 'be around Americans'; by which she means, I presume, people who support America's war against terror.

Shame on you, Chelsea. There are millions of people, every bit as American as you, who have every reason to question whether or not this is really a 'war for democracy', a 'war against terror' that will 'keep Americans safe'. I am speaking about the millions of us who are Americans of African descent, and the millions of others, in England and elsewhere, who oppose this war.

While many black Americans felt wounded after the September 11 attacks – indeed, only one of the 38 blacks in Congress voted against giving Bush war powers – we're far more circumspect than our white compatriots. Fully 20 per cent of blacks opposed Bush's response, compared to only 6 per cent of whites (64 per cent of blacks were in support, compared with 83 per cent of whites). As bombs fell, black opposition rose. We're less enthusiastic about America's wars in the Third World because we are aware, to borrow a phrase from Muhammad Ali, that no Iraqi ever called us ni**er.

Don't misunderstand me: many black Americans are (surprisingly) patriotic. We've fought in all of America's wars. But, 20 years after we helped liberate Nazi death camps, we still could not vote in our own country. When black Freedom Riders challenged America's apartheid laws, they were firebombed and beaten. The police and FBI did not hunt down the 'evil-doers' responsible for these crimes; indeed, more often than not they assisted them.

Mind you, just because the FBI broke the law in the 1960s does not mean that they're wrong about bin Laden. But we have every right to question US 'intelligence' when the same FBI and CIA now chasing bin Laden also once trained their sights on Martin Luther King and Malcolm X. (When both men were shot, the first people to rush to their sides were the undercover policemen who had infiltrated their entourages to spy on them.)

In a country that refuses to pay reparations for slavery, the FBI spent the equivalent of $500m (in today's dollars) to 'neutralise' black leaders – with frightening success, as the mothers of Black Panther activists Fred Hampton and the exiled Assata Shakur can attest. (The former was killed in his sleep in a police raid in 1969, for which the government, admitting wrongdoing, was forced to pay $1.85m in damages.) White supremacist murders and police killings have claimed the lives of thousands of blacks, most notably in the Tulsa Massacre of 1921, and the prisons house nearly one million more.

So you see, Chelsea, African-Americans are not much less safe now than we were before September 11. Even if we found out who was sending the anthrax tomorrow, innocent black males in LA and New York and Cincinnati would continue to have fatal allergic reactions – to bullets fired by white cops.

Do you expect blacks to line up to fight the Taliban? How can we, when one of our own senators (ex-Klansman Robert Byrd of West Virginia) once vowed that he would never fight 'with a Negro by my side', preferring instead to 'die a thousand times'? Even now, while our FBI is arresting anyone whose first name rhymes with Osama, groups like the Klan operate openly and legally in all 50 states. Next time you're in Tennessee, Chelsea, come visit Nathan Bedford Forrest Park, named after the founder of America's al-Qaida, the KKK.

Absurdly, we're supposed to breathe a sigh of relief now that we think the anthrax was sent, not by Arabs, but by white supremacists.

But why were the (mostly black) postal workers treated a week after the whites on Capitol Hill? Has US Attorney-General John Ashcroft detained 1,000 Christians without charge? Is everyone with links to Oklahoma City bomber Timothy McVeigh now under surveillance? And what terrorist-harbouring state will be bombed next? Alabama?

And have you thought, Chelsea, why so many Britons oppose the bombing? As I write this, I sit only one mile from a people at war with America. They are not poor, illiterate, or Muslim. In fact, they are mostly white, Christian, and middle class. They are students at Oxford University. Wadham College (which is part of Oxford) declared war with the United States when America started carpet-bombing Vietnam. The stately, ancient Oxford hall boasts a well-kept, manicured lawn, which the students still call Ho Chi Minh Quad.

Of course, the state of hostilities is mostly facetious (Oxford's Trinity College and Balliol College have also declared war – against each other), but not entirely. The English philosopher and mathematician Bertrand Russell, one of the most renowned thinkers of the twentieth century, convened a war crimes tribunal in the 1960s, in which he accused the United States of crimes against humanity. They may not be shouting, 'Death to America', but Brits have long scoffed at American imperiousness.

Since September 11, Americans have been asking, 'How could anybody hate us so much?' And they have mostly been coming to the wrong conclusions. (Novelist Salman Rushdie recently said that Islamists hate America because we eat bacon sandwiches!) I'm not an eloquent writer like Mr Rushdie, but as a mathematician I can put two and two together; and I'd like to opine why the British feel 'they' hate 'us'. That reason is American state-sponsored terrorism.

America has long accused nations like Iraq, Sudan and Cuba of sponsoring terrorism. But, according to a major American television network, it was the Joint Chiefs of Staff of the US military who, in the 1960s, drafted plans to commit terrorist attacks. 'We could blow up a US ship in [Cuba's] Guantanamo Bay and blame Cuba', read one report, codenamed Operation Northwoods. The militarists would then have an excuse to topple Castro.

During the 1980s, the US fought a secret war in Central America, supporting murderous regimes in El Salvador and Honduras that used death squads to terrorise civilians, murder priests and rape nuns. Many of the generalissimos who conducted this reign of terror were trained in the School of the Americas – in Georgia. Their training manuals included instructions on how to torture.

Chile's dictator, Pinochet, who specialised in dropping his political opponents out of airplanes, came to power after a CIA-orchestrated coup, during which the democratically elected president, Salvador Allende, was murdered. The Congo was plunged into 40 years of chaos after the US-backed dictator, Mobutu, seized power, following the murder of the democratically elected prime minister Patrice Lumumba.

The US government occupied Haiti for decades and, later, supported that country's brutal dictators, the Duvaliers. It sustained the dictator of the Philippines, Ferdinand Marcos, even after his people overthrew him. The Shah of Iran persecuted his own people with our tax dollars; yet we pretend that Iranian anti-Americanism is unprovoked.

When the US stops sponsoring terrorism, and starts cracking down on terrorism at home (the KKK and the LAPD), the English may start respecting our moral leadership. That's why British newspapers are as likely to call George W Bush 'the mad bomber' as they are Osama bin Laden. And that's why so many Britons are saying, America's not at war with terrorism: it's in bed with it.

The charge has been laid that the left predicted a long war. 'Look how they got it wrong, big-time!' as Vice-President Dick Cheney might say (from his 'secret location'). But this phase of the war – the massacres, the continued bombing, the infighting as returning warlords reassert themselves – is far from over; and who knows what is likely to happen once Bush turns his attention to Iraq. The irony is that it was the right, especially the military, which expected the Taliban regime to hold out. In late October, Defense Secretary Donald Rumsfeld predicted that the war in Afghanistan would take 'years, not weeks or months'.

So the real question is: why did the military and the CIA get it so wrong so badly? After all, we're paying them $300bn a year to (a) predict the fall of the Berlin Wall, (b) predict the invasion of Kuwait, (c) not bomb Chinese embassies when we're not at war with China, (d) not train and fund Osama bin Laden when he will later use our own weapons against us. Maybe we deserve to be laughed at, left and right, for giving the military and the CIA so much money when they've done such a hopeless job.

Unlike them, I'll admit that I don't know who is responsible for the attacks. But there are only a few men in the world sick enough and evil enough to be happy over what happened. I'm not simply talking about Osama bin Laden, Saddam Hussein and Gary Condit.

I'm talking about the shadowy masters of the defence and intelligence industry, the alarmists. 'We are at war', the alarmists cried on September 12. But against whom? As George Bush said so eloquently, 'We may not know who "they" are, but we know they're there.'

'We should be prepared for massive security measures', I heard a commentator say on television, his bow tie a stand-in for a toothbrush moustache. In other words, we need to curtail freedom in the name of freedom. His co-panelist chimed in, as excited as a puppy, 'We need to track down who did it, kill them, and remove the governments of those states [harbouring the terrorists].' So much for international law. That's how terrorists think: Get them, and I don't care who's in the way, just get them!

'If there is one purpose for a government to exist, it is to protect its people', Mr Bow Tie said, adding that a 'feeling of vulnerability is [now] present'. But people of colour feel vulnerable every day: Amadou Diallo was shot 41 times by a government sworn to protect him. I don't feel any less safe because of the attack on the Pentagon; I feel less safe because of the anti-democratic alarmists in the Pentagon.

In 1933, soon after Hitler came to power, the German parliament building burned down. Hitler blamed the Communists. He used the fire as an excuse to lock up minorities and anyone who disagreed with his politics. Will our government do the same? 'Impossible!' you harrumph. 'We have checks and balances.' But those checks disappear in times of war.

The 'they' we need to worry about are the alarmist militarists, who will use this tragedy to extort billions of dollars from us for the intelligence industry (which failed to predict the attack) and for Nuclear Missile Defence (which couldn't have prevented it). By scaring us out of our socks, they hope to get into our wallets, too. Mark my words, future peaceful protests will be heavily curtailed 'in the interests of national security'. In other words, we won't have the right of assembly, we will only have the right to remain silent.

The Statue of Liberty was not struck by a plane, Chelsea, but it is already crumbling. If the alarmists are serious about conducting 'business as usual', then there must be no security crackdown, no eavesdropping on the Internet, no restrictions on the right to dissent. Is our freedom merely a privilege, which can be taken away when it is inconvenient? You fight terrorism by fighting terrorists, not by persecuting the American people. If the alarmists have their way, the next 'they' could be us, and then 6,000 men and women, who believed in American democracy, will have died in vain.

So, Chelsea, please do not corral all Americans into the pro-war camp. The Stars and Stripes your friend draped across his back remind too many of us of the bloody stripes that once laced our own. One of Bill Clinton's redeeming traits is the fact that, when he studied at Oxford, he opposed America's war. Maybe some time, Chelsea, you will too.

NEITHER PURE NOR VILE

Mike Marqusee

I was visiting New York when the news of the massacre of 15 Christians in Bahawalpur flashed up on CNN. It was a brief item, included in an update on the war, and all that the casual viewer would know was that 'Islamic fundamentalists' had struck again. As I had once spent some balmy days in Bahawalpur, I was touched and disturbed by the news, which was both one more horror among so many others in recent weeks, and at the same time something more intimate. I draped myself in the tie-dyed shawl I had purchased for one hundred Pakistani rupees in Bahawalpur's eighteenth-century bazaar, and ventured out into the brisk autumn air of the traumatised city.

The weather in New York was not that different from the late January week I had spent in Bahawalpur 20 months earlier. It's a small city in deepest southern Punjab, perched on the edge of the desert that stretches across the border with India. Years ago, a series of Anglophile Nawabs ornamented the old walled city with a fine fringe of palaces, colleges, hospitals and administrative buildings in various styles of late Victorian Mughal-Italianate-Gothic, as well as one of the country's most disgracefully underused cricket grounds, the placid Dring Stadium. In recent decades, development has sprawled across the vast adjacent plane, and the armed forces now occupy huge encampments outside the city, side by side with an industrial complex dominated by Novartis, the agro-chemical multi-national. Nonetheless, Bahawalpur retains a pleasantly provincial air. The streets are lined with trees and, by Pakistani standards, the traffic is calm.

Since it is no longer (post-partition) on the way to or from anywhere of importance, Bahawalpur attracts few casual visitors. Like most tourists who make it this far, I had come in part to see the fifteenth-century blue-glazed tile-clad tombs in nearby Uch Sharif. Once upon a time, before the river Chenab altered course, Uch was a major centre of Islamic study. Today it is a dilapidated rural outpost, distinguished by the exquisite remains of shrines and mosques built to honour Sufi saints – some from as far away as Bokhara in Uzbekistan and Tabriz in Iran. In Europe or even in India, monuments of such delicate magnificence would become the hub of a tourist industry. There would be hotels and restaurants and guides. Here, in a region largely neglected by central government, one is left to enjoy the elegant ceramic décor and the classically pro-portioned domes and arches in tranquillity. Women labouring in the neatly irrigated fields surrounding the shrines meet an intrusive male foreigner with relaxed smiles and confident chatter. There are no veils. The taste is for bold, eye-catching colours – including the scarlet, gold and azure tie-dye pattern, a prize specimen of which I later purchased in Bahawalpur's bazaar.

They call this region southern Punjab, but it feels a very long way from Lahore, the Punjabi provincial capital. The people here speak their own language, Seraiki, which boasts its own poetry and song and its own patron saints, commemorated in the shrines that everywhere dot the landscape. After a few days in Bahawalpur, I drove out into the Cholistan desert – an extension of the vast Thar desert through which the India–Pakistan border is drawn. Next to a wind-blown hamlet of mud-walled square-sided dwellings, there was a sand dune, now covered with green-painted concrete, venerated as the burial site of Chanon Pir, a mythic figure whose cult harks back to the centuries long before Islam, or even Hinduism or Buddhism, reached these parts. On the day I visited, people from settlements across Cholistan were assembling for the beginning of the Pir's annual festival. The skies were blue, the air was temperate and the mood was cheerful. Devotees were performing rites around the shrine, accompanied by the drone of harmonium and patter of tabla. Men dressed as women danced and laughed and begged. Peddlers set out stalls of cheap plastic trinkets. And there was not a mullah in sight.

Watching the merry interaction of cross-dressers and camel-herders, truck-drivers and sweet-sellers, I wondered what on earth it meant to dub ourselves Muslim or Hindu, Pakistani or Indian, or Jew or American or New Yorker or Londoner. And I thought of the classic lyric of Bullah Shah, the eighteenth-century Punjabi poet-sufi: 'Bullah, what do I know of myself? I am no believer in mosque or temple. I am not pure. I am not vile. I'm no Moses and I'm no Pharaoh. Bullah, what do I know of myself?'

Back in New York City, on the day I learned of the Bahawalpur massacre, I dined with my sisters and brother, nieces and nephew, who live scattered across the United States. It was a sombre gathering. My mother had just passed away and there was a shared horror at the unfolding 'war on terrorism'. I was still wearing the tie-dyed shawl, now twisted, most un-Pakistani style, into a scarf around my neck. My ten-year-old Californian niece admired its vibrant colours, and I promised that the next time I went to Pakistan I would buy her one. She frowned. 'In Pakistan, if you're American, they chop off your hand.'

What the CNN report did not ask was just how a war being fought across a border some 400 miles away could overflow into a place like Bahawalpur. But to ask that question would have been to invite some discomforting answers.

A report into the massacre by investigators from the Commission on Peace and Justice, an independent human rights organisation, chronicles the events and the context. Early on the morning of Sunday, October 28, some 50 local Protestants were singing the final hymn in their service at St Dominic's Catholic church (the two local Christian communities are so small that they share the single church). Five men, said to be aged between 20 and 25, rode up on two motorcycles. Three of them entered the church, quietly closed the door, shot dead the Muslim policeman stationed there, and sprayed the church with gunfire, killing 15, including the pastor, and injuring another seven. They then fled the scene, with their waiting accomplices, on the two motorcycles. Among the dead were six men, seven women and two children.

At 11 a.m. the following day, a mass funeral took place at the church. The entire city shut down as a mark of respect. According to local newspapers, 5,000 people took part in the ceremony. Muslims easily outnumbered Christians in the ranks lining both sides of the road leading from the church to the graveyard.

The killings were immediately condemned by General Musharraf and politicians of all stripes. Even the right-wing Urdu press, in a break from its more inflammatory habits, joined the condemnations and the calls for national unity. Eight members of two groups were quickly arrested – press reports said three belonged to Jash-e-Muhammad and five to Harkat-ul-Mujahidine, two of the numerous jehadi factions that have proliferated in Pakistan over the last 20 years, with support from the army and the intelligence services. Critics noted that, although the local police had been warned about potential sectarian violence, and specifically asked to station an additional guard at the church in Bahawalpur, no precautionary measures had been taken. Government sources muttered darkly about 'the foreign hand', and in some quarters it was openly alleged that RAW, India's intelligence agency, had masterminded the killings in an attempt to destabilise Pakistan – at the very moment that Pakistan was consolidating its new relationship with the United States.

In the aftermath of September 11, faced with enraged and peremptory demands from the US government, the military regime in Islamabad had chosen the carrot over the stick, and signed up for the 'war against terrorism'. As a result, an intimate and powerful nexus that had flourished for more than two decades came under severe pressure. That nexus bound together the military and the multifarious outfits of the Islamist right – a force that has attracted few voters in any of Pakistan's intermittent democratic elections, but has prospered thanks to sponsorship from Pakistan's state-within-a-state. In places like Bahawalapur, there was no history of anything like Islamic fundamentalism until the 1980s, when, as part of the US-sponsored war against the Soviets in Afghanistan, and with full US government cognisance and approval, a new form of highly organised and belligerent religious intolerance, completely at odds with Seraiki and Sufi traditions, made its appearance.

Although the Bahawalpur massacre is probably the worst atrocity to be inflicted on Pakistan's Christian community, it is by no means an isolated incident. The 2.2 million Pakistani Christians comprise the country's largest non-Muslim minority. They are descendants of lower caste Hindus who sought in conversion – but did not find – relief from age-old oppression. They remain among the poorest and most abused people in Pakistani society, and as a result of the military-Islamist tie-up their situation over the last 20 years has deteriorated. Under Zia's dictatorship, Christians were effectively disenfranchised, forced to vote in an apartheid-like 'separate electorate'. They were also subject to discrimination in the courts because of

'Islamic' legal reforms and to prosecution under the blasphemy laws. The latter proved a handy tool for pursuing personal vendettas as well as for jehadi demagogues looking to provoke communal conflict. As the jehadi groups received increasing aid and succour from Zia's regime in the 1980s, sectarian violence – against Shias, other Muslim minorities, and Christians – rose steadily, and did not abate with the return of democracy in the late 1980s. In 1995, Manzoor Masih, a Christian on trial in a blasphemy case, was shot dead on the premises of the Lahore high court. In 1996, Shanti Nagar, a Christian village near Khanewal (also in southern Punjab), was burnt to the ground, with the apparent collusion of the local police.

The authors of the Commission for Peace and Justice report ask 'why a community, the majority of which is already leading a vulnerable life, and whose loyalty to the country is indisputable, should be targeted in any organised violence'. In answering that question, they place the Bahawalpur attack in an international context. 'The wrong notion of some people, relating the interests of Pakistani Christians with the West, should be put to an end now ... After September 11, the change in the international scenario also affected the atmosphere of Pakistan and the extremists got a boost, especially after October 7 with the US attacks on Afghanistan ... and if the war continues for long, this is not going to be rooted out.' The authors of the report conclude that until state-sponsored discrimination against Christians is eliminated, and until the police take a firmer grip on the sectarian terrorists, Christian communities will remain vulnerable.

On CNN, the massacre in Bahawalpur was just another headline atrocity, another example of the violence wracking the Muslim world and Pakistan in particular. There was, inevitably, no mention of the decisive role that the US had played in nurturing the sources of this violence, nor of the discriminatory policies of the Pakistani state. No indication that long-standing traditions of secularism and religious tolerance had been slapped aside by remote geopolitical interests. No reference to the persecution of Christians across the border, in India, under the Hindu fundamentalist BJP government, the US ally in 'the war against terrorism'. No hint of the real meaning, the resonant tragedy, of these deaths. And therefore no illumination of the succession of horrors – the villages carpet-bombed, the prisoners executed, the refugees forever on the move – that make up this war.

In the week following the Bahawalpur massacre, as the B52s pounded Afghanistan, the New York Yankees played the Arizona Diamondbacks in the World Series. As a long-time Yankee fan I would normally have welcomed this rare chance to watch my childhood favourites in action. But there was something about the way a wartime USA had repackaged the Yankees that deterred me. Suddenly 'those damn Yankees' were 'America's team', bearers of the cause of the thousands killed in the World Trade Center. It was conveniently forgotten that, until September 11, Yankee-hating was the norm across the rest of the country, as was a muted suspicion and hostility to New York in general. When the Yanks lost the series opener in Arizona by 12–1, the *New York Post*, under an image of the WTC ruins, ran a front page headline reading: YANKEES SLAUGHTERED IN THE DESERT. Can you blame me for getting muddled about what was at issue here – baseball or war?

Feeling increasingly alienated from my native city, I found myself in a taxi heading downtown for a meeting with a local anti-war activist. Like nearly all the cabs in New York, and certainly all those driven by people from south Asia or the Middle East, this one was festooned with American flags. I asked the driver where he was from. 'Pakistan', he answered, in a defensive whisper. 'A beautiful country', I said. 'You have visited there?' he asked. I explained that I'd worked in Pakistan as a journalist and also travelled around as a tourist. Soon we were agreeing about the various attractions of Pakistan, and particularly of Lahore, his home city, and in no time we moved on to the subject of the war, its impact on Pakistan, and the mad brutality of the US response to September 11.

Remember, this man was a New Yorker. He'd been driving a cab in the city for ten years. He was proud of his detailed knowledge of its road map. But he also had knowledge of other worlds – not only of Pakistan, and the role the US had played there, but also of Iraq, Palestine, Indonesia. He talked about how the US's promotion of big-time heroin production along the Afghanistan border in the 1980s had led to an outflow of heroin across south Asia and into the cities of America itself. 'People in New York have been living with the problems caused by these policies for many years, they just don't know it.'

I must have expressed over-forcefully my dismay and disgust with much of what I had seen and heard in New York, for he urged me to be patient. 'These people,' he said, and he indicated the human swarm surrounding us in the mid-afternoon traffic, 'have never experienced this kind of violence before. All they know is what is on their televisions and this tells them nothing about what has happened and why it has happened. Give them time. They will understand.'

Once again, that verse from Bullah Shah ran through my head: 'Bullah, what do I know of myself? I am no believer in mosque or temple. I am not pure. I am not vile. I'm no Moses and I'm no Pharaoh. Bullah, what do I know of myself?'

THE LION, THE WITCH AND THE WARMONGER: 'GOOD', 'EVIL' AND THE SHATTERING OF IMPERIAL MYTH

Howard Davis

'It was just like a Hollywood movie.' There have been so many words said or written since September 11 about what happened that day. But I remember hearing those particular words many times. I remember saying them myself. It *was* just like a movie. What else did we have to compare it to except a scene from some blood and thunder blockbuster? In one of the first camcorder pieces, at the moment the second aircraft flew into the tower, a voice off-screen screamed in delight, 'This is great!' In the chat rooms of the aftermath one person relayed how the moment had taken her back to previous confusion when she had mistaken a screening of the movie *Independence Day* for a real catastrophe. It had 'looked so real. I live[d] in Manhattan so I went to my roof to look downtown and see if there was anything there.' Now, as a 'real' blockbuster unfolded, she thought that 'this was something like [that] experience ... someone in the lobby had a camera, so I thought maybe this was "Candid Camera". I quickly realised, however, that this was all too real. I cried and shook all over.'

The screenplay to this real disaster spectacular had no superhero to single-handedly save the day. His (*sic*) absence at the moment civilisation needed him was incomprehensible, he should have been there. But, of course, the superhero is a myth. And if shattering lives, steel and concrete were enormous achievements for al-Qaida, the prime-time shattering of Western myths was, perhaps, even more stunning.

Imperial systems have always generated powerful mythologies. These have been expressed historically in many ways, in stories and statues, pageantry and uniforms, music and pictures. They have emphasised power, grandeur and, not least, righteousness. In an age of 'reason' it is tempting to place ourselves above myth and impression. But more than ever, they surround us. Media and cultural studies courses rightly assert their ubiquity, sophistication and power. But if nothing else, September 11 and the days that followed attested to their fragility.

Television viewers worldwide watched as the impregnability of American superpowerdom collapsed in an instant. In the US, viewers watched, incredulous, images not of mourning, but of jubilant celebration from those 'outside'. Their leaders floundered. What 'should' have been the very clear moral basis to their emerging plans for war were clearly rejected by millions, possibly hundreds of millions, abroad. When movie madmen conspire to destroy civilisation it is completely taken for granted that 'evil' will be opposed by all 'right thinking' people. We have been brought up to believe this, indeed, to know this.

In the aftermath I was struck how the words and tones of 'our' leaders echoed the stereotypes and moralities of children's TV. It was as if, with the superheroes gone AWOL, President George W Bush turned to Disney. Successive, excruciating performances – hailed as 'Churchillian' – could have been written by those scripting the videos that grip my four-year-old son. In both, intricate problems are simply a case of 'good' versus 'evil'. With these simplistic categories the most powerful leader on earth dismissed the myriad complexities, ambiguities and resentments of a world created out of his nation's own imperial *realpolitik*.

While I listened to Bush's words my son continued his socialisation into the same myths. As children we become practised in their use and as adults, in the face of complexity, we are exhorted by our opinion-formers to return to their comforting simplicities. Such myths are deeply held. We don't know, of course, that they are myths, rather they are our beliefs, our assumptions. My first exposure to 'evil' was the Witch Queen in *Snow White and the Seven Dwarves*. I had nightmares afterwards. My son watches *The Lion King* instead. It is more sensitive to the tastes and sensibilities of a modern audience – it is less misogynistic and it doesn't stereotype dwarves.

It even soothes away the moral delicacy around lion kings eating their loyal subjects. The Lion King, Mufasah tells Simba, his son, that we are all part of the same 'circle of life'. But what remains a constant is that the villain is clearly established from the very first frames. He is the wicked uncle, Scar, lurking in his cave, snatching and eating a mouse. His first tones are arrogant, sneering. By the time Mufasah enters the cave, we are in no doubt which is on the side of 'good' and which on the side of 'evil'.

Our attitudes to Scar or to the Witch Queen are not partial or 'half-hearted'. Nor are they elicited primarily through moral reasoning. Certainly, we discover disagreeable aspects of Scar's personality, most notably (in the context of George W Bush, ironically) his devious lust for power. But, in truth, we have begun to despise and fear him well before this. There is no 'reason' here. Mufasah's 'right' to kingship, after all, is based on archaic notions of heredity, and physical prowess. Scar's deficiency, as he bitterly complains, derives only from the arbitrariness of the 'shallow end of the gene pool'. We applaud and deride not according to reasoned notions of 'good' and 'evil', but to visual and auditory cues.

We have been schooled to recognise and use concepts of 'good' and 'evil'. As media multinationals have encircled the globe they have invited us to share the same archetypes. Seldom have I heard so many different languages, or seen so many different shaped and shaded faces as when visiting EuroDisney. And everybody, African, Asian and European shared the same reference points. We all cheered as our Disney favourites paraded past us. We pointed out the characters for our children, and they did the same for us, calling out their names in their respective languages. It seemed like a global experience. If McDonald's 'golden arches' are the symbol of US economic imperialism then Disney's magic kingdom symbolises its cultural hegemony.

But if the propagandising of 'good' and 'evil', 'right' and 'wrong' is global, we have now (re)discovered that their specific interpretations, the contents with which we fill them are not. Presidential assertions of right and wrong, while they have convinced many, have not convinced all. Where the historical realities of Western imperialism are more biting than its myths are soothing, populations have remained unconvinced. For many in these worlds 'war' did not begin on September 11. For all its barbarity, the destruction of aircraft, buildings and lives was not regarded as an unprovoked assault, but as a response.

This has been a major blow to Western leaders. When they stated that those not 'with us' were 'against us', 'we' were supposed to know instinctively what they meant, why they were right and how to react. In truth, total cultural dominance eludes the West, in children's entertainment as in politics. A vice-president of one Disney subsidiary states that the 'plan is to think globally but to customise locally'. The heroes and heroines of the newer animations attempt to appeal to 'other' traditions. Mulan, for example is a Chinese woman who, disguised as a man, saved the imperial, feudal 'civilisation' from the 'barbarous' Huns. It is the familiar myth in fact, repackaged. But, for all its complex marketing strategies, the company is forced to concede that it is 'in the ironic position of being one of the best known brands on the planet ... with too little of its income ... generated outside of the United States'. With only 5 per cent of the world's population, the US homeland accounts for 80 per cent of company revenues.

For a right-wing US president, whose election defeat had been predicated on withdrawal from the hostile, un-American outside world, it has been particularly difficult to escape the imagery of 'childish' cinema fantasy. When he finally appeared in public after the tragedies of September 11, it was to declare war on 'terrorism'. As in the 'old west' the perpetrators would be brought back 'dead or alive'. Oblivious to those not sharing his gun-slinging Christian heritage, he called his war a 'crusade', codenamed 'Infinite Justice'. This could hardly have been designed to cause greater offence to the very Muslims whose support the US needed. *Raison d'état* took second place to Hollywood swagger. This was a war of the 'civilised' against the 'uncivilised'. The attacks of September 11 were, he perversely asserted, motivated by a hatred of America's freedom. That they may have had some roots in the historic subjugation of the freedom of others inflicted by the US was not in the script. As bombing began, he pronounced, with a straight face, that donations of one dollar by American children to buy Afghan children food proved that the US was on the side of 'civilisation'. This was not the sort of 'compassionate' behaviour, he assured us, that could be expected of the Taliban.

If the division of humanity into 'good' and 'evil' is a myth, so is the inevitable triumph of the former. In one manifestation, this myth is the 'American Dream'. It asserts individualised triumph, not only over evil, but over any type of random or structural adversity. In another, harder version, it is the masculine John

Wayne or Bruce Willis myth. Here, strength, courage and killing power are required to prevail not over life's misfortune but over demonised, ruthless evil. It is nonsense. But, like the bifurcation of 'good' and 'evil', the inevitable triumph of the 'good' the 'deserving' or the 'heroic', often through violence, becomes part of our mental software at an early age.

My son's Disney heroes sometimes fail. They are humanised by their failings, or through some transgression of the norms. But they too, ultimately and heroically, prevail. It has been suggested by post-trauma therapists that we each internalise a residual faith in 'deservingness'. If we behave well, we will come to no harm – that, at least in this limited sense, life is fair. We may even 'get on' in life and if we do, we will claim our success to be a reflection of our worthiness. Individuals and communities afflicted by calamity, however, come to know that this is not true. Virtue does not always win through; struggle and honest toil are not usually rewarded. Those bereaved by, or surviving, the terror in the Pentagon, New York, or Pennsylvania will in an important sense become outsiders. They represent what an individualistic, materialistic and shallow society does not wish to confront: that life is not fair or just. But they will not be outsiders quite like the surviving poor of Palestine, Afghanistan, Iraq, or any other of the sinks of misery created by globalised greed. These are Zygmunt Bauman's 'faraway locals', associated in the minds of the wealthy with 'the pictures of inhumanity which rules [their] lands'. Their dangerous otherness allows Blair and Bush to bomb their countries and sustain their oppressors while turning them away as refugees.

The myths of 'good' and 'evil' and the triumph of 'right' are, of course, implicitly about superiority and security. Western élites take it upon themselves to define what is 'good' and 'evil' or, as pertinently, 'force' and 'terror'. As the decision to attack Afghanistan was made, British newspapers overdosed on pictorial and diagrammatic displays of military hardware. 'Right' became welded with 'might'. The *Daily Star* and *Daily Mail* were not so much mimicking Disney or Schwarzenegger as *The Victor,* an old 'comic' that I am old enough to remember. Like today's comics for adults, it graphically presented the heroism of 'our boys', blacked up and camouflaged, ready to run untouched into hails of enemy bullets to mete out heroic, spectacular 'justice'.

But even this martial myth has been subverted. One epithet, dropped almost as soon as it was first mentioned, was that terrorists were 'cowards'. Terrorists? Maybe. But cowards? Their very danger-ousness derives from their willingness to sacrifice themselves. And they have succeeded, spectacularly. If the US bombing of Hiroshima and Nagasaki remain defining images of the twentieth century, it is difficult, indeed terrifying, to conceive of one more iconic for the twenty-first than of the aircraft and the towers. The terrorists 'out-Hollywooded' Hollywood. The United States has manufactured and consumed images like the September 11 attacks for decades, selling them as products for universal titillation. Al-Qaida did it for real. Hollywood's thriller screenwriters were recruited and relegated to assisting the Pentagon anticipate the next likely scenarios of terror attack.

Some weeks after the September tragedies the Pentagon began a war the US had already lost. No victory would reclaim its myths of military, economic and ideological impregnability. Whether Osama bin Laden was to be delivered dead or alive, different realities had been forced on the world. The fearsome technologies and intricate infrastructures of the West, for so long the key to its dominance have been exposed as its Achilles heel. Nuclear, biological and chemical authorities explain how 'nobody could have imagined' the sort of scenarios that even they now concede are all *too* imaginable.

How these new realities come to be understood remains to be seen. If there is an opportunity here it lies in dismantling the bankrupted 'good'/'evil' dichotomy, replacing it with sophisticated analyses, of power and politics and also of the duplicitous 'moral' bases to which the powerful in all societies, not only the West, have laid claim. The 'linkage' of Palestine with September 11, to which, initially, it was unacceptable even to allude for a time, moved to centre stage. Then domestic clampdowns and international realignments in the interests of security reasserted élite fixation with 'security'. Tony Blair, although reportedly frustrated at US reluctance to seize the opportunity to tackle the Palestinian question, intensified his moral exposition of the basis of his foreign and military policies. Recourse to the security agenda is a familiar reflex for Western leaders. As, in their reflex to frame social ills in terms of 'good' and 'evil', it has a well-proven history of political, if not social, efficacy. Major vested interests have much to gain from the construction of 'evil empires'. 'The problem' may easily become retrenched once again as one of 'security', ideologically framed by a renewed emphasis on the morality of the state's monopoly of violence.

The incredible dangerousness of this approach lies in the massively enhanced scale of 'our' vulnerability. Al-Qaida demonstrated the immense destruction now achievable by well-organised, but relatively small, networks. Military destruction of the Taliban regime does nothing to overturn this 'new' reality. The real lesson of this stage of the 'war' has been that our intelligence and security experts, for all their wealth and technology failed to see what was coming. In an age of suitcase bombs, chemical and biological agents and hijackers armed with knives, it is this disastrous failure of intelligence that terrifies. As Jonathan Farley observes in this book, 'We're paying [the military and CIA] $300bn a year to (a) predict the fall of the Berlin Wall, (b) predict the invasion of Kuwait, (c) not bomb Chinese embassies when we're not at war with China, (d) not train and fund Osama bin Laden when he will later use our own weapons against us.' The military-industrial complex, assimilates only selective lessons of its 'last wars'. But deterrence and civil safety are bankrupted by the deadly combination of mass destruction for the masses and individual aspirations to martyrdom. If there is one old military dogma that should be exhumed it is the inter-war mantra that 'the bomber will always get through'. The trouble is (for 'us') that the bomber might be riding a bicycle rather than an F-16.

It has been suggested that the events of September 11 have discredited the 'anti-globalisers', 'the pacifists' and the 'left'. But the triumphalists make two key errors. They understate the costs of their war, in terms of death and injury, but also in terms of broader goodwill. And they miss the fact that the key lessons from September 11 dovetail precisely with warnings made by the derided radicals, 'fainthearts' and 'traitors'. Major structural changes are required in the relationships between powerful and the powerless to tackle the profit-driven proliferation of deadly weapons and the complex roots of grievance. Goodwill among the dispossessed, upon which adequate intelligence is based, needs to be established as a matter of urgency. Without these changes we will need to place infinite faith in our superheroes to save the world for 'good'. A happy ending is not inevitable. When Simba dethrones Scar, the 'evil-doer', the devastated pride lands are rejuvenated by rain and life returns. My son is happy. But the lands and lives of millions of real people remain devastated. The abiding legacy of September 11 is not of subsequent American military success. It is that for the first time the dispossessed, the grief-stricken and the angry have seen that they have the means to strike back. At 'us'. His father finds it harder to smile.

BEYOND SEPTEMBER 11: CERTAINTIES AND DOUBTS

Barbara Hudson

Introduction

Replying to the invitation to contribute to this collection of short reflective essays on the events of September 11 and their aftermath was easy: like everyone else I know, these events were dominating my thoughts and conversations, so the opportunity to have an outlet for my feelings was welcome. Moreover, opinion polls and most media editorialising and reporting did not seem to be at all consistent with the views of the people I talked to. So, yes please, a chance to express my reactions to the events, and more importantly, a chance to contribute to such a key debate.

My interests and feelings coalesce round three of my 'identities'. As a citizen of one of the 'coalition against terrorism' nations, bombs are being dropped in my name, military action is being undertaken allegedly to protect the values which are fundamentally important to me and mine. As someone who has spent time in Beirut and Gaza, who has Palestinian friends and friends working for UNRWA, the organisation providing services to Palestinian refugees, I have a keen interest in Middle Eastern affairs and a long-standing sympathy with the Palestinian people. As a criminologist, and more particularly as a critical criminologist, I am interested in my discipline's ability to encompass these crimes; moreover, as someone who has specialised in control rather than crime, how can one disentangle crime and control here, still less how can one theorise and critique these entangled occurrences of terrorism, war crimes and states' crimes?

Sitting down to write, though, I discovered unexpected difficulties. My thoughts were indeed numerous, but lacked any coherence. What struck me most of all were the balances of certainties and doubts whenever I tried to think through the issues. The things of which I am certain are questions of basic values to do with rights to self-determination (in this case, raised in relation to Afghanistan, Islam, women, and Palestine); life and liberty (violated by the September 11 terrorists, but also by Western bombing, Israeli actions, and proposed restrictions on human rights in the UK); and with prohibition on torture, punishment without fair trials and arbitrary detention of any kind (again, in danger of breach by proposals for anti-terrorism legislation in the UK, and by suggestions of allowing torture of terrorism suspects in the USA). The doubts rise mainly in relation to the balance between some of the fundamental rights (religion and women's rights, for example); the extent to which I support Western intervention (unease in the case of Afghanistan, wanting more intervention in Bosnia, East Timor and Sierra Leone, for example). What struck me most was the difference between my own tentative, highly qualified thinking and the strident certainties of Blair, Bush and most other Anglo-American politicians and commentators, and how objectionable I find this breathtaking lack of self-doubt on the part of those who order military action and seek to reorder the world along the lines of their own uncritical thinking.

Western values and military intervention

For several years I have been working on theories of justice, and for the last two I have been researching and writing a book which looks at communitarian, feminist and poststructuralist critiques of Enlightenment philosophies of justice and tries to assess the extent to which such philosophies and the institutions based on them continue to be valid and viable. I see the problems not so much in terms of the universal and the situated (which I see as a false dichotomy), or of rival philosophies, but in the threats posed to justice by the politics of risk and safety. What one sees, across the globe and across the ages, is that understandings of justice are undermined by understandings of what (or, more precisely, who) threatens the community among whom that justice obtains. From the veiling and even mutilation of women, through the ghettoisation or 'cleansing' of minority groups, to the internment of suspects and strengthening of barriers against immigrants, the key issue is not rival ideas of what justice is, but denial of justice to certain groups of people. The drawing of boundaries around the community of justice, with the expulsion of (it seems) ever-increasing categories of people outside the bounds, is the principal source of injustice. Once a people (the Palestinians, the Tutsis, the Roma), or a group (women, immigrants, dissidents, non-citizens, non-co-religionists) are described as a threat to order, culture, economic prosperity or physical integrity, they are denied any claims on justice.

There is, of course, nothing new about this. What is new is the way that the ending of the Cold War has changed the discourse of intervention. In Cold War times (or any time when there has been more than one global power), interventions in the affairs of other nations were usually advocated in the cause of 'defending the interests' of the power or alliance supposedly threatened. Other interventions – in defence of 'justice' or 'human rights' – were clearly the province of the United Nations, or of regional organisations such as the Organisation of African Unity. It was easy to distinguish, for example, the US role in Vietnam from Vietnam's intervention to depose the Pol Pot regime. The former involved no genuine defence of national interests; whereas the latter removed a regime that violated human rights in the most gross way, and did not produce territorial gain for Vietnam. Similarly, Tanzania's overthrow of Idi Amin was clearly legitimate, and very different from Western support for its client regimes in Africa and the Middle East.

Now that the Cold War has ended and there is only one global superpower, American interests and 'the democratic way of life' are fused. The US in its unchallenged military and economic supremacy is able to decline to intervene if it does not perceive any interests worth defending, or present itself as the champion of freedom and democracy if it does intervene. Human rights violations are likely to be ignored if they take place in a country that does not have any material or strategic importance for the US, but threats to America will be severely dealt with on the basis that they are threats to the civilised world.

The US not only bypasses international organisations and sets itself up as the defender of all that is good and true, it also undermines those organisations that should be acting as neutral defenders of fundamental values. For years the US has withheld contributions to the UN; it will not place its soldiers under UN control; it opposes UN resolutions and recognises governments that violate rights and freedoms, and of course it arms and finances such regimes. It also undermines the importance of due process and ethical principles in law enforcement by refusing to support the establishment of an International Criminal Court. It substitutes might for right by bombing Afghanistan rather than insisting that bin Laden and those who are suspected of being involved in the events of September 11 are brought to trial, either in the US or in an international court. This is the established US response – remember the bombing of the pharmaceutical depot after the American embassy bombings in Africa.

In terms of my theme of doubts and certainties, I am certain that I do not like the US fusing of the *realpolitik* discourse of interests with the moral discourse of rights and freedoms. I am certain that I do not want the bombing to continue and that I do not see any justification for one Afghan civilian being killed, for one person to have to flee their home, or for one food convoy to be delayed. I also think there is no justification for killing the Taliban, or even (though here the doubts creep in) assisting in their overthrow. Certainly they are a thoroughly objectionable regime, but even if (as seems unlikely) their replacement regime were very much better, I cannot see that the Americans have any right to bring about the downfall of a government they – for the moment – dislike.

My area of doubt is – what do I want done and by whom? If Western and Cold War powers, in successive waves of imperialism and rivalry, have destabilised much of Africa and the near and Middle East, when does 'withdrawal' (good) amount to 'abandonment' (bad)? What I certainly want is no-strings-attached economic and humanitarian aid, but does this include 'peacekeeping' and 'nation-building'? What I certainly want is a strengthened United Nations and strengthened regional organisations, but what their criteria for intervention should be, and whether there should be some sort of democratic test for influence in such organisations, are questions that bring me back to the morass of doubt.

The problem of Palestine

One thing of which I am certain is that bin Laden and his network are not fighting for Palestine. They seem solely concerned with fighting the 'great Satan' of Western secularism and Middle Eastern departures from their fundamentalist version of Islam. Another thing of which I am certain is that there is a difference between Palestinian groups such as Fatah, Hamas and Hezbollah, who see themselves as resistance fighters, and the al-Qaida terrorists.

Another of my certainties is that Israel should withdraw from the lands it has occupied since 1967. I have been angered by the way in which Israeli incursions have shifted the demands away from this to withdrawal from land occupied since September 11, and also towards a cessation of settlement expansion rather than abandonment of settlements outside pre-1967 boundaries.

My area of doubt here is around the definition of terrorism, and the extent to which violence is legitimate in defence of one's territory and rights to self-determination. I was outraged by a BBC *Newsnight* feature on definitions of terrorism, which gave a respectful hearing to Benjamin Netanyahu, former prime minister of Israel, and a very aggressive interrogation to Michel Massih, chairman of the Association of the Palestinian Community. This interview was bad journalism in that it allowed no illumination on the Palestinian view of what constitutes terrorism, and what they see as the limits on justifiable actions in resisting occupation, and it doubtless reinforced the impression among Palestinians that they cannot get a fair hearing in the West.

I have no doubt that for me, living in a democratic country, any act of violence in support of a political cause would be indefensible: I have no doubts about opposing violence in Northern Ireland, in the Basque region, or anywhere else with the possibility of bringing about peaceful change. But Palestine is an occupied territory, with an occupation which has become increasingly harsh over the years; where the people have no rights to freedom of movement; where they suffer from collective punishments and arbitrary arrests; and where the occupying power assassinates people, destroys property and occupies further territory at will. The Palestinians have used the 'proper channels' of UN resolutions, negotiations and diplomatic campaigns to no avail, and while there are obviously limits to what could be considered justifiable action in pursuit of their cause, these limits may well be different from limits in the West.

Criminology and terrorism

As a criminologist, I am torn between the need to include war crimes, crimes of the state, and terrorism, and my doubts about how to do this. If criminology cannot encompass these topics, how can it move beyond the confines of the official crime definitions of 'administrative criminology'? Although some excellent, critical, material is emerging, I am conscious of the need to include non-Western material, and doubtful of my own ability to go beyond my own cultural standpoint in selecting student reading material and writing lectures. Doubts about unconscious cultural relativism, about trying to fit events into theoretical categories that cannot properly encompass them, are formidable. Writing this essay, letting my own doubts and confusions surface, has shown me how well founded my anxieties are; reading the other contributions and participating in meetings of critical criminologists to try and think through some of the issues is the only way of coming to terms with these events criminologically. Putting the issues arising from my different identities together also reminds me that injustices and conflicts demand both criminological and political work, and of the importance of not letting the demands of the daily work routine be an excuse for a retreat from political engagement.

COULD OSAMA BIN LADEN HAVE BEEN A WOMAN? MASCULINITY AND SEPTEMBER 11[1]

Martti Grönfors

I am writing this piece in Sri Lanka, where I am finishing work on a book on the culture of masculinity and violence in this country. Sri Lanka is a nation with a violent past and a violent present. The ongoing civil war between Sinhalese and Tamil factions has claimed up to 100,000 lives in the past 20 years. In 1989, in another internal conflict, the ultra-left Sinhalese party killed thousands of civilians. When the tide turned, the government of the day killed up to 50,000 young people, mainly young men, in vicious reprisals. In present-day Sri Lanka, bombs go off at regular intervals, killing and injuring people. In my own work on violence, I am mainly concentrating not on the institutional violence that takes place as part of the political struggle, but on the violence at the intimate, everyday level of ordinary people's lives. Of course the two levels are connected, but I feel that to understand violence as a phenomenon, we have to look at it at the grass-roots level first and foremost.

From my extensive study of masculinity and its relationship to violence, it is clear to me that the link between those two is indisputable. Being a man and being violent inherently go together. I go even further by saying that being a man and being violent is totally normal. Male privilege, male socialisation, and institutional support for male dominance guarantee that. All systems of power require at least the potential use of violence as the means of maintaining that power. The male power system is no exception.

Violence is seen too easily as something that only 'bad', 'deviant', 'sick' and 'criminal' people commit. By viewing it in that light, violent behaviour is removed from the everyday arena to exceptional areas of life where no 'normal', 'decent' people enter. By the same token, 'ordinary' men are safe when violent behaviour is considered the characteristic of only a few deviant and evil people. Our understanding of male violence is distorted. Ordinary men can be released from responsibility when attention is drawn to those who are on the margins of society. As a mental game, let us try to imagine bin Laden as a female, al-Qaida as a network of women. In that event their gender would certainly have become an issue. But when men commit these terrible acts of violence, their gender is never mentioned. So normal is the fact of violence carried out by men that it requires no comment.

September 11 shocked the world. It did so probably because it was so spectacular. CNN and other media outlets made sure that everybody knew more or less in real time what happened on that fateful day. The shock was also on such a scale because the event did not take place in darkest Africa, where a million people could be clubbed to death without too much coverage and interest in the West. The attack on the World Trade Center struck at the very heart of Western values – commercialism and trade. It actually shook its very foundations. The attacks on the World Trade Center and the Pentagon were also strikes against the very centres of male dominance; the temples of monetarism and war.

Of course, it was an immeasurable tragedy for those affected by the loss of loved ones in the terrorist attacks. But in time they will get over it; people have that ability when they are faced with personal loss, even loss of such magnitude. Grief often brings the best out in people, compassion and forgiveness. This was evidenced in the numerous pleas by some of the relatives of those killed: that there be no acts of revenge. But will the world ever get over it? Will the world ever be allowed to get over it? Or more, will the male institutions of power ever get over it? Will they ever let others get over it? These are the huge questions here. It has become evident to many that we are nearer, perhaps more than ever before, the destruction of our civilisation, at least in the form we now know it. Ominous threats are voiced in support of the escalation of the American-led attack, confirming initial fears that this is not 'just' an issue to do with September 11.

We have been watching the other side too. We have seen the men in Pakistan, in Afghanistan and in many other Muslim countries showering their testosterone over our television screens. This is not a war between religions. It is not a war between West and East either. It might be a war between the rich and the poor. But it is most certainly a man-made war, men on both sides committed *as men* to wage terrible acts of violence on other men, but in so doing, also on innocent women and children. We hear the US president talking about 'revenge', about a 'crusade', about a 'just war' against 'evil-doers'. We hear from the other side similar proclamations in the name of jihad, holy war. This is not only rhetoric, not even just male rhetoric, but it is justification for action. The calls are excuses, needed to justify the murder of innocent people and the terrible pillage that has occurred. The real reasons, if they were to be established, are not all that important. What is important are the excuses.

During the Gulf War, I met a US rear admiral socially in Vermont. I asked him why Americans seem to be fighting always so far away from the USA, on other people's soil, involved in other people's fights. The answer came quickly: 'We don't want to, but we have to. No other nation cares. We do.' Care about what? Care about Western interests, perhaps? Care that governments which support Western interests stay in power, or are put in power, in strategic non-Western countries? Care that certain commercial and political and military interests of the USA and the Western world are safeguarded? Care that the interests of the central male institutions of power, commerce, politics and the military are safeguarded? There is no evidence of care about the poverty, hunger and epidemics which ensure the suffering of hundreds of millions – these do not create such passion. That is partly because they are not particularly masculine interests. As an anthropologist, I have learned – and many feminist researchers confirm this – that in many if not most societies, loving and caring are generally classified as female attributes. In those same societies, the interests of women are usually classified as secondary in importance and prestige, whereas males engage in 'real' issues. Waging war to secure commercial, political or military interests is, to use the popular vernacular, 'sexy', while caring for human needs is not.

What is it that the men in Afghanistan, Pakistan, Sri Lanka and other poor nations, not only poor Muslim nations, are guarding? My study of men and masculinity in Sri Lanka shows that in this Buddhist country, poor and uneducated men become very articulate when their status as males is being discussed. As of one mind, they relate that they were born as males in this life as a reward for good deeds in their previous lives. Conversely, they are able to say that to have been born a woman is punishment for ill deeds committed in previous lives. Although at the time of writing Sri Lanka still has a woman president, she too is regarded by these poor men as handicapped because she is a woman. Such is the strength of feeling about gender that they would prefer to be poor and male rather than powerful, rich and female! From that 'original sin' in Buddhist society stems the justification for the privileged position of men and the excuses to keep women under their control. Out of this comes the pride of poor men – they may be poor, but at least they are men. That realisation gives them a confidence which finds no counterpart in the West. They feel that they can change their own lives, those of their families, and the fate of the nation. They take action, often violent action, against each other and against 'their' women and children. They take action as a group against successive governments, in various uprisings, only to get themselves killed. This confidence, justified on religious grounds, is drummed into them through their system of socialisation, which favours boys and men over girls and women.

What happens if the supreme confidence in the all-powerful abilities of males fails them, as it so often does? It is mainly men who are killed in personal conflicts, in civil strife and in wars. Among the Liberation Tigers of Tamil Eelam, fighting for an independent Tamil country in Sri Lanka's northern and eastern districts, the leader gives suicide bombers his personal blessings and assurances of the glory that they will receive in their next lives. In the event of losing their lives, Buddhists can rely on being born males again, if the cause of the death was honourable. Muslims go straight to heaven when they become martyrs for their causes. It is a powerful incentive for acting. And it is also totally understandable why men in poor countries want to hang on to male privilege. It is just about the only one they have in the world.

Although the extreme form of male privilege, especially in poor countries, is understandable, it is not justifiable. It is maintained by the material conditions in those poor countries, and in turn, affects the mental condition of their people – men and women. It is only through improving the material and social conditions that change can be attempted. However, it suits Western interests to keep these countries poor. The West gets cheap oil, cheap labour and other resources by doing so. Men in the West secure their dominant position by maintaining poverty throughout the world. However, it is not politically appropriate to state that, and the messages have to be couched in acceptable rhetoric. Fighting a war requires a certain rhetoric to sell it to people. All wars need enemies – bad, evil people whom the good and just need to fight. Real interests and circumstances have no part in this rhetoric.

It is this kind of rhetoric, together with the division of the world into simple black and white, good and evil, that makes me suspect that we are not going to see a quick conclusion to the war in Afghanistan. This has been both hinted at and stated overtly by US spokesmen as they seek to justify escalation elsewhere. When my own country, Finland, went into severe economic recession in the early 1990s, many scores were settled in the name of the recession. Suddenly it became acceptable that in a welfare state we had record levels of unemployment. This had been in the wings for a long time, as Finland was one of the most automated industrialised nations in the world at that time. Until then, however, it had found no decent way of getting rid of the surplus labour. The recession provided that needed excuse.

What is also certain with the events following September 11 is that much more is at stake than bringing terrorists to meet their justice. This was made apparent by the US Secretary for Defense, Donald Rumsfeld, when he said that it would be preferable to have bin Laden killed than to have him captured. It would be 'convenient', as summary justice has always been. But this also shows – at least to me – that bin Laden is just a small factor in this entire war. Also, I wonder whether there are concerns about what could come out in the investigations should bin Laden, being CIA-trained, be caught alive! Understandably bin Laden is a terrorist, but it is questionable whether this is merely a war against him and terrorism.

Will this, for example, provide the much wanted excuse to rekindle the unfinished business with Saddam Hussein? Will this provide Saddam Hussein a welcome opportunity to launch another war with the US, the country which humiliated him? Men do not suffer public humiliation lightly. Some time ago I studied the institution of blood feuding. In that system, the only way to restore lost male honour is *revenge*. Maybe the only way of restoring the honour of the male institution of presidency is revenge.

So the war was used to settle scores, it was used to strengthen and weaken systems and institutions. It is not long ago that George W Bush was the butt of numerous jokes. Now he is a father figure for most Americans; a tower of strength in these dreadful days following the terrorist acts. Instantly he changed from being Mr Bush, the president, to Mr President, George W Bush. It ceased to matter who occupied that bastion of male power. The US presidency is an all-powerful male institution which has changed the lives of millions of people, not only within the USA but also *outside* it. If terrorists are playing their game at the expense of innocent people, politicians of the Western capitalist nations are doing the same, albeit supported by a different rhetoric. If the terrorists and their supporters call all Muslims to support their cause, so is President Bush calling out to the rest of the world: 'If you are not with us you are against us.' With its economic and military power it is difficult for less powerful nations, such as Finland, to make a free and considered choice on how to react and/or participate. Finland has a female president who initially refused to accept categorically the call by the US but as the weeks rolled on her tone changed. The men in the Parliament and government probably made sure that her initial doubts were drowned.

Any fundamental change is slow, and it is particularly slow when the powerful are asked/demanded to share power more equally. People in power do not usually relinquish power voluntarily. It either has to be taken from them, or they have to be convinced that the benefits accruing from power-sharing are greater than hanging on to their former position. In the West over the last few decades there have been certain changes at the individual level in the male–female relations; small but decisive changes. But I would say that the changes at the institutional level for more equal sharing of institutional power between men and women have been negligible. The age-old male ideas about power and subjugation dominate and are put into effect regardless of the gender of the person wielding that power. However, I am convinced that in order to begin a change in the course of the world to a more peaceful and equal place for all, there has to be a change in men. What is needed especially is to examine and challenge the ideas of masculinity to serve construction rather than destruction, to serve building rather than tearing down, to serve co-operation rather than conflict and competition, to serve peace rather than war.

1. In preparing this article I am very much indebted to Jill Abigail in New Zealand for having not only checked the language and style but also having made many constructive suggestions for the content, including the title. As an ardent, 'old-school' feminist and a person who has most expanded my awareness of gender issues, she knows what I am trying to say here. Sari Vesikansa in Finland as my partner has provided a much needed sounding board in issues brought out here and as a sociologist has been able to comment on the piece both from the ideological and sociological aspects. With Peter Davidson in London we have been able to live through and interact as men of two different generations, to grow together in our struggle to understand ourselves, other men and the world for three decades. He has also provided valuable comments for this piece of writing.

AN ATTACK ON TRUTH?
Elizabeth Stanley

The people clutch the faces, hold on to the names of their kin. In the midst of placards and candles, the relatives seek to have their questions answered; they want to know where their loved ones are, to find out what happened to them. They want the 'truth'.

This scene continues to be played out around the world from Santiago to Buenos Aires, Guatemala City, Belfast and San Salvador. In their grief, people want to understand the history of how certain events happened, they want to know who did what and to whom, and why. Invariably, they disregard the impunity of state officials and seek justice, a 'day in court', some symbolic restoration or societal change.

For the 'Families of the Disappeared' in Chile, September 11 is a date never to be forgotten. It signifies the start of repression. From this point in 1973, the Pinochet dictatorship began to strip away freedom, justice and equality. Throughout the following 17 years, thousands were subject to state-enforced torture, brutality and exile; 2,279 individuals were officially 'disappeared'. Under the political and economic patronage of the UK and the US, among others, Pinochet and his associates have, for the main part, enjoyed free rein ... those who survived the regime's activities continue to march for 'truth'.

Twenty-eight years later, the Chilean families are connected to more grieving families and friends who hold similar cards in their hands and the same date on their lips. In New York, groups congregate with their own questions; they link implicitly with others across the globe in their experience of terror. They understand the pain of not knowing, of not yet understanding.

For bystanders, those of us who watch from a distance, the pain and suffering caused by the recent attacks on the US have been clear to see. From the movie-like 'live' destruction of the twin towers on television screens to the detailed press reports of the heroic behaviour and last words of those caught in the buildings, the personal accounts of such experiences are widely acknowledged. And, indeed, these experiences should be commonly represented and explored; in their detail of individual 'truths' they form the basis of our understanding of the social world.

Such truth-telling, as truth commissions, their participants and their commentators note, can pave the way to promote healing, restore human dignity, demonstrate censure for horrific acts, encourage democratic ideals and promote reconciliation. In sum, truth-telling can underpin societal awareness and transformation. To listen to and, more importantly, acknowledge personal narratives (that confront common-sense assumptions and challenge stereotypical/ historical perceptions) is the first step, following trauma, to collectively deal with the past and plan for the future.

Yet, within this truth-telling framework, two pertinent rules should also be advocated if such positive outcomes are to be reached: (i) truth needs to come from all sides; (ii) individual experience has to be historically contextualised within wider societal and structural relations. Without adherence to these rules, as knowledge from transitional states demonstrates, truth-telling at best loses its value and, at worst, can encourage further conflict. Within Chile, for example, campaigners continue to demand that the military expose their truth of the whereabouts of the disappeared; similarly, others have recently sought to identify how the right-wing repression under Pinochet was supported and guided by CIA activity. For these people, the Chilean National Commission on Truth and Reconciliation did not go far enough in exposing how human rights violations were structured, undertaken and maintained. It is clear, then, that the way 'truth' is told bears resonance over many years; people do not just forget. Memories live on and ensuing conflict, underpinned by feelings of 'injustice' and marginalisation, may intensify over generations.

These rules are worth remembering, particularly in the midst of war when events are susceptible to distorted representation. Indeed, two months after the attacks on the US, the prognosis for 'truth' does not look good. Within the UK, this could be appreciated within days as the BBC gave a public apology for its live transmission of a programme, *Question Time*, which (in its own words) caused offence 'by the ... language and ... attitudes of a small part of the audience'.[1] The 'offensive' remarks, made by a member of a chosen audience, had detailed some reasons why the US, and its foreign policy, was not so universally liked. In the immediate aftermath of the US attacks, structural concerns of neo-colonialist, capitalist agendas could not be drawn on as an explanation for 'terrorism' within mainstream reporting; rather, the focus of 'truth' within the media clamped on individual causation ... the *'evil terrorists'* and, more recently, the *'enemy within'*.

Such disqualification of wider debate has also continued within political frames. With the UK prime minister, Tony Blair, in the principal cheerleading role, there has been little political opposition to the military retaliation against Afghanistan. Those politically elected individuals who have attempted to speak out, raise their concerns and promote alternative responses have been faced with coercive tactics to 'keep the party line'. The most obvious case in point here is that of Labour MP Paul Marsden who, following his request for a parliamentary vote on the bombing of Afghanistan in October 2001, was personally 'pulled back into rank' by government chief whip, Hilary Armstrong. Armstrong is noted as declaring, 'Those that aren't with us are against us ... War is not a matter of conscience ... it is government policy.' Such personal bullying, negating the democratic process, reflects the wider governmental desire to maintain a façade of parliamentary cohesion to political strategy.

In the US, the neutralisation of alternative voices has also extended into the academic community. With more than a whiff of Pinochet practice, US academics who have spoken out against government policy have been threatened and attacked by their own universities. The City University of New York, MIT and the University of Texas, among others, have each made attempts to silence criticism and denounce academics for 'making excuses' for 'terrorists'.

These events, establishing the boundaries of liberal democratic truth-telling, expose the sharp reality of the everyday management of state-accepted discourse. In the context of the current conflict, explanations that legitimise the interests and intentions of Western powerful élites while authorising depictions of the 'enemy' as *the* propaganda merchants are to be coercively maintained if not accepted with consent. Alternative analyses, detailing the historical, political, economic and cultural underpinnings of conflict and violence are subject to official denigration and dismissal.

However, these dominant ideological constructions cannot, and should not, be upheld. After all, the falsely claimed clear distinction between who is deemed to be a 'victim' and who is designated as a 'perpetrator' of violence does not stand up to scrutiny. Two months after the attacks on the US, the police maintained a dead/missing figure of approximately 5,000 people while the companies and organisations, which resided in the twin towers, settled at a figure below 2,500. Conversely, the *New Internationalist*[2] illustrated the point that on September 11 (assuming annual deaths were evenly spread) 24,000 people died of hunger, 6,020 children were killed by diarrhoea and 2,700 children were killed by measles. The latter 'mundane' and preventable deaths, related to the structural imple-mentation of Western 'liberal democratic' agendas, do not serve to delineate a hierarchy of pain or 'victimhood'; rather they allow us to understand that, in some instances, the distinctions between 'per-petrators' and 'victims' overlap.

As a rule, deaths caused by everyday social injustice do not fit neatly into the established categorisation of 'violence'. In their clear link with inequality, discrimination and long-term suffering they are too complex and difficult in their 'truth' to be easily accepted and represented as forms of violence. Classifications of 'violence', 'crime' and 'terrorism' have traditionally reiterated the interests of economic and cultural powers, and the designated 'violence' of September 11 has been no exception. In repeated political rallies, the only pain and suffering to be associated with is that felt within the US. As Tony Blair emotionally urged the UK population, '... Never forget how we felt as we watched planes fly into the trade towers, never forget those answerphone messages ...', he simultaneously dampened the memory of the violence suffered by 'others' on that day and in the continued bombing of Afghanistan.

This construction of violence, however, is not a hard and fast category as, when they have a use value, experiential truths from all sides can be called on to legitimise politically difficult decisions. For example, with growing public concern about the social conditions in Afghanistan, the war became detailed as the means by which 'the starving, the wretched and the dispossessed will be saved' and human rights for Afghani women, in particular, would be secured. In a bizarre twist of (hypocritical) logic, the experiences of Afghani people have been ideologically deployed to maintain legitimacy for the continued bombing in the area. Certainly, an evaluation of previous Western 'support' for the women of Afghanistan would indicate that, far from showing a concern to change their experience, Western foreign policies have maintained the status quo of human rights violations and patriarchal repression. Yet, these sorrowful tales are now used to claim a further elevation in the 'moral high ground' on which retaliatory violence can be undertaken. Here, 'truth' is made to fit.

Clearly, the representational management of 'victims' is one means by which the Western alleviation of responsibility for the broader reality of global suffering can be maintained. In addition, this designation of who is authorised to be a 'victim' underpins decisions on what is deemed to be an appropriate response to a perceived 'perpetrator'. And, here, the implicit links that could be drawn between the diverse forms of violence experienced by those in Chile and the United States are officially destroyed. With just a casual glance at the international collaboration and military action following events in the US, against the uncomfortable belated legal quibbles on the Pinochet case, one issue is clear: violence undertaken *against* the state is subject to far more regulation and 'punishment' than violence undertaken *by* the state.

This is not to argue that truth-telling is closely affiliated to criminal justice. Indicators would actually suggest otherwise, particularly in cases where perpetrators are state officials. All too often the power of the defendants in such cases ensures that they are rarely brought to book within the legal system. Truth-telling, however, is implicitly linked with issues of social justice. After all, the processes of detailing how events occurred, of knowing who did what, to whom and why are quite pointless if they are not followed by some positive response, some form of structural, societal or institutional change. Given the global backdrop of neo-colonialist, capitalist patriarchies which contextualises violence, in its many forms, there is much to be considered here.

An agenda that avoids a challenge to the status quo will serve to consolidate problems and negate possibilities in the future. The promotion of healing, human dignity, democratic ideals and reconciliation each require careful support. They do not occur in a vacuum, nor do they emerge out of short-term fixes. Following his October visit to the 'rogue state' Syria, in which leader Bashar al-Assad condemned the bombing of Afghanistan, Tony Blair commented, 'You can either stay out of the dialogue, or you can try and get into it and build a bridge of understanding for the future.' These words, made in an attempt to curb criticism and embarrassment for misjudged PR, tell an essential truth – that it is only through the exchange of subjective, difficult and diverse viewpoints that change, based on peace-making rather than war-making, may be activated.

1. The BBC apology also included the view that the programme should not have been transmitted 'live'. The programme makers should, in the BBC's view, have had the foresight to allow for the 'editing' of 'offensive' remarks.
2. *New Internationalist*, No. 340, p. 19.

MY BEATING BY REFUGEES IS A SYMBOL OF THE HATRED AND FURY OF THIS FILTHY WAR[1]
Robert Fisk

They started by shaking hands. We said, 'Salaam aleikum' – peace be upon you – then the first pebbles flew past my face. A small boy tried to grab my bag. Then another. Then someone punched me in the back. Then young men broke my glasses, began smashing stones into my face and head. I couldn't see for the blood pouring down my forehead and swamping my eyes. And even then, I understood. I couldn't blame them for what they were doing. In fact, if I were the Afghan refugees of Kila Abdullah, close to the Afghan-Pakistan border, I would have done just the same to Robert Fisk. Or any other Westerner I could find.

So why record my few minutes of terror and self-disgust under assault near the Afghan border, bleeding and crying like an animal, when hundreds – let us be frank and say thousands – of innocent civilians are dying under American air strikes in Afghanistan, when the 'War of Civilisation' is burning and maiming the Pashtuns of Kandahar and destroying their homes because 'good' must triumph over 'evil'? Some of the Afghans in the little village had been there for years, others had arrived – desperate and angry and mourning their slaughtered loved ones – over the past two weeks. It was a bad place for a car to break down. A bad time, just before the Iftar, the end of the daily fast of Ramadan. But what happened to us was symbolic of the hatred and fury and hypocrisy of this filthy war, a growing band of destitute Afghan men, young and old, who saw foreigners – enemies – in their midst and tried to destroy at least one of them.

Many of these Afghans, so we were to learn, were outraged by what they had seen on television of the Mazar-I-Sharif massacres, of the prisoners killed with their hands tied behind their backs. A villager later told one of our drivers that they had seen the videotape of CIA officers 'Mike' and 'Dave' threatening death to a kneeling prisoner at Mazar. They were uneducated – I doubt if many could read – but you don't have to have a schooling to respond to the death of loved ones under a B-52's bombs. At one point a screaming teenager had turned to my driver and asked, in all sincerity, 'Is that Mr Bush?'

It must have been about 4.30 p.m. that we reached Kila Abdullah, halfway between the Pakistani city of Quetta and the border town of

Chaman; Amanullah, our driver, Fayyaz Ahmed, our translator, Justin Huggler of the *Independent* – fresh from covering the Mazar massacre – and myself.

The first we knew that something was wrong was when the car stopped in the middle of the narrow, crowded street. A film of white steam was rising from the bonnet of our jeep, a constant shriek of car horns and buses and trucks and rickshaws protesting at the roadblock we had created. All four of us got out of the car and pushed it to the side of the road. I muttered something to Justin about this being 'a bad place to break down'. Kila Abdullah was home to thousands of Afghan refugees, the poor and huddled masses that the war has produced in Pakistan.

Amanullah went off to find another car – there is only one thing worse than a crowd of angry men and that's a crowd of angry men after dark – and Justin and I smiled at the initially friendly crowd that had already gathered round our steaming vehicle. I shook a lot of hands – perhaps I should have thought of Mr Bush – and uttered a lot of 'Salaam aleikums'. I knew what could happen if the smiling stopped. The crowd grew larger and I suggested to Justin that we move away from the jeep, walk into the open road. A child had flicked his finger hard against my wrist and I persuaded myself that it was an accident, a childish moment of contempt. Then a pebble whisked past my head and bounced off Justin's shoulder. Justin turned round. His eyes spoke of concern and I remember how I breathed in. Please, I thought, it was just a prank. Then another kid tried to grab my bag. It contained my passport, credit cards, money, diary, contacts book, mobile phone. I yanked it back and put the strap round my shoulder. Justin and I crossed the road and someone punched me in the back.

How do you walk out of a dream when the characters suddenly turn hostile? I saw one of the men who had been all smiles when we shook hands. He wasn't smiling now. Some of the smaller boys were still laughing but their grins were transforming into something else. The respected foreigner – the man who had been all 'Salaam aleikum' a few minutes ago – was upset, frightened, on the run. The West was being brought low. Justin was being pushed around and, in the middle of the road, we noticed a bus driver waving us to his vehicle. Fayyaz, still by the car, unable to understand why we had walked away, could no longer see us. Justin reached the bus and climbed aboard. As I put my foot on the step three men grabbed the strap of my bag and wrenched me back on to the road. Justin's hand shot out. 'Hold on', he shouted. I did.

That's when the first mighty crack descended on my head. I almost fell down under the blow, my ears singing with the impact. I had expected this, though not so painful or hard, not so immediate. Its message was awful. Someone hated me enough to hurt me. There were two more blows, one on the back of my shoulder, a powerful fist that sent me crashing against the side of the bus while still clutching Justin's hand. The passengers were looking out at me and then at Justin. But they did not move. No one wanted to help.

I cried out, 'Help me, Justin', and Justin, who was doing more than any human could do by clinging to my ever loosening grip, asked me – over the screams of the crowd – what I wanted him to do. Then I realised. I could only just hear him. Yes, they were shouting. Did I catch the word 'kaffir' – infidel? Perhaps I was wrong. That's when I was dragged away from Justin.

There were two more cracks on my head, one on each side and for some odd reason, part of my memory – some small crack in my brain – registered a moment at school, at a primary school called the Cedars in Maidstone more than 50 years ago when a tall boy building sandcastles in the playground had hit me on the head. I had a memory of the blow smelling, as if it had affected my nose. The next blow came from a man I saw carrying a big stone in his right hand. He brought it down on my forehead with tremendous force and something hot and liquid splashed down my face and lips and chin. I was kicked. On the back, on the shins, on my right thigh. Another teenager grabbed my bag yet again and I was left clinging to the strap, looking up suddenly and realising there must have been 60 men in front of me, howling. Oddly, it wasn't fear I felt but a kind of wonderment. So this is how it happens. I knew that I had to respond. Or, so I reasoned in my stunned state, I had to die.

The only thing that shocked me was my own physical sense of collapse, my growing awareness of the liquid beginning to cover me. I don't think I've ever seen so much blood before. For a second, I caught a glimpse of something terrible, a nightmare face – my own – reflected in the window of the bus, streaked in blood, my hands drenched in the stuff like Lady Macbeth, slopping down my pullover and the collar of my shirt until my back was wet and my bag dripping with crimson and vague splashes suddenly appearing on my trousers.

The more I bled, the more the crowd gathered and beat me with their fists. Pebbles and small stones began to bounce off my head and shoulders. How long, I remembered thinking, could this go on? My head was suddenly struck by stones on both sides at the same time – not thrown stones but stones in the palms of men who were using them to try and crack my skull. Then a fist punched me in the face, splintering my glasses on my nose, another hand grabbed at the spare pair of spectacles round my neck and ripped the leather container from the cord. I guess that at this point I should thank Lebanon. For 25 years, I have covered Lebanon's wars and the Lebanese used to teach me, over and over again, how to stay alive: take a decision – any decision – but don't do nothing.

So I wrenched the bag back from the hands of the young man who was holding it. He stepped back. Then I turned on the man on my right, the one holding the bloody stone in his hand and I bashed my fist into his mouth. I couldn't see very much – my eyes were not only short-sighted without my glasses but were misting over with a red haze – but I saw the man sort of cough and a tooth fall from his lip and then he fell back on the road. For a second the crowd stopped. Then I went for the other man, clutching my bag under my arm and banging my fist into his nose. He roared in anger and it suddenly turned all red. I missed another man with a punch, hit one more in the face, and ran.

I was back in the middle of the road but could not see. I brought my hands to my eyes and they were full of blood, and with my fingers I tried to scrape the gooey stuff out. It made a kind of sucking sound but I began to see again and realised that I was crying and weeping and that the tears were cleaning my eyes of blood. What had I done, I kept asking myself? I had been punching and attacking Afghan refugees, the very people I had been writing about for so long, the very dispossessed, mutilated people whom my own country – among others – was killing, along with the Taliban, just across the border. God spare me, I thought. I think I actually said it. The men whose families our bombers were killing were now my enemies too.

Then something quite remarkable happened. A man walked up to me, very calmly, and took me by the arm. I couldn't see him very well for all the blood that was running into my eyes but he was dressed in a kind of robe and wore a turban and had a white-grey beard. And he led me away from the crowd. I looked over my shoulder. There were now 100 men behind me and a few stones skittered along the road, but they were not aimed at me – presumably to avoid hitting the stranger. He was like an Old Testament figure or from some Bible story, the Good Samaritan, a Muslim man – perhaps a mullah in the village – who was trying to save my life.

He pushed me into the back of a police truck. But the policemen didn't move. They were terrified. 'Help me', I kept shouting through the tiny window at the back of their cab, my hands leaving streams of blood down the glass. They drove a few metres and stopped until the tall man spoke to them again. Then they drove another 300 metres.

And there, beside the road, was a Red Cross-Red Crescent convoy. The crowd was still behind us. But two of the medical attendants pulled me behind one of their vehicles, poured water over my hands and face and began pushing bandages on to my head and face and the back of my head. 'Lie down and we'll cover you with a blanket so they can't see you', one of them said. They were both Muslims, Bangladeshis, and their names should be recorded because they were good men and true: Mohamed Abdul Halim and Sikder Mokaddes Ahmed. I lay on the floor, groaning, aware that I might live.

Within minutes, Justin arrived. He had been protected by a massive soldier from the Baluchistan Levies – true ghost of the British Empire – who, with a single rifle, kept the crowds away from the car in which Justin was now sitting. I fumbled with my bag. They never got the bag, I kept saying to myself, as if my passport and my credit cards were a kind of Holy Grail. But they had seized my final pair of spare glasses – I was blind without all three – and my mobile telephone was missing and so was my contacts book, containing 25 years of telephone numbers throughout the Middle East. What was I supposed to do? Ask everyone who ever knew me to re-send their telephone numbers?

'Goddamit', I said and tried to bang my fist on my side until I realised it was bleeding from a big gash on the wrist – the mark of the tooth I had just knocked out of a man's jaw, a man who was truly innocent of any crime except that of being the victim of the world.

I had spent more than two and a half decades reporting the humiliation and misery of the Muslim world and now their anger had embraced me too. Or had it? There were Mohamed and Sikder of the Red Crescent and Fayyaz who came panting back to the car incandescent at our treatment and Amanullah who invited us to his home for medical treatment. And there was the Muslim saint who had taken me by the arm. And – I realised – there were all the Afghan men and boys who had attacked me who should never have done so but whose brutality was entirely the product of others, of us – of we who had armed their struggle against the Russians and ignored their pain and laughed at their civil war and then armed and paid them again for the 'War for Civilisation' just a few miles away and then bombed their homes and ripped up their families and called them 'collateral damage'.

So I thought I should write about what happened to us in this fearful, silly, bloody, tiny incident. I feared other versions would produce a different narrative, of how a British journalist was 'beaten up by a mob of Afghan refugees'. And of course, that's the point. The people who were assaulted were the Afghans, the scars inflicted by us – by B-52s, not by them. And I'll say it again. If I were an Afghan refugee in Kila Abdullah, I would have done just what they did. I would have attacked Robert Fisk. Or any other Westerner I could find.

1. First published in the *Independent*, December 10, 2001.

IN THE NAME OF A 'JUST WAR'
Phil Scraton

The politics of atrocity

> It is our hope that they [Northern Alliance] will not engage in negotiations that would provide for the release of al-Qaida forces; that would provide for the release of foreign nationals leaving the country and destabilising neighbouring countries ... So my hope is that they will either be killed or taken prisoners.
>
> Donald Rumsfeld, US Defense Secretary
> November 19, 2001

> These things happen in war. Just remember that these people in the prison were al-Qaida fighters ... We do not see a need for an inquiry. Nasty things happen in war.
>
> Peter Hain, UK Foreign Minister
> BBC Radio 5, November 29, 2001

The prosecution of the 'war on terror' in Afghanistan was constructed to maximise the destruction of the Taliban regime and to minimise the possibility of US and allied soldiers returning home in body bags. Aerial bombardment, using cruise missiles, carpet and cluster bombing, guaranteed a war offensive without retaliation. The lack of effective anti-aircraft defences, or anything resembling an air force, enabled bombing virtually without risk. On the ground the war was conducted by the notoriously fractured Northern Alliance whose own history of human rights violations made it an uneasy bedfellow for Western democratic governments espousing a rhetoric peppered with the vocabulary of 'freedom', 'justice', 'community' and 'rights'. Whatever its claims of special forces' intelligence directing the military action, as the war progressed it became increasingly clear that Northern Alliance commanders were instrumental in defining targets and establishing priorities.

With the trenches and caves no match for sophisticated, deadly ordnance, the Taliban forces – despite media and political hype to the contrary – could not withstand the bombing. The full extent of the casualties inflicted by the air strikes remains unclear but it became obvious that once the ground war developed there would be little effective resistance to the advance of the Northern Alliance. The US military command could not but have anticipated that the Northern Alliance would show no mercy to the Taliban forces, particularly the hated foreign recruits. US Defense Secretary Donald Rumsfeld must have known that his preference for the imprisonment or killing of foreign nationals would be interpreted as tacitly condoning torture, brutality and summary execution. It also appeared to locate al-Qaida forces beyond the reach of the Geneva Conventions.

In this climate what ensued at the Qala-I-Jhangi fortress close to the northern town of Mazar-I-Sharif seemed as inevitable as it was appalling. Towards the end of November the Northern Alliance closed in on the northern city of Kunduz, a Taliban stronghold with 12,000 soldiers supported by 2,000 foreign nationals. A cessation in the fighting was negotiated, exchanging a safe passage for the Taliban command and élite guard for unconditional surrender. The fate of the foreign nationals, however, was unclear. Despite open divisions in its regional leadership, the Northern Alliance guaranteed fair treatment of prisoners of war in accordance with international law and conventions. Yet Rumsfeld issued a statement making it clear that the US was 'not inclined to negotiate surrender'.[1] A British defence source judged Rumsfeld's comment 'belligerent'. The UK foreign secretary, Jack Straw, asserted his government's commitment to avoiding 'a massacre'. Professor Adam Roberts considered it 'shocking' that the Pentagon had been 'unclear on the basic and simple point that if the fighters in Kunduz surrender, they will not be massacred'.[2]

Following their surrender several hundred Taliban fighters, of whom only a small number were Afghan, were imprisoned by the Northern Alliance, supported on the ground by a handful of US Special Forces personnel, at the Qala-I-Jhangi fortress near to the town of Mazar-I-Sharif. This would allow US forces the opportunity to conduct intelligence-gathering interrogations. Within two days of their surrender possibly as many as 400 lay dead. A group of prisoners, assuming they were about to be executed as guards tied their hands behind their backs, rebelled and seized weapons. In the ensuing panic, and following the shooting of a CIA interrogator, another US agent called in helicopters and troops. Within hours, 'American missiles plunged into the area ... killing hundreds of prisoners in an inferno.' The bombardment, to the displeasure of the Northern Alliance command, killed and injured many of its soldiers. Having accessed the fort's armoury a group of Taliban fighters dug in and British SAS soldiers assumed co-ordination of the operation. Eventually the insurrection was ended. There were few survivors and many of those who died did so with their hands tied. Bodies were desecrated as Northern Alliance soldiers removed gold teeth.

As Jonathan Freedland reflected, 'Many will baulk at calling this a massacre because the Taliban seemed to bring their fate upon themselves by rebelling, thereby forfeiting their right to Geneva Convention protection as prisoners of war.'[3] Certainly this was the British government position; a source was quoted as stating that Qala-I-Jhangi had been a 'situation in which prisoners tried to break out with grenades and Kalashnikovs' which 'had to be dealt with and you cannot be too squeamish'.[4] Yet significant questions required answers. Why, in an impromptu decision, were so many prisoners incarcerated in a compound known to house heavy weaponry? Why were so many killed when only a few rebelled? In what circumstances did prisoners die while remaining bound? What was the relationship on the ground between US personnel and the Northern Alliance? Was the force used, particularly the aerial bombardment, proportionate?

As international criticism of the circumstances surrounding the deaths at the fortress mounted, the US attempted to distance itself, claiming that the prisoners were a Northern Alliance responsibility.

Amnesty International and the UN High Commissioner for Human Rights, Mary Robinson, called for a full inquiry. But UK foreign minister, Peter Hain, responded that an inquiry was 'unnecessary' given that those killed were 'al-Qaida fighters' and '[n]asty things happen in war'. He appeared to suggest that because of the prisoners' status or because of the war's status, the rules and conventions of engagement and incarceration could be abandoned. Yet Jack Straw's assessment at the outset indicated that a massacre was on the cards. After all, it would not have been without precedent.

Just two weeks earlier at a school in Mazar-I-Sharif independent eyewitnesses reported that many of the 520 Pakistani recruits to the Taliban cause had been killed while trying to surrender.[5] Allegedly they were attacked by US airplanes and those who survived were taken prisoner by the Northern Alliance. The Red Cross claimed that 250 were killed either by the bombardment or by execution. As Kunduz was taken confirmed reports emerged of wounded prisoners being shot and left to die in the streets. This followed similar summary executions and fatal beatings administered after the fall of Kabul. According to a Northern Alliance commander, in the aftermath of a battle at Takteh Pol in southern Afghanistan, and apparently in the presence of US military personnel, his soldiers lined up and machine-gunned 160 Taliban prisoners.

On December 23 the inauguration of the interim administration took place in Kabul. The previous day, based on unattributed 'intelligence', US warplanes destroyed a convoy claimed by the Afghan Islamic Press to comprise delegates to the inauguration. Over 60 people were killed, offering no defence against the attacks. US military sources justified the use of force, stating that those killed were Taliban or al-Qaida leaders. As the war continued into January 2002 the US deployed the 'vacuum' bomb used previously against Iraq in the Gulf War. Designed to suck oxygen from confined areas, such as dug-in trenches, tunnels and caves, it kills through depletion of lungs and haemorrhaging of vital organs.

A war without end

Despite the progress in Afghanistan, the global war against terror is still in its early stages. The terrorist networks that threaten us operate in dozens of different countries, and terrorist threats against both of our nations' citizens and interests continue.

Meeting the challenges ahead will require sacrifice, determination and perseverance.

Donald Rumsfeld, US Defense Secretary
December 2, 2001

From the onset of military action the US made it clear to the world that regardless of 'progress' in Afghanistan the 'war on terror' would be taken to other nation-states. As the BBC veteran war reporter, John Simpson, marched liberation-style into Kabul it was apparent that Taliban military defences, regardless of the resilience and tenacity of individuals, were fragile. It should not have taken military analysts much concentrated thought to realise that the Taliban would not last long. The sheer weight and relentlessness of the bombing meant that the Northern Alliance ground offensive would meet with little sustained opposition.

Those who planned and supported the bombing of Afghanistan hailed the Taliban's fall a great success. They heaped derision on anti-war campaigners and presented the Bush administration as heroic. Amid this triumphalism, however, the more detailed and profound consequences of the military action were neglected. The two primary objectives of the 'war on terror' were not achieved. Osama bin Laden had been neither killed nor captured and al-Qaida's network had not been broken. The Taliban regime had been overthrown but, however pernicious its rule, the US/allied role in the forcible removal of a government set a troubling contemporary precedent. As Rumsfeld inferred, by naming a state as supportive of or involved with proscribed terrorist groups, it would become a legitimate target for US-led military intervention, its government deposed and a replacement regime negotiated. The US had claimed for itself the power to intervene with impunity in the domestic affairs of regimes which, by its own imposed criteria, did not meet with approval.

That impunity extended to denying responsibility for contributing to or investigating atrocities, and also to the infliction of civilian casualties. The US media showed little interest in the deaths of Afghan civilians, occasionally noting 'regret' over 'collateral damage'. Such deaths were 'rare', 'accidental' casualties of war. US and allied audiences were reminded of the thousands killed in the World Trade Center and Pentagon attacks, about the inhumanity of the Taliban and about 'who started the war' in the first place. Yet, casualties were high. Independent research by University of New

Hampshire economics professor, Marc Herold, estimated civilian deaths between October 7 and December 10 at 3,767.[6] Herold's methodology and findings have been contested but disputes over calculating civilian deaths are perverse, given the indiscriminate and persistent bombardment.

Herold's research was based on 'corroborated reports from aid agencies, the UN, eyewitnesses, TV stations, newspapers and news agencies' applying 'conservative assumptions ... to each incident'. It did not include those who died subsequently from their injuries, those killed after December 10 and those dying from cold, hunger or homelessness. Neither did it include military victims nor the prisoners killed at Mazar-I-Sharif, Qala-I-Jhangi, Takteh Pol, Kandahar and in other incidents. Seumas Milne, questioning the morality of civilian deaths in the context of a 'just war' concluded that they were not 'an accidental by-product of the decision to overthrow the Taliban regime, but because of the low value put on Afghan civilian lives by US military planners'. Milne's argument is well-illustrated by his chilling account of 93 villagers killed at Chowkar-Karez, randomly strafed by US gunships. He quotes a Pentagon official: 'The people there are dead because we wanted them dead.'

These were the very issues which created sustained political opposition to the 'war on terror' throughout Western democracies. Yet, as Law Professor Patricia Williams noted, 'student demonstrators, global justice workers, civil libertarians, animal rights and peace activists' throughout the US had 'become characterised as terrorist sympathisers'.[7] By late November over one thousand people in the US had been 'arrested and held, approximately 800 with no disclosure of identities or location or charges against them'. Widespread public support was polled for the use of torture to extract information relating to terrorism and the US PATRIOT Act, enabling law enforcers to 'gather information with few checks and balances from the judiciary', was introduced.

Williams argued that state-legitimated 'righteous lawlessness', previously institutionalised and 'practiced in oppressed communities', had a substantial constituency in contemporary America. Given the rise and consolidation of excessive imprisonment over the last two decades, the denial of 'natural justice' embodied in draconian legislation and the show-boating of capital punishment, the post-September 11 attack on rights and liberties is unsurprising. The enthusiasm to 'embrace profiling based on looks and ethnicity; detention without charges; searches without warrants; and even torture and assassination', however shocking, is the inevitable consequence of what Christian Parenti astutely names 'Lockdown America'.[8]

In the UK on December 14, 2001, just three months after the September 11 attacks the Anti-Terrorism, Crime and Security Act became law. Focusing on the investigation of crime and the use of surveillance the Act enables the unlimited detention of those suspected of terrorism who cannot be removed from the country. Grounds for suspicion lie with information provided by the security and intelligence services, with no right of disclosure of that information. All telecommunications providers are required to hold all data (internet, emails, telephone calls) for twelve months with access granted for 'safeguarding national security' and 'for the purposes of prevention or detection of crime' or the 'prosecution of offenders' relating 'directly or indirectly to national security'. National security is threatened not only by acts of 'terrorism' but also through acts of 'subversion'. Among the range of powers granted to the police, customs and immigration services are the exchange of personal data and the retention for ten years of fingerprints taken from asylum seekers and refugees.

Mary Robinson, the UN High Commissioner for Human Rights, was so troubled by the domestic impact of the 'war on terror' that she requested 'all governments to refrain from excessive steps which would violate fundamental freedoms and undermine legitimate rights'.[9] Anti-terrorism measures, she stated, should 'protect human rights and democracy' and not 'undermine these fundamental values of our societies'. Yet the die had been cast. As in the US, a moral climate founded on righteous indignation and a calculus of retribution enabled the introduction of authoritarian powers and punitive sanctions. If the 'war on terror' was to succeed abroad, its elimination would begin at home.

Prisoners of the states

Prison expansionism in the US, although uneven across states, has left England and Wales – Europe's primary carceral state – in the shade. It did not happen by chance. As Elliott Currie states, in the late 1960s successive commissions into crime and urban disorders 'called for a *balanced* approach to crime' wanting 'a strong and efficient criminal justice system' alongside broader social reform. Their message was that 'we could never imprison our way out of

America's violent crime problem'. To defeat violent crime and urban unrest would mean 'attacking social exclusion'. The alternative, the 'second road' at 'the crossroads', was to neglect social disadvantage, the material reality of poverty and marginalisation and hit offenders hard with harsher laws, zero-tolerance policing and uncompromising prison regimes. Successive US administrations took the second road resulting in 'bursting prisons, devastated cities and a violent crime rate still unmatched in the developed world'.[10]

In his excellent book, *Crime Control as Industry*, Nils Christie reflects on the 1980s' explosion in US incarceration, the harsh treatment of prisoners, the 'new techniques' and instruments of containment and the consolidation of super maximum security prisons. The latter use chains, manacles, isolation, natural light deprivation, 'non-lethal' weapons and ritual humiliation to impose confinement in the supposed 'free world'. Reading *Corrections Today*, the official publication of the American Correctional Association, Christie was 'close to not trusting my own eyes'. Images of prisoners – 'who would love to stab, slash, pound, punch and burn' their captors – were 'unbelievable'. Yet the Association, its interests fully integrated with large multinationals as providers of the fabric and means of imprisonment, was 'the organisation with the mandate to administer the ultimate power of society ... an organisation for the delivery of pain ... sponsored by those who make the tools'.[11]

Christian Parenti's detailed exposé of the institutionalised violence endemic in California's maximum-security prisons demonstrates chillingly that it is 'an extreme expression of the nationwide campaign to degrade and abuse convicts'. The issue being that in order to prove their hard-line credentials politicians have perfected a 'rhetoric' which demonstrates to the electorate that 'going to prison is no longer punishment enough'. In this volatile context of public clamour and political opportunism has risen 'a wave of political fads: from chain gangs and striped uniforms, to the stunning evisceration of prisoners' legal rights'.[12] It amounts to a 'bureaucratic abuse' with the terrifying outcomes of deprivation, rape, torture and even death. Parenti's research shows that prisons, the industrial-penal complex, expanded dramatically over four decades – functioning 'to terrorise the poor, warehouse social dynamite and social wreckage'. The pathologising of the poor and the marginalised, supported by academic constructions of the 'underclass', justified and legitimated 'state repression and the militarisation of public space ...'.[13]

Within the UK the excesses of US incarceration, either in numbers imprisoned or in the sheer viciousness of regimes, their forms of containment and use of weapons, have not developed throughout the system, the exception being the conditions and practices endured by Irish prisoners. More broadly, the social and political climate has produced and sustained a popular commitment to longer sentences, harsher conditions and reduced prisoner rights. Certainly there has been no effective challenge to the Conservative slogan 'Prison Works' and no discernible concern about the escalation in imprisonment since the Labour Government's election in 1997. Despite much evidence to the contrary, the incarceration of children as young as ten and the catastrophic failure of prisons 'on their own terms', the public perception is that of 'holiday camps' where prisoners enjoy rehabilitation and education programmes at the taxpayers' expense. That the Prison Service Inspectorate has condemned the conditions and regimes suffered by those imprisoned in the main young offenders' and women's jails and has criticised the squalor of Victorian prisons is of little consequence to a media locked into a 'soft-on-crime' mindset. With virtually no public concern expressed over the appalling conditions inflicted on those sentenced for minor criminal offences, it follows that apathy is exchanged for outright hostility towards those convicted of 'terrorist' offences.

Intimidation, abuse and degradation have characterised the incarceration of Irish nationalist prisoners, men and women, held in British jails for over a quarter of a century. Yet it was early in 1997, following two aborted trials of high security prisoners who had escaped from Whitemoor prison, that a judge abandoned proceedings because he deemed them mentally unfit to stand trial. The conditions in which they had been held since recapture had made them ill. The UK government's chief medical officer found that secure regimes within the special units were so 'cramped' and 'claustrophobic', lacking in 'meaningful work ... social contact and incentives', that 'it was likely over a course of years that a proportion of them [prisoners] would develop significant adverse effects to mental health'. This was, he concluded, unacceptable. All prisoners, regardless of their offence, were entitled to the 'same rights as regards health and healthcare as any other person in the country'.[14]

Taken together the UK court ruling and the chief medical officer's findings represent a damning indictment of regimes which, however politically expedient and popular with sections of the media, gradually weaken the resolve and break the spirit of individuals through inhumane and degrading treatment. It is against this backcloth, both in the US and the UK, that the punishing regime inflicted on alleged al-Qaida or pro-Taliban soldiers, taken prisoner in Afghanistan and incarcerated 8,000 miles away in Camp X-Ray at the US naval base, Guantanamo Bay, has to be considered. The arrival of the first 20 prisoners immediately raised serious questions about the application of 'justice' pursued by the US administration. Denied prisoner-of-war status they were held and transported without the protection of international law or the Geneva Conventions. Incarcerated outside US sovereign territory, they were unprotected by the US Constitution and, in the event of prosecution, had no right to jury trial.

Donald Rumsfeld was unbending: 'They will be handled not as prisoners of war, because they are not, but as unlawful combatants.' By classifying them as unlawful combatants he enabled their prosecution through military commissions thus providing more permissive rules of evidence and a lesser burden of proof to secure conviction than obtains in regular criminal courts. Yet within the terms of the Geneva Conventions Rumsfeld did not have the authority to reclassify them as unlawful combatants. The legal status of those captured in armed conflict can be determined only by an appropriate, recognised court or tribunal. The 'war on terror', according to Rumsfeld, was not a war. In the military conflict the only legitimate 'military' personnel belonged to the US and its allies. Having defined the parameters and theatre of war the US now designated the status of combatants and the forums of justice.

As the first consignment of 'unlawful combatants' arrived at Camp X-Ray the consequences of reclassification became apparent. Dressed in bright orange boiler suits, wearing caps, taped-over goggles and surgical masks they were bound, shackled and, in some cases, sedated. Other than masks and enforced blindness, however, their state was little different to that of regular prisoners in transit throughout the US penal system. Sensory deprivation and sedation were justified by the senior officer in charge of the security operation: 'We asked for the bad guys first.' These prisoners were the 'worst of the worst' and, according to Rumsfeld, would be 'perfectly willing to kill themselves and kill other people'. According to the US Joint Chief of Staff they 'would gnaw through hydraulic lines in a C-17 [troop carrying aircraft] to bring it down'. Bound, manacled, blindfolded and shackled, they were then caged. Their 'cells' were 8 foot by 8 foot outdoor chain-link cages, affording little protection from the weather or from mosquitoes. They slept on mats, sheets for bedding, under halogen floodlights. As a direct affront to their cultural and religious beliefs their beards were shaved.

Within days of the international outcry over the classification and treatment of the prisoners the Pentagon embarked on a spectacularly incompetent public relations exercise. It issued full colour photographs of the detainees, manacled and masked, kneeling before their armed captors. Their humiliation was palpable and the US soldiers' physical domination clearly more than symbolic. Presumably published to demonstrate the uncompromising response of the US administration to terrorism, the photographs not only caused grave concern throughout Western democracies, but they fuelled the deep resentment of US double standards prevalent within Muslim nations and communities. As Richard Norton-Taylor commented, the photographs showed a 'complete disregard, not to say contempt, [within] the Bush administration ... for international opinion'. The prevalent view of the US government, he concluded, was 'that the US does not need to be bound by international law, any more than it does by international arms control treaties, and that military might is enough'.[15]

It was the informed opinion of the International Red Cross that whatever the status ascribed by the US, all prisoners taken in Afghanistan should have been held under the terms of the Geneva Conventions, including the international standards prohibiting 'cruel, degrading and inhumane treatment'. While it is not policy for Red Cross inspection teams to publicise their findings it soon became clear that the organisation was at odds with the US administration over status, conditions and practices at Camp X-Ray. Others did voice their opinion. Kenneth Roth, executive director of Human Rights Watch, raised the paradox inherent within the US procedures: 'Terrorists believe that anything goes in the name of their cause. The fight against terror must not buy into that logic. Human rights principles must not be compromised in the name of any cause.'[16]

Typically and predictably, Donald Rumsfeld dismissed the allegations of inhumane treatment at Camp X-Ray as 'utter nonsense'. America, he said, 'is not what's wrong with the world'. He continued: 'Let there be no doubt, the treatment of detainees is proper ... humane ... appropriate ... and fully consistent with international conventions.' The 'truth ultimately wins out' and 'the truth of the matter is they're being treated humanely'.[17] Within days of this robust, uncompromising statement, following an inspection by the

International Red Cross and rumours of Colin Powell's concern over the classification and treatment of the prisoners, the US authorities announced a review of the conditions of containment.

In the UK such unease began to surface within government. Initially willing to go along with the US classification of prisoners, the Foreign Office stated that legal status was a matter solely for the US. Within days, however, Defence Secretary Geoff Hoon commented that they had to be detained 'with proper respect for international law'. As it emerged that British citizens were among those imprisoned in Camp X-Ray the mood shifted to one of returning those prisoners to the UK to stand trial. Yet all was not well in Britain concerning 'terrorist' suspects incarcerated under the terms of new legislation.

At Belmarsh high security prison those held without charge endured inappropriate conditions. Locked in isolation without natural light for 22 hours each day, initially denied access to solicitors or families, their detention became a cause for concern. Human rights lawyer, Gareth Peirce stated, 'These men have been buried alive in concrete coffins and have been told the legislation provides for their detention for life without trial.'[18] Complaints included intimidation, abuse, strip searches and refused medication. None of the detainees were charged with any crime but were, in effect, internees technically innocent and held on suspicion of unspecified involvement in terrorist activities.

Given the circumstances and the protection afforded by international law and conventions, the treatment meted out to prisoners held at Camp X-Ray and within the US and UK could not be defended. It amounted to degrading and inhumane imprisonment. The unwillingness of the US administration to have the issue of prisoner status settled by an appropriate court or tribunal provided unequivocal evidence of political, and military, interference in the judicial process. Shifting definitions of 'war' made mockery of the much trumpeted legitimacy of this first and frightful stage of the 'war on terror'. Yet public opinion in the US and the UK remained content that the status, conditions and treatment afforded to prisoners held without charge were reasonable. So powerful had been the 'moral panic' around 'terrorism' that the very civilised values that Bush and Blair had been so eager to defend in rhetoric were lost in practice. It amounted to a dreadful end game, the rules of which were justified through constant reference to the attacks on the US and its vengeful, hateful 'war on terror'. Frustrated by their seeming inability to locate

Osama bin Laden or the al-Qaida leadership, the US administration used those held captive as the tangible manifestation of the terrorism responsible for the deaths at the World Trade Center and the Pentagon. By labelling those 'innocent until proven guilty' as the 'worst of the worst' the moral high ground was finally vacated.

Defending the 'civilised world'

On January 29, 2002 George W Bush gave his State of the Nation address. A president whose popularity bordered on the unelectable just a year earlier, whose credibility at home and abroad had seemed torn beyond repair, now enjoyed an 82 per cent rating within the US. The key to this remarkable turnabout was in his first sentence: 'As we gather tonight, our nation is at war ... '[19] Forget the economic recession, ignore the criticisms of US global domination and reject the growing alienation of populations throughout the Middle East and Asia, 'the State of our Union has never been stronger'. As Bush was constantly interrupted by waves of enthusiastic applause, 77 times in all, his triumphalism was unrestrained: 'Our nation has comforted the victims ... rallied a great coalition, captured, arrested, and rid the world of thousands of terrorists, destroyed Afghanistan's terrorist training camps, saved a people from starvation, and freed a country from brutal oppression.'

Thanks to the US military 'we are winning the war on terror'. The message of the Afghanistan intervention was 'now clear to every enemy of the United States: even 7,000 miles away, across mountains and continents, on mountaintops and in caves – you will not escape the justice of this nation'. Yet the 'war' on terror was in its infancy as 'tens of thousands of trained terrorists ... schooled in the methods of murder, often supported by outlaw regimes' remained at large. The twin objectives for the US and its allies were the elimination of terrorist training camps and the bringing of terrorists to justice alongside the prevention of regimes 'who seek chemical, biological or nuclear weapons from threatening the United States and the world'. While 'training camps operate' and 'nations harbour terrorists, freedom is at risk'. And so, 'our war against terror is only beginning'. It represented 'the civilised world' against the rest.

Bush named the states and their 'terrorist allies' which 'constitute an axis of evil', the regimes that 'pose a grave and growing danger'. The US knew 'the true nature' of North Korea, Iran, Iraq and Somalia. Iraq was 'a regime that has something to hide from the civilised world'. Meanwhile, the US remained operational in Bosnia, the

Philippines and off the coast of Africa 'acting' to 'eliminate the terrorist parasites'. Whatever proved 'necessary to ensure our nation's security' would be done without hesitation or further provocation for 'the price of indifference would be catastrophic'. As has been the habit of many contemporary US senior politicians, Bush transformed collective responsibility for waging war into one of destiny and honour: 'History has called America and our allies to action, and it is both our responsibility and our privilege to fight freedom's fight.'

History and freedom become self-evident determinants that seemingly release the US and its allies from voluntarism and choice. Perhaps Sir Paul McCartney, with an equally uncomplicated lyric written in support of the post-September 11 military action, more succinctly caught the populist mood that projected Bush's poll ratings into the stratosphere: 'This is my right/A right given by God/To live a free life/To live in freedom/Anyone who tries to take it away/Will have to answer/For this is my right/Talkin' about freedom/Talkin' about freedom/I'll fight for the right/To live in freedom'. Concert hall or Congress hall, the audience was ecstatic; a president and a Knight of the Realm together in perfect harmony. What was remarkable, perhaps not when Thatcher's Falklands/Malvinas War is remembered, was how Bush became elevated to major league statesman and presidential hero while the US economic recession deepened and international markets recoiled from the spectacular collapse of Enron. His State of the Nation speech pressed the right buttons, making spurious yet convincing connections between the necessity of costly military interventions abroad and swallowing the bitter pill of economic downturn.

Apparently subjected to 17 redrafts, the speech sabre-rattled its way through to the 'billion dollars a month' cost of the 'war on terror' and the promise of a pay rise for the 'men and women in uniform'. Bush justified the 'largest increase in defence spending', stating that 'while the price of freedom and security is high, it is never too high. Whatever it costs to defend our country, we will pay.' Not only was this a commitment to bankrolling the 'war', but also to doubling the funds available to establish 'a sustained strategy of homeland security' focused on 'bioterrorism, emergency response, airport and border security, and improved intelligence'. Built on the twin foundations of the 'war on terror' and 'homeland security' would be the 'final great priority ... economic security for the American people'.

Thus the three objectives were successfully interwoven: winning the war, protecting the homeland and revitalising the economy. The 'priorities' were 'clear' and the 'purpose and resolve we have shown overseas' would succeed 'at home': 'We'll prevail in the war, and we will defeat this recession.' Bush's knockabout one-liners on jobs, energy, trade, tax cuts, welfare reform, teaching and health security represented a cynical exercise mobilising ideologies and rhetoric of patriotism and freedom to demand public acceptance of unemployment, low-pay long-term poverty and social exclusion.

The carefully choreographed and interminably rehearsed delivery sought and received endorsement from the newly liberated, from the bereaved and from the heroes. During the address he welcomed to Congress Chairman Hamid Karzai, the Afghanistan interim leader, and Dr Sima Samar, the new minister of women's affairs. At the moment of remembrance to those who had died at Ground Zero he introduced Shannon Spann, the wife of the CIA officer killed at Mazar-I-Sharif. And while affirming his commitment to homeland security he acknowledged the two flight attendants who had apprehended the British 'heel-bomber' in flight. His final introduction, as he reflected on the 'courage and compassion, strength and resolve' of the American people, was 'our First Lady, Laura Bush'. She had brought 'strength and calm and comfort' to 'our nation in crisis'.

Bush made a commitment to the expansion of the US Freedom Corps (homeland security) and the Peace Corps, encouraging 'development and education and opportunity in the Islamic world'. This expansion would be at the heart of 'a new culture of responsibility'. The US had taken the lead, 'defending liberty and justice because they are right and true and unchanging for people everywhere'. There was 'no intention' to impose 'our culture' but the 'demands of human dignity: the rule of law; limits on the power of the state; respect for women; private property; free speech; equal justice; and religious tolerance' were 'non-negotiable'. He concluded: 'Steadfast in our purpose, we now press on. We have known freedom's price. We have shown freedom's power. And in this great conflict, my fellow Americans, we will see freedom's victory.'

On the long march to freedom Bush was not celebrating a war won. He was not winding down a reactive and reactionary operation which had deposed a brutal and brutalising regime. Rather, he was proclaiming the initial success of what would be an enduring military offensive which 'may not be finished on our watch ...'. The US had taken it upon itself to use its superpower, lone ranger status to police globally and engage selectively according to its criteria for establishing terrorism, its definitions of lawful combat and its acceptance of international conventions regarding war. The shame and guilt of Vietnam finally had been buried deep in the rubble of Afghanistan. A 'just' war was a war so labelled; 'justice' was justice according to the US administration. And the primary enemies, comprising a 'terrorist underworld', were offered to the American nation: Hamas, Hezbollah, Islamic Jihad, Jaish-i-Mohammed.

As Bush was widely criticised for cranking up the volume of war, particularly his endorsement of populist assumptions about 'civilisation', 'evil' and 'terrorism', he fiercely condemned 'nations that developed weapons of mass destruction' that might 'team up with' or give shelter to terrorist groups.[20] These were the nations on the US 'watch list'. He continued, 'People say, well, what does that mean? It means they had better get their house in order is what it means. It means they better respect the rule of law. It means they better not try to terrorise America and our friends and allies or the justice of the nation will be served on them as well.' So that was what carpet-bombing, cluster bombs, collateral damage, atrocities, civilian deaths and Camp X-Ray together amounted to: US justice.

While Bush appeared to enthuse at the projection of 'tens of thousands of trained terrorists' on the loose, providing him and his administration with their calling, a real and present danger was inspired by US words and deeds. Throughout Asia and the Middle East the deep distrust of the US, the hate directed against its military-industrial complex and cultural imperialism and its open disdain for human rights while mouthing rhetoric of the 'civilised' against the 'uncivilised', emphasised a profoundly riven world. For 'Third World' nations already knew to their cost that the US had never promoted globalisation – politically, economically or culturally – as an arena for equal participation, equal shares or equal opportunities.

Five months on from the September 11 attacks and many deaths beyond those at the World Trade Center, the Pentagon and in the Pennsylvania countryside, the enduring casualty – as so often the case – is truth. The struggle for truth is about making public and private institutions accountable for their definitions, policies, strategies and actions. It is about challenging what Foucault analysed as 'regimes of truth' through the critique of power relations. Power that has the ability, capacity and ideological appeal to harm with political confidence and legal impunity. Power that has the authority to confer legitimacy on external military action and on internal law enforcement. To this end it can establish partial investigations, deny disclosure of information and evidence and place restrictions on findings.

Conversely, it is formidable in its capacity to deny legitimacy, neutralise opposition and disqualify knowledge – ruling alternative accounts out of court. It pathologises victims, survivors and campaigners, using patriotism, loyalty and ostracism as means of silencing. The condemners become condemned. The demonisation and vilification at first directed towards the 'terrorists' is redirected towards 'sympathisers', 'appeasers' and 'traitors'. Within this distorted world of 'with us or against us' the casualties of war, regardless of their status as military or civilian, are held responsible; their losses, their injuries, their suffering reconstructed as self-inflicted. With so much reporting and commentary derived in the manufacture and selection of news through spin and manipulation, it is not difficult for states and their administrations to deny responsibility for their part in atrocities, their part in the long-term consequences of war. 'Refusal to acknowledge' reveals the power within advanced capitalist states at its most cynical, its most self-serving. History soon becomes rewritten, truth becomes degraded, the pain of death and destruction heightened by the pain of deceit and denial. It is from within this experience that the next generation of terror strategists will emerge and develop their consciousness. And the 'sacrifice, determination and perseverance' demanded by Rumsfeld in the US global 'war on terror' will be matched.

1. *Guardian*, November 24, 2001.
2. Roberts, Adam, 'Crisis at Kunduz', *Guardian*, November 24, 2001, p. 20.
3. Freedland, Jonathan, 'Playing the Great Game', *Guardian*, November 28, 2001, p. 21.
4. *Guardian*, November 29, 2001.
5. *Guardian*, November 24, 2001.
6. Quoted in Milne, Seumas, 'The innocent dead in a coward's war', *Guardian*, December 20, 2001.
7. Williams, Patricia J, 'By Any Means Necessary', *The Nation*, November 26, 2001.
8. Parenti, Christian, *Lockdown America: Police and Prisons in the Age of Crisis*, New York: Verso, 1999.
9. *Guardian*, November 30, 2001.
10. Currie, Elliott, *Crime and Punishment in America*, New York: Holt, 1998, pp. 185–6.

11. Christie, Nils, *Crime Control as Industry*, London: Routledge, 1994 (2nd edn) pp. 99–100.
12. Parenti, *Lockdown America*, p. 174.
13. Ibid p. 169.
14. Editorial, *Asylum*, Special Issue on Prisons, vol. 10, No. 3, Winter, 1997–98.
15. Norton-Taylor, Richard, 'The war against terror is making villains of us all', *Guardian*, January 22, 2002.
16. *Guardian*, January 17, 2002.
17. *Guardian*, January 23, 2002.
18. *Guardian*, January 20, 2002.
19. All quotes taken from *The President's State of the Union Address* issued by the Office of Press Secretary, The White House, January 29, 2002.
20. *Guardian*, February 1, 2002.

Notes on Contributors

Eileen Berrington is Lecturer in Critical Criminology at the Centre for Studies in Crime and Social Justice, Edge Hill University College, and has written on media and journalist responses to disasters and other traumatic events.

Ben Bowling is Reader in Criminology and Criminal Justice, School of Law, King's College, London, and author of *Racism, Crime and Justice*, Longman, 2002.

Madeleine Bunting is a columnist for the *Guardian*.

Noam Chomsky is Institute Professor at the Massachusetts Institute of Technology, USA, and is a world-renowned linguist, philosopher and political analyst. His most recent books include *The New Military Humanism: Lessons From Kosovo*, 1999, *Fateful Triangle: The United States, Israel and the Palestinians*, 1999 (2nd edition) and *Rogue States: The Rule of Force in World Affairs*, 2000 (all Pluto Press).

Howard Davis is Research Fellow and Senior Lecturer at the Centre for Studies in Crime and Social Justice, Edge Hill University College. He is co-author of *Disaster, Trauma, Aftermath*, Lawrence and Wishart, 2002.

Jonathan D Farley is Professor and Fulbright Distinguished Scholar at Oxford University and a Green Party Candidate for the US Congress.

Liz Fekete is Principal Researcher for the Institute of Race Relations European Race Audit and a member of the Campaign Against Racism and Fascism. Her recent writing is on xeno-racism and she is the author of *Racism: The Hidden Cost of September 11*, IRR, 2002.

Robert Fisk is a renowned foreign affairs, award-winning journalist specialising in conflict in the Middle East. He writes for the *Independent*.

Paul Foot is a campaigning and investigative journalist whose publications have exposed numerous miscarriages of justice. He is a regular columnist for the *Guardian*.

Penny Green is Professor of Law and Director of the Graduate Centre at the University of Westminster.

Martti Grönfors is Professor of Sociology and Criminology at the Universities of Kuopio and Helsinki, Finland. He is currently working on a primary research text on masculinity and violence.

Paddy Hillyard is Professor of Social Administration and Policy, University of Ulster and author of *Suspect Community: People's Experiences of Terrorism Acts in Britain*, Pluto Press, 1993.

Russell Hogg is Senior Lecturer in Criminology in the School of Sociology and Justice Studies at the University of Western Sydney. His most recent publications are *Rethinking Law and Order* , 1998, and *Critical Criminology: issues, debates, challenges*, Willan Publishing, 2002 (co-editor).

Barbara Hudson is Professor of Law at the University of Central Lancashire. She writes extensively on criminal justice and human rights issues and her books include *Penal Policy and Social Justice*, Macmillan, 1993, and *Understanding Justice*, Open University Press, 1996.

Naomi Klein is an award-winning journalist and best-selling author who contributes regularly to *The Nation*, the *New Statesman,* the *Guardian,* the *New York Times* and *Newsweek*. Her book *No Logo*, Flamingo, 2000, was published to universal acclaim.

Thomas Mathiesen is Professor of Sociology of Law at the University of Oslo, Norway. He is author of the revised and updated *Prison on Trial*, Sage, 2002, and of *On Globalisation of Control: Towards an Integrated Surveillance System in Europe*, Statewatch, 1999.

Michael Mandel is Professor of Law at the Osgoode Law School of York University, Toronto, Canada, specialising in international criminal law. He is co-chair of Lawyers Against the War (Canada) formed to oppose America's so-called 'War on Terrorism'.

Mike Marqusee is a London-based writer and activist. His most recent book is *Redemption Song: Muhammed Ali and the Spirit of the Sixties*, Verso, 2000, and was voted one of twenty-five 'Books to Remember' by New York Library. He is a member of the Steering Committee of the Stop the War Coalition.

Jude McCulloch is Lecturer in Police Studies at Deakin University, Australia, and author of *Blue Army: Paramilitary Policing in Australia*, University of Melbourne Press, 2001.

Mick North has worked in the UK and the international gun control movements since 1996, the year his daughter was shot dead at Dunblane Primary School, Scotland. He is the author of *Dunblane: Never Forget*, Mainstream, 2000, and writes and speaks on gun control and disaster response issues.

Cecilia O'Leary is Associate Professor of History and Co-Director of the Oral History and Community Memory Institute at California State University, Monterey Bay. She is the author of *To Die For: The Paradox of American Patriotism*, University of Princeton Press, 1999, and guest editor of the forthcoming *Social Justice* special edition, *New Pedagogies for Social Change*.

Christian Parenti teaches at the New College of California, San Francisco, and is a regular contributor to *The Nation*. He is author of *Lockdown America: Police and Prisons in the Age of Crisis*, Verso, 1999.

Tony Platt is Professor of Social Work at California State University, Sacramento, and has been on the editorial board of *Social Justice* since its inception in 1974. His books include, *The Child Savers: The Invention of Delinquency* and *The Politics of Riot Commissions, 1917–1970*.

John Pilger is an international, award-winning broadcaster, writer and journalist. His books include *Heroes, Distant Voices* and *A Secret Country* (all Verso). His latest book is *The New Rulers of the World*, Verso, 2002.

Bill Rolston is Professor of Sociology at the University of Ulster. His most recent book is *Unfinished Business: State Killings and the Quest for Truth*, Beyond the Pale Publications, 2000.

Herman Schwendinger is Emeritus Professor at the State University of New York, New Paltz, USA. He has been at the forefront of radical criminology and civil rights struggles in the USA since the 1960s and is co-author of *Sociologists of the Chair: A Radical Analysis of the Formative Years of North American Sociology*, 1974, and *Who Killed the Berkeley School of Criminology?* (forthcoming).

Julia Schwendinger is Courtesy Professor in the Department of Criminology at the University of Southern Florida, Tampa, USA. A human rights and feminist activist since the 1960s, her work includes *Sociologists of the Chair: A Radical Analysis of the Formative Years of North American Sociology* and, most recently, *Who Killed the Berkeley School of Criminology?*

Phil Scraton is Professor of Criminology and Director of the Centre for Studies in Crime and Social Justice, Edge Hill University College. His most recent books are *Hillsborough: The Truth*, Mainstream, 2000, and *Disaster, Trauma, Aftermath*, Lawrence and Wishart, 2002 (with Howard Davis).

A Sivanandan is a political activist, writer and founding editor of *Race and Class*. He is Director of the Institute of Race Relations and his most recent publications include *When Memory Dies*, Arcadia, 1997, and *Where the Dance Is*, Arcadia, 2000.

Elizabeth Stanley is Lecturer in Critical Criminology at the Centre for Studies in Crime and Social Justice at Edge Hill University College and has researched and written on storytelling, torture and truth commissions.

Philip A Thomas is Professor of Law, Cardiff Law School, Cardiff University. He has published widely in socio-legal studies, human rights and social justice and is Editor of the *Journal of Law and Society*.

Steve Tombs is Professor of Sociology at Liverpool John Moores University. He is co-author of *Corporate Crime* and *Toxic Capitalism* and co-editor of *Risk, Management and Society* and *Researching the Crimes of the Powerful* (forthcoming).

Leanne Weber is a freelance researcher in human rights and criminal justice, most recently researching the detention of asylum seekers in Britain.

Dave Whyte is Lecturer in Criminology at Manchester Metropolitan University. He has researched and written on the regulation of corporate crime, worker safety and is co-editor of *Researching the Crimes of the Powerful*, Peter Lang, (forthcoming).

Tunde Zack-Williams is Professor of Sociology at the University of Central Lancashire, author of *Africa in Crisis*, Pluto Press, 2001, and a member of the Editorial Working Group of the *Review of African Political Economy*.

Index

Compiled by Sue Carlton